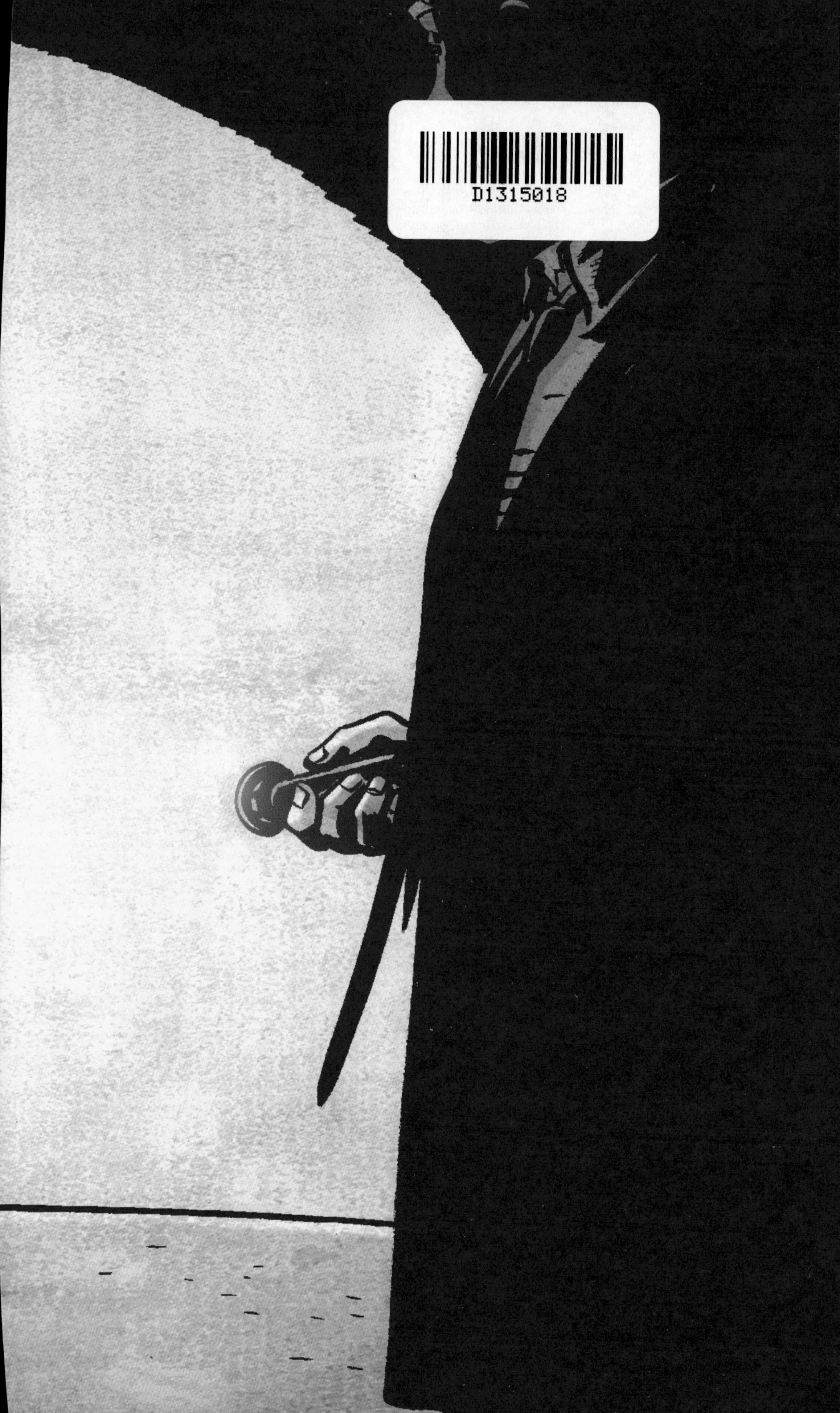

ROSS RICHIE
chief executive officer

ANDREW COSBY
chief creative officer

MARK WAID
editor-in-chief

ADAM FORTIER
vice president,
publishing

CHIP MOSHER
marketing director

MATT GAGNON
managing editor

THE UNKNOWN — September 2009 published by BOOM! Studios. The Unknown is Copyright Boom! Studios. BOOM!
Studios™ and the BOOM! logo are trademarks of Boom Entertainment, Inc., registered in various countries and categories. All
rights reserved. The characters and events depicted herein are fictional. Any similarity to actual persons, demons, anti-Christs,
aliens, vampires, face-suckers or political figures, whether living, dead or undead, or to any actual or supernatural events is
coincidental and unintentional. So don't come whining to us.

Office of publication: 6310 San Vicente Blvd, Ste 404, Los Angeles, CA 90048-5457.

FIRST EDITION: SEPTEMBER 2009
　10 9 8 7 6 5 4 3 2 1
　PRINTED IN KOREA

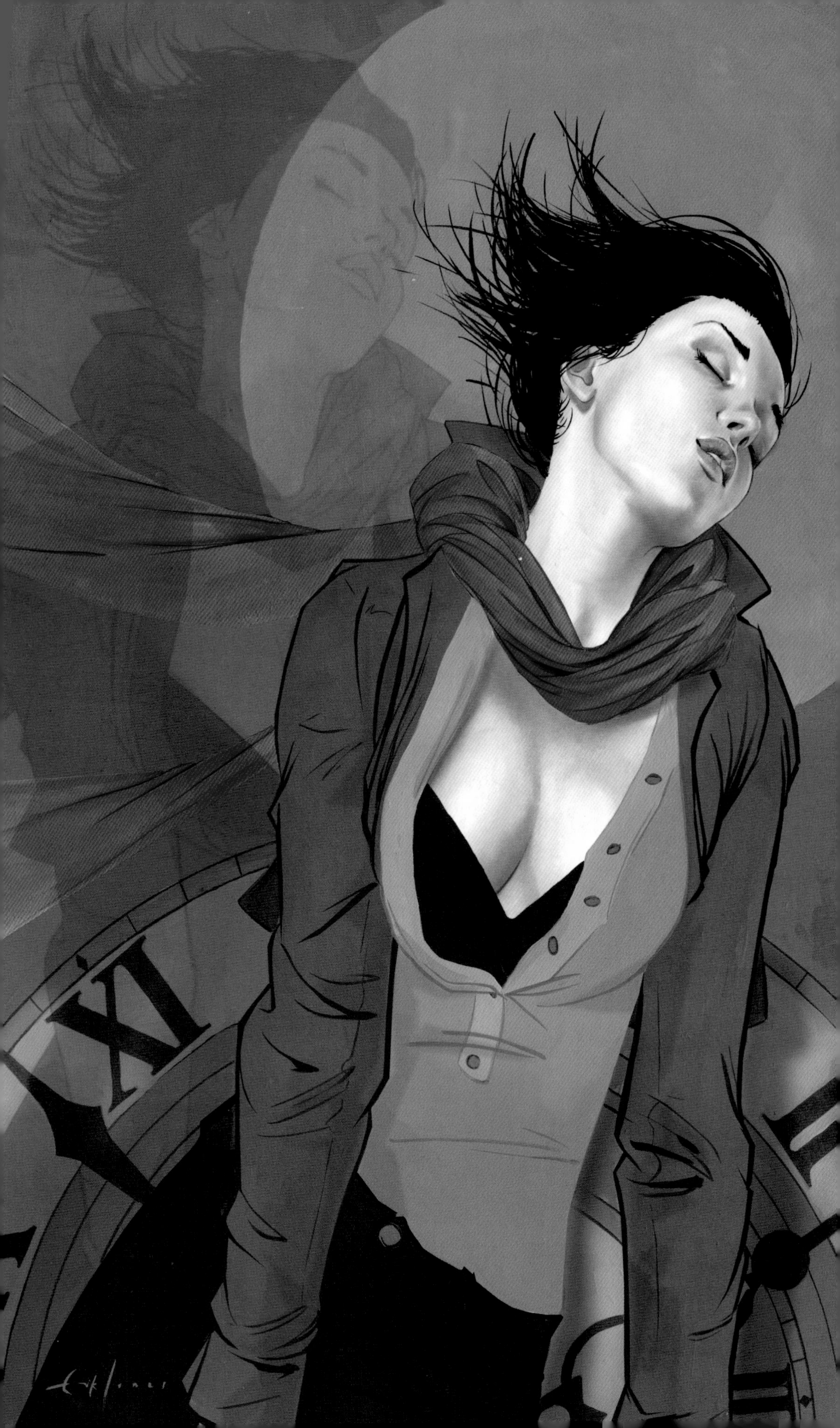

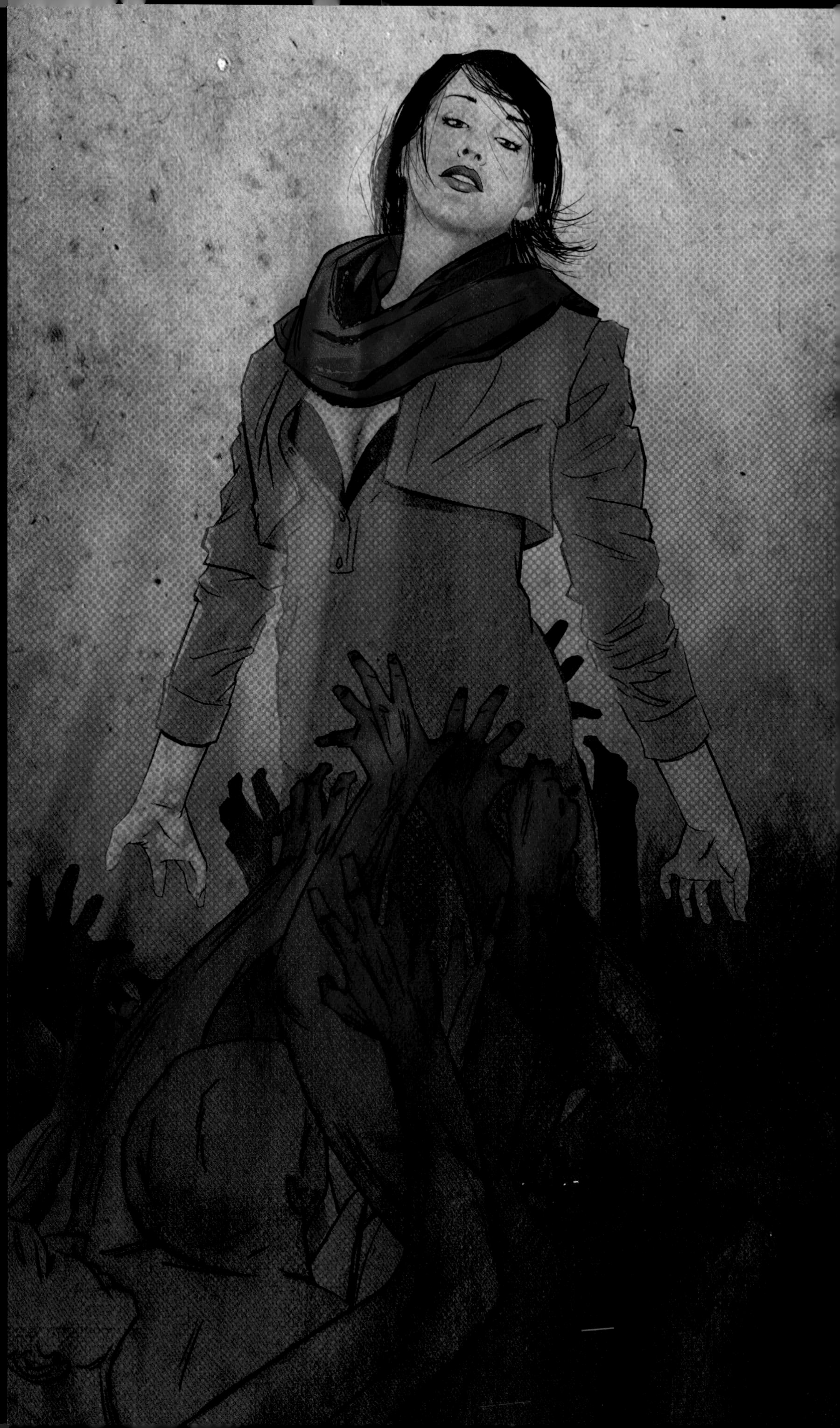

The UNKNOWN

WAID · OOSTERVEER

STORY **MARK WAID** ART **MINCK OOSTERVEER**

LETTERED BY **MARSHALL DILLON** EDITED BY **MATT GAGNO**

COVER BY **ERIK JONES** TRADE DESIGN BY **ERIKA TERRIQUE**

COLORS BY **FELLIPE MARTINS** • **RENATO FACCINI** • **ANDRES LOZAN**
ISSUE 1-3, 4 (1-4)   ISSUE 4 (5-10, 18-22)   ISSUE 4 (11-17)

Quite by accident, my lovely and brilliant sister recently stumbled across an internet message b
about my work, and she, being sensibly inexperienced with the perils and pratfalls of such pl
was very surprised at the range of topics raised and questions asked: everything from horrid in
to grand praise and every possible permutation in between. After that eye-opening experience
called me with an interesting question, one that I'd never heard before:

"What is the most gratifying comment a reader has ever given you?"

Now, the truth is, accepting praise on the internet is a dicey proposition. If you accept
accolades with gracious eagerness, then you are equally obliged to accept the comments of t
who feel you "raped their childhood." And as entertaining as that can be, it's not exactly he
to the writing process.

Nevertheless, there are observations that brighten the day and lift the spirits: when a critic
respect found your work compelling; when a reader felt terribly moved in some unexpected
or perhaps when a peer takes the time to let you know you did it, you got it right. All of t
comments have a way of spinning the world a little bit more in your direction.

"I love your work."

"This story helped me through some tough times."

And again, from anyone, really…"You did it, you got it right."

All of those kind phrases are likely to put a little more starch in your step (I'm not sure
that metaphor right, but humor me). But I think the answer to my sister's question is
sentence, even more lovely to the writer's ear:

"I didn't know you could do that."

That's the one, that's the one that makes the heart sing. "I didn't know you could do that
means you did the best thing a writer can do, you confounded and demolished expectat
They might have loved your work, but they had a box around it, they had a series of notior
what you were capable of, and you bloody well proved them wrong. That's worth all the sta
reviews and "thumbs up" ratings imaginable. They expected taffy, you gave them poison.
expected sunshine, you gave them gunpowder. They expected darkness, and you gave then
full brightness of the sun.

"I didn't know you could do that."

think of writers like James Bond creator Ian Fleming, who one day got it in his head to v
a children's book about a flying car and gave us CHITTY CHITTY BANG BANG. Or Ja
Dickey, who, after winning tremendous acclaim as a poet, wrote one of the greatest Amer
novels of all time in his first try at bat, DELIVERANCE. And people who knew Roald
only for his charming and fanciful children's novels, like CHARLIE AND THE CHOCOL
FACTORY, must have been downright befuddled upon their discovery of his much darker a
fiction, and vice versa.

That's what THE UNKNOWN is like for me, regarding Mark Waid. Make no mistake, I am as big a Waid fan as likely exists anywhere. I've read with great pleasure almost every single printed word the man has written. I follow his works and I read his interviews.

I knew he could write game-changing super-hero stories, like KINGDOM COME and THE FLASH. I knew he could write sparkling new twists on the Sherlock Holmesian mystery story, as in the sadly short-lived RUSE. I knew he had a killer's instinct for science fantasy, in books like LEGION OF SUPER-HEROES. And I knew he had the disturbing knack of writing evil in IRREDEEMABLE and EMPIRE. In short, I thought I knew his bag of tricks.

But I didn't know he could do *this*.

I didn't know he could write one of the most thrilling, expectation-crushing, genre-bending, knuckle-biting thrill rides of the last few years.

It's a story that's part classic chase, part detective, part speculative science, part metaphysical, part crime drama, part buddy flick, and oh, hell, let's just throw in the damn kitchen sink while we're at it and God knows how he did it but it all *works*. It's four issues of thriller comic heaven, with characters that scare and delight and amuse and you know what? I'm getting a little sick of Mark Waid parading his talent around all the time. He ought to have the decency to stink up the joint once in a while with a complete failure now and then, but is Mark nice enough to do that?

No, he is not. Really, he should be flogged, just on principle.

I love this story. I love the main characters, I love the dream-like villains, I love the brilliant nerdiness of the maguffin. It has heart and brains and originality, and every issue aspires to and delivers more than most comics do in a year of trying.

So, while I couldn't have predicted this beautiful mishmash, it doesn't *really* come as a surprise to me that Mark Waid has written another ripping story unlike anything else out there.

Because I *did* know he could do *that*.

Before I end this introduction, I want to comment on the art of Minck Oosterveer. I confess I'd never heard of this Dutch artist, but what a find this guy is. His work reminds me of the polish and wit of one of my all-time favorites, Eduardo Barreto, but with a fascinating gloss that makes the creepy segments all the more unsettling. As someone who has had many an action sequence fall flat on the printed page, it's a delight to see an artist who can actually convincingly convey the dynamics of a fight with a monster aboard a train hurtling through the Austrian countryside. Mark, you'd better lock this guy down for the sequel, or I'm stealing him. Sorry, it's already decided.

Now please get comfortable, grab some chips and a drink if you like, because it's very likely you're not getting up until you've read the whole thing, like I did.

Because it's the *unknown* in a writer that's the most fun bit of all.

Gail Simone

Gail Simone is an award–winning comics, animation and prose writer and, in the 21ˢᵗ century, established herself as one of the best new voices in the comics/graphic novel medium. Her works include WONDER WOMAN, WELCOME TO TRANQUILITY, THE SIMPSONS, KILLER PRINCESSES, and many more.

CHAPTER ONE

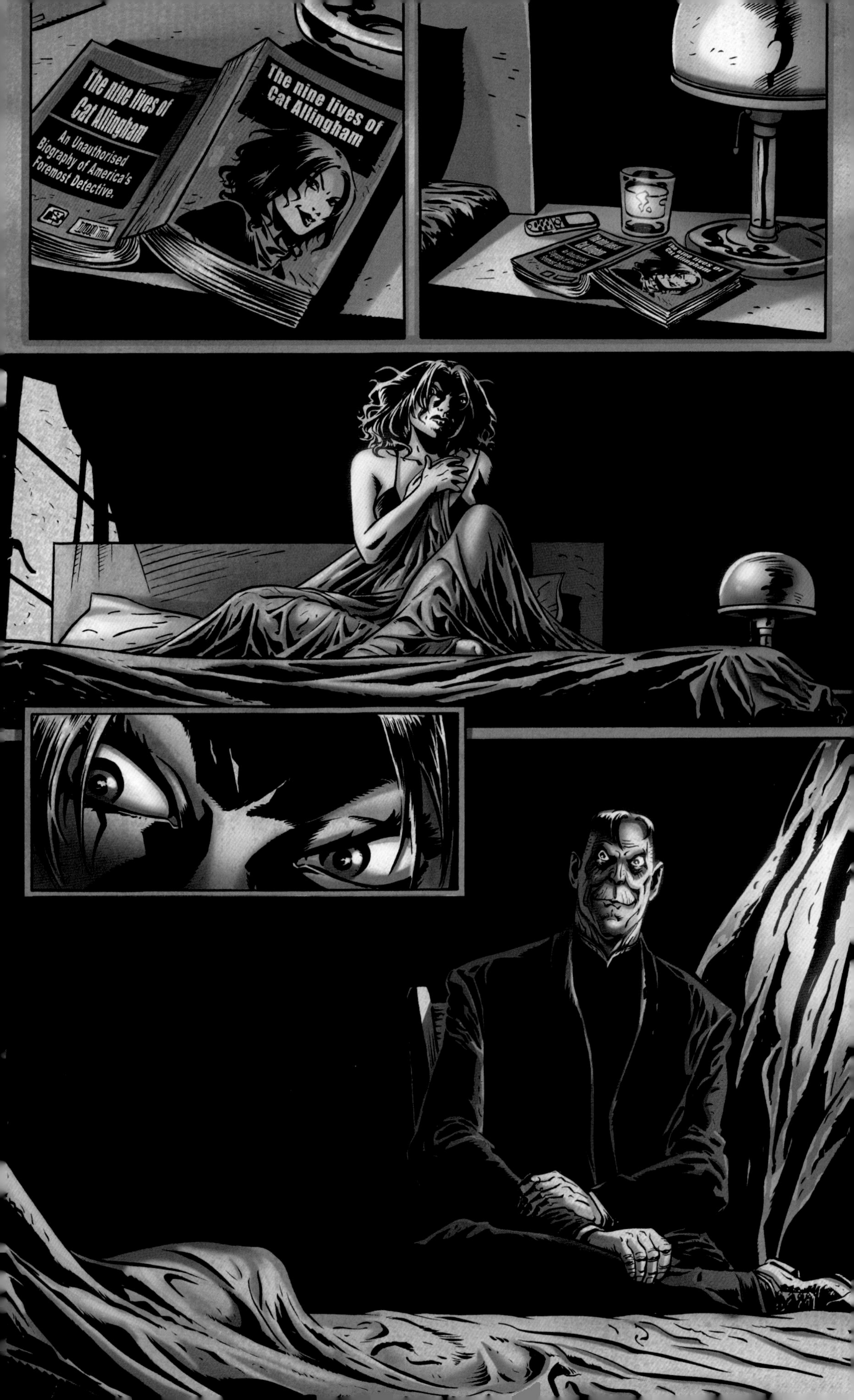
The nine lives of Cat Allingham
An Unauthorised Biography of America's Foremost Detective.
The nine lives of Cat Allingham

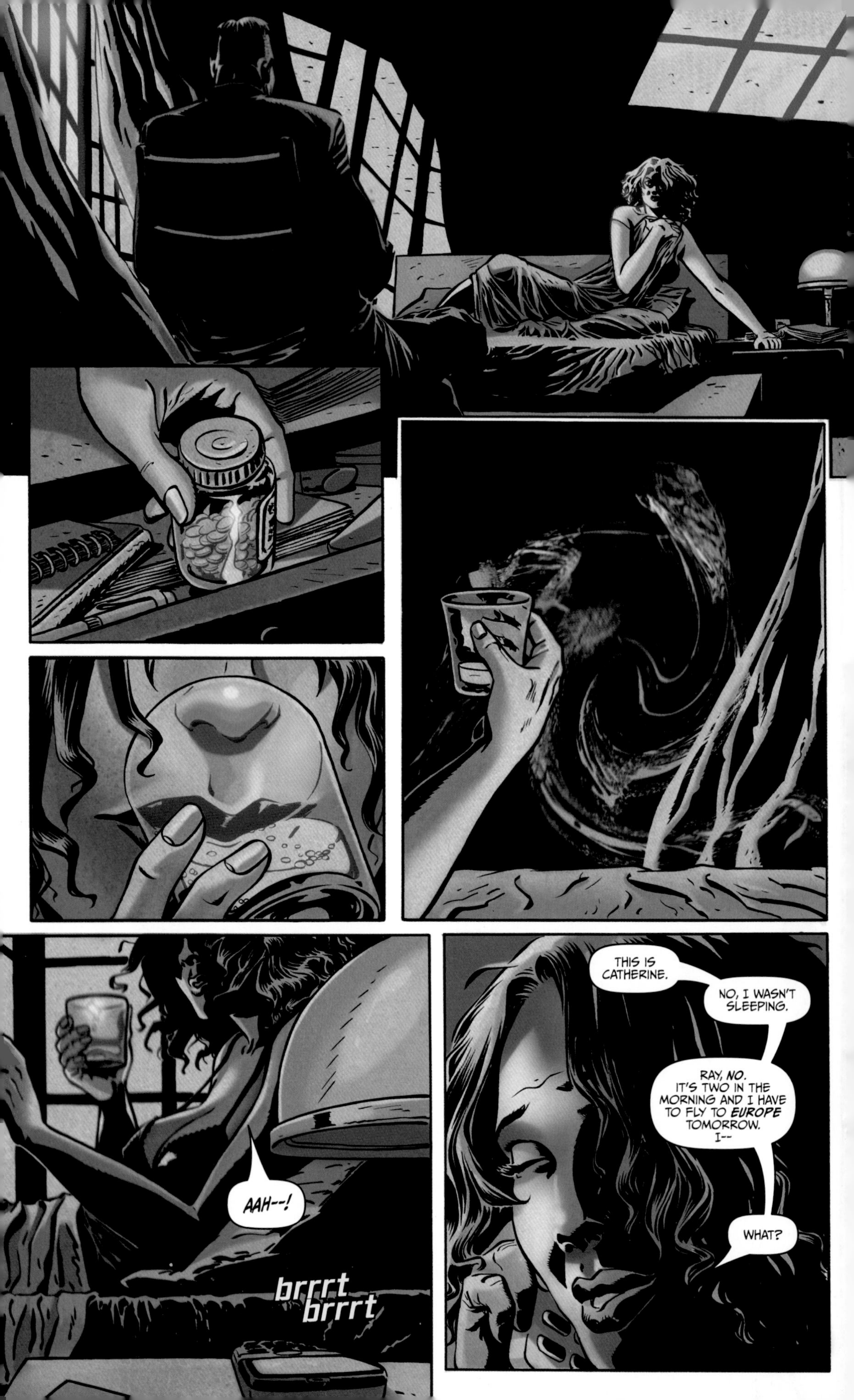
AAH--!
brrrt brrrt
THIS IS CATHERINE.
NO, I WASN'T SLEEPING.
RAY, NO. IT'S TWO IN THE MORNING AND I HAVE TO FLY TO EUROPE TOMORROW. I--
WHAT?

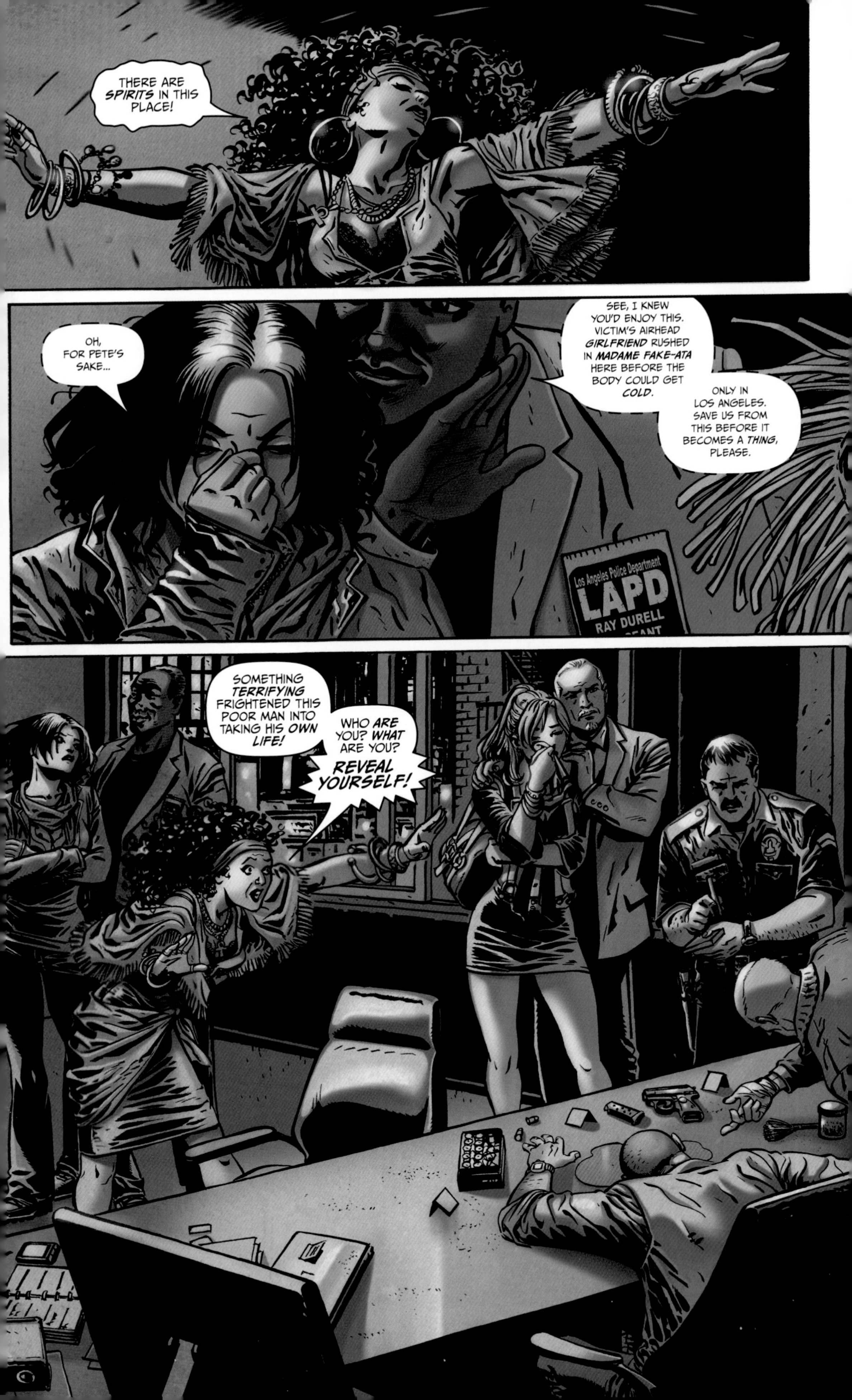
THERE ARE SPIRITS IN THIS PLACE!
OH, FOR PETE'S SAKE...
SEE, I KNEW YOU'D ENJOY THIS. VICTIM'S AIRHEAD GIRLFRIEND RUSHED IN MADAME FAKE-ATA HERE BEFORE THE BODY COULD GET COLD.
ONLY IN LOS ANGELES. SAVE US FROM THIS BEFORE IT BECOMES A THING, PLEASE.
Los Angeles Police Department
LAPD
RAY DURELL
SOMETHING TERRIFYING FRIGHTENED THIS POOR MAN INTO TAKING HIS OWN LIFE!
WHO ARE YOU? WHAT ARE YOU?
REVEAL YOURSELF!

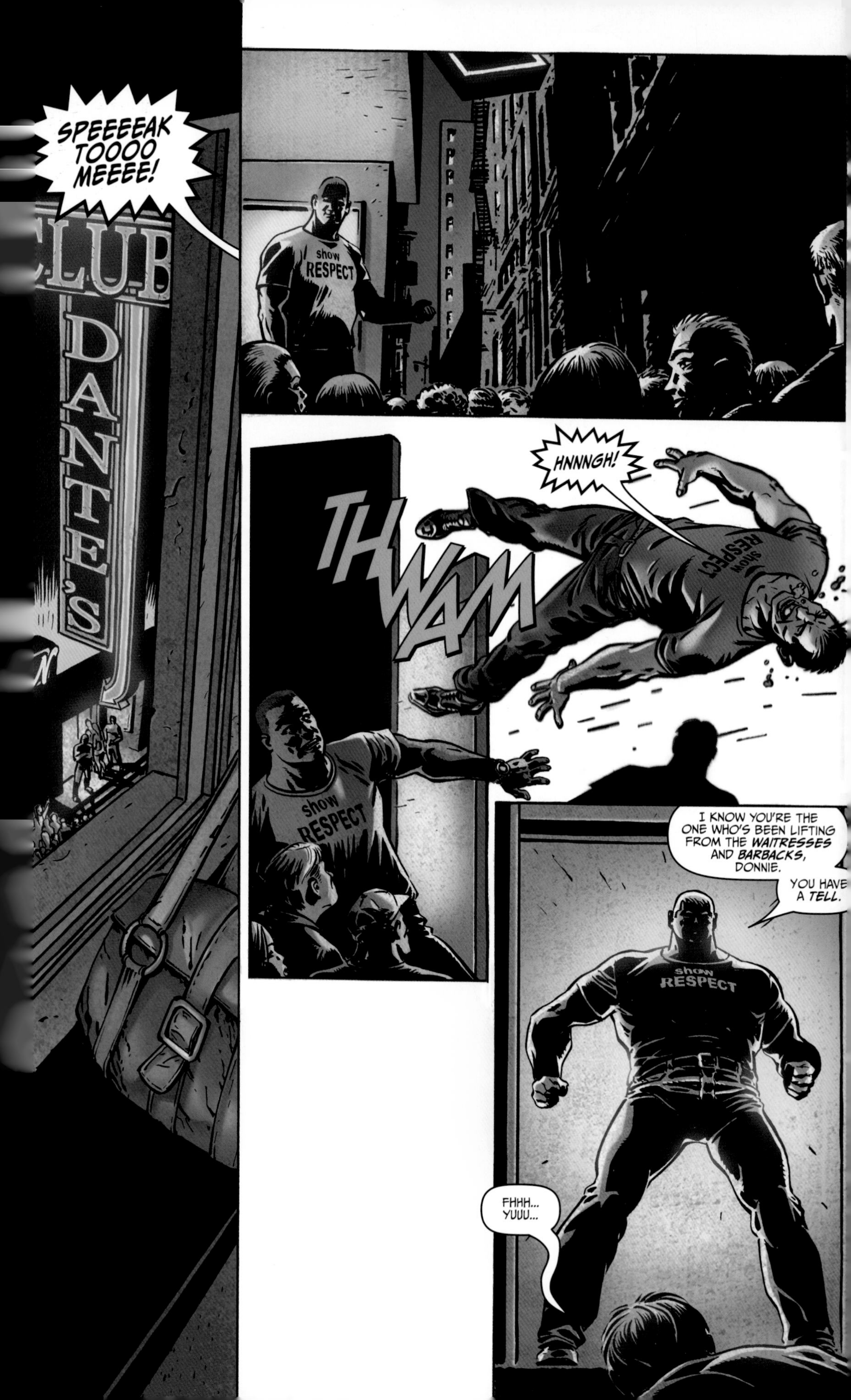

SPEEEEAK TOOOO MEEEE!
CLUB DANTE'S
show RESPECT
HNNNGH!
THWAM
show RESPECT
show RESPECT
I KNOW YOU'RE THE ONE WHO'S BEEN LIFTING FROM THE WAITRESSES AND BARBACKS, DONNIE.
YOU HAVE A TELL.
show RESPECT
FHHH... YUUU...

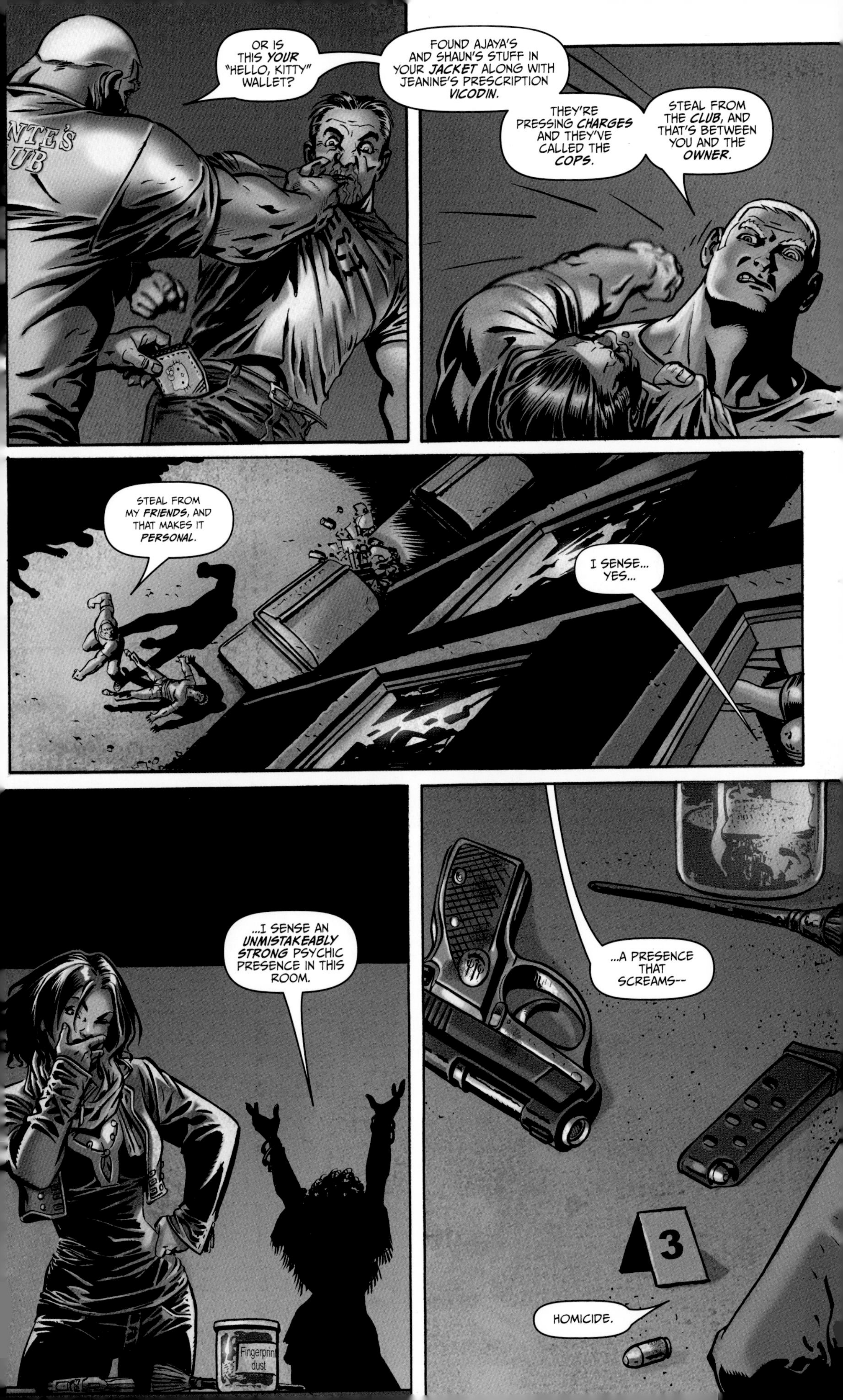
OR IS THIS YOUR "HELLO, KITTY" WALLET?
FOUND AJAYA'S AND SHAUN'S STUFF IN YOUR JACKET ALONG WITH JEANINE'S PRESCRIPTION VICODIN.
THEY'RE PRESSING CHARGES AND THEY'VE CALLED THE COPS.
STEAL FROM THE CLUB, AND THAT'S BETWEEN YOU AND THE OWNER.
STEAL FROM MY FRIENDS, AND THAT MAKES IT PERSONAL.
I SENSE... YES...
...I SENSE AN UNMISTAKEABLY STRONG PSYCHIC PRESENCE IN THIS ROOM.
Fingerprint dust
...A PRESENCE THAT SCREAMS--
3
HOMICIDE.

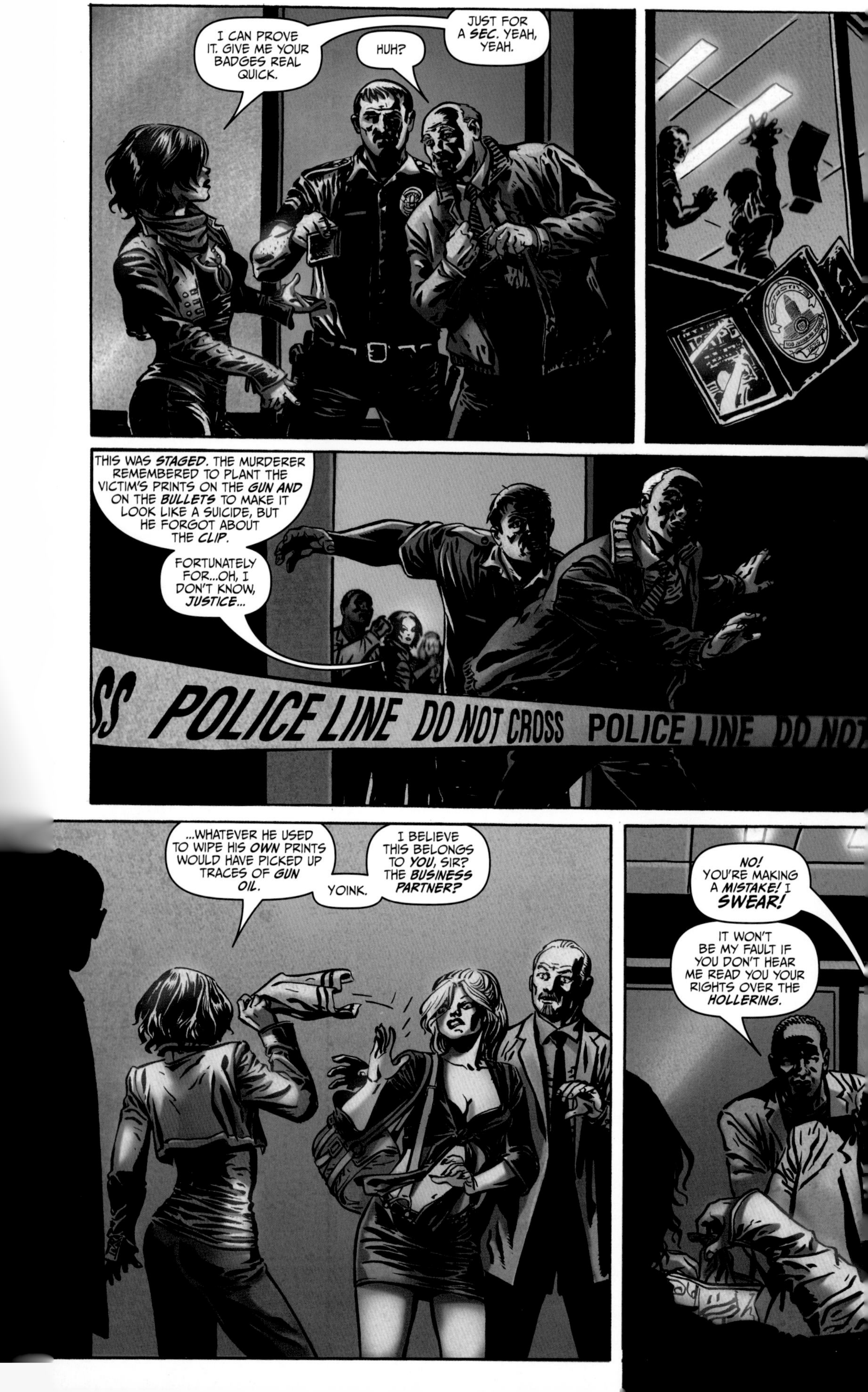
I CAN PROVE IT. GIVE ME YOUR BADGES REAL QUICK.
HUH?
JUST FOR A SEC. YEAH, YEAH.
THIS WAS STAGED. THE MURDERER REMEMBERED TO PLANT THE VICTIM'S PRINTS ON THE GUN AND ON THE BULLETS TO MAKE IT LOOK LIKE A SUICIDE, BUT HE FORGOT ABOUT THE CLIP.
FORTUNATELY FOR...OH, I DON'T KNOW, JUSTICE...
POLICE LINE DO NOT CROSS POLICE LINE
...WHATEVER HE USED TO WIPE HIS OWN PRINTS WOULD HAVE PICKED UP TRACES OF GUN OIL.
YOINK.
I BELIEVE THIS BELONGS TO YOU, SIR? THE BUSINESS PARTNER?
NO! YOU'RE MAKING A MISTAKE! I SWEAR!
IT WON'T BE MY FAULT IF YOU DON'T HEAR ME READ YOU YOUR RIGHTS OVER THE HOLLERING.

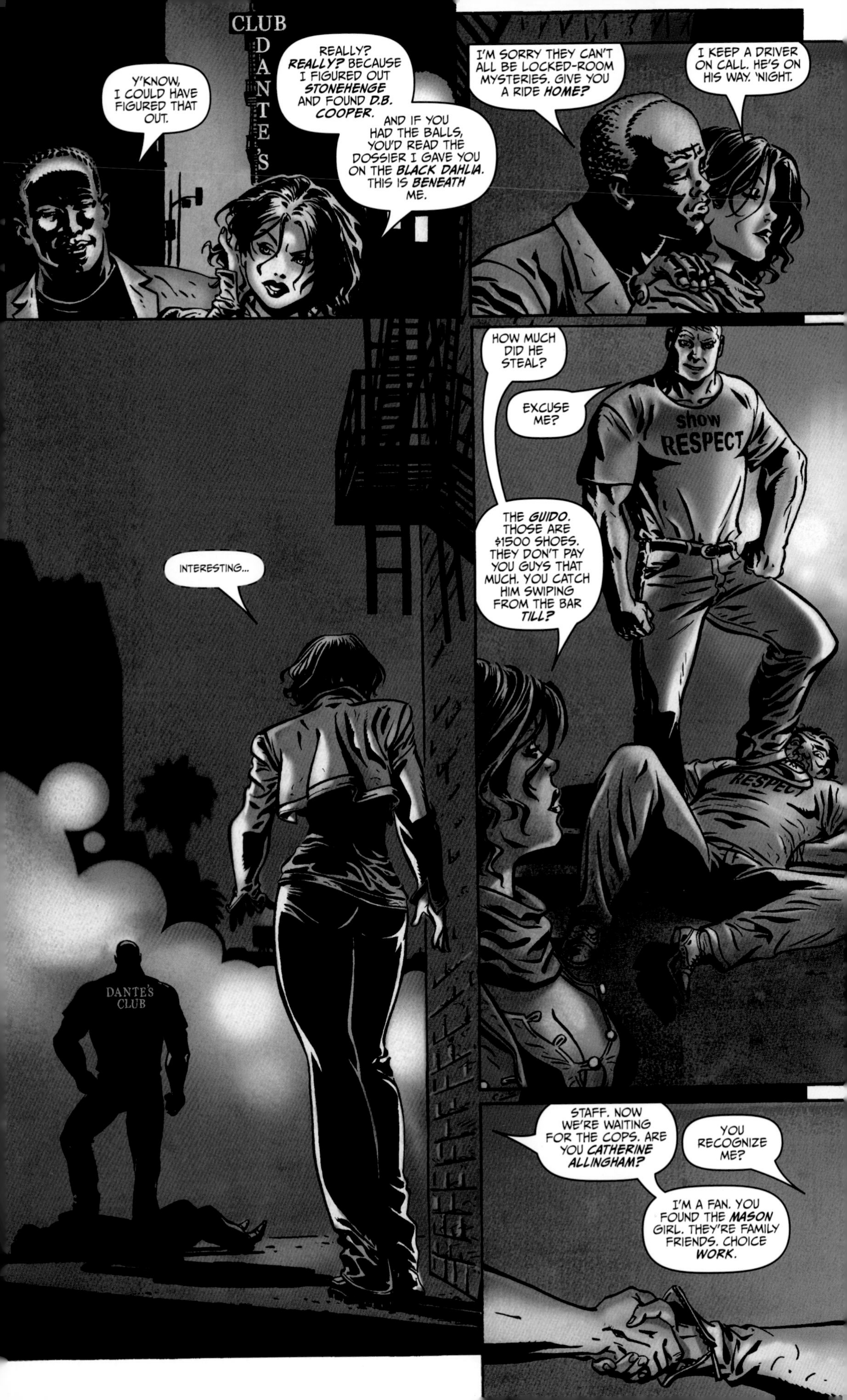
CLUB DANTE'S
Y'KNOW, I COULD HAVE FIGURED THAT OUT.
REALLY? REALLY? BECAUSE I FIGURED OUT STONEHENGE AND FOUND D.B. COOPER.
AND IF YOU HAD THE BALLS, YOU'D READ THE DOSSIER I GAVE YOU ON THE BLACK DAHLIA. THIS IS BENEATH ME.
I'M SORRY THEY CAN'T ALL BE LOCKED-ROOM MYSTERIES. GIVE YOU A RIDE HOME?
I KEEP A DRIVER ON CALL. HE'S ON HIS WAY. 'NIGHT.
INTERESTING...
DANTE'S CLUB
HOW MUCH DID HE STEAL?
EXCUSE ME?
show RESPECT
THE GUIDO. THOSE ARE $1500 SHOES. THEY DON'T PAY YOU GUYS THAT MUCH. YOU CATCH HIM SWIPING FROM THE BAR TILL?
RESPECT
STAFF. NOW WE'RE WAITING FOR THE COPS. ARE YOU CATHERINE ALLINGHAM?
YOU RECOGNIZE ME?
I'M A FAN. YOU FOUND THE MASON GIRL. THEY'RE FAMILY FRIENDS. CHOICE WORK.

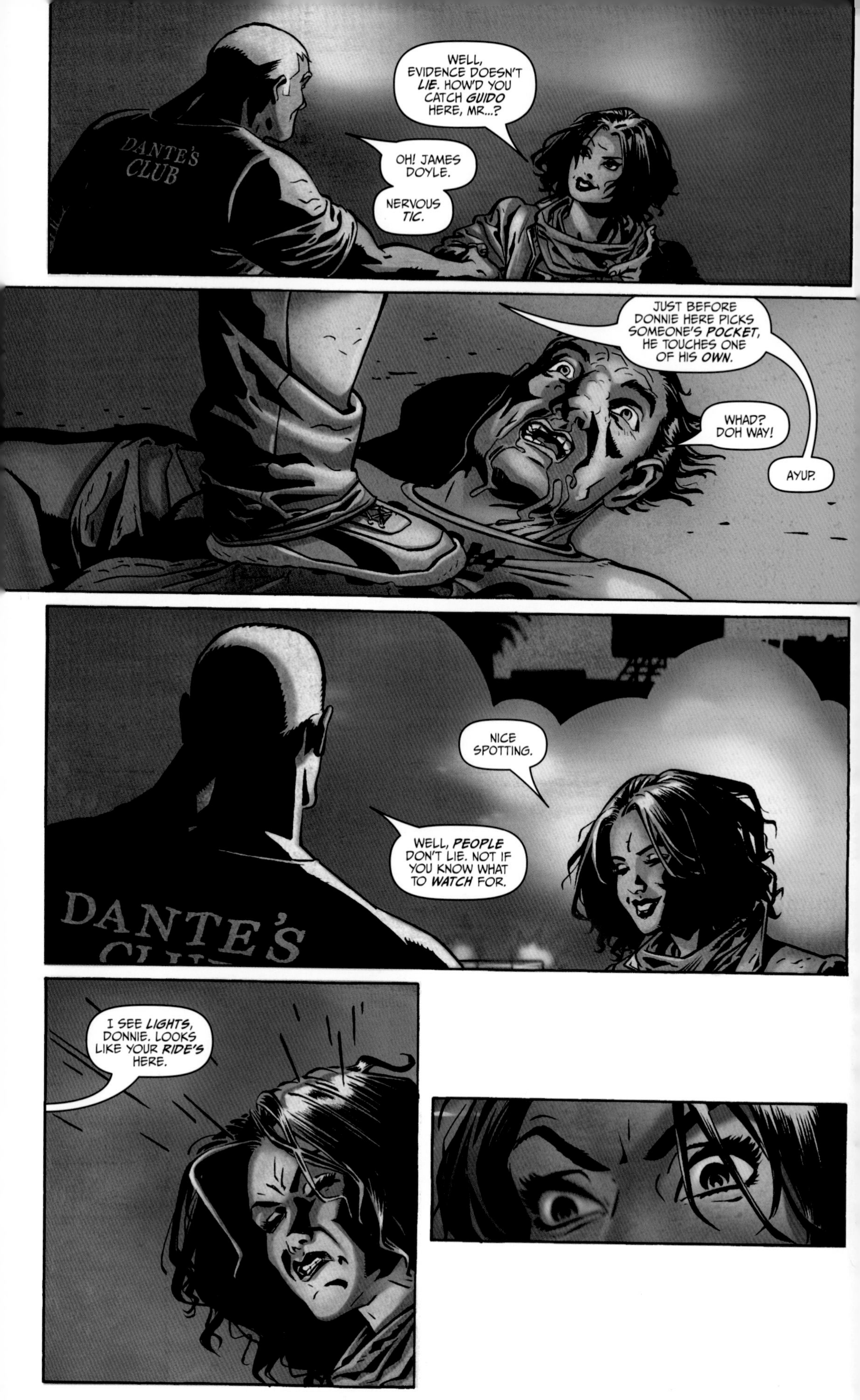
WELL, EVIDENCE DOESN'T LIE. HOW'D YOU CATCH GUIDO HERE, MR...?
DANTE'S CLUB
OH! JAMES DOYLE.
NERVOUS TIC.
JUST BEFORE DONNIE HERE PICKS SOMEONE'S POCKET, HE TOUCHES ONE OF HIS OWN.
WHAD? DOH WAY!
AYUP.
NICE SPOTTING.
WELL, PEOPLE DON'T LIE. NOT IF YOU KNOW WHAT TO WATCH FOR.
DANTE'S
I SEE LIGHTS, DONNIE. LOOKS LIKE YOUR RIDE'S HERE.

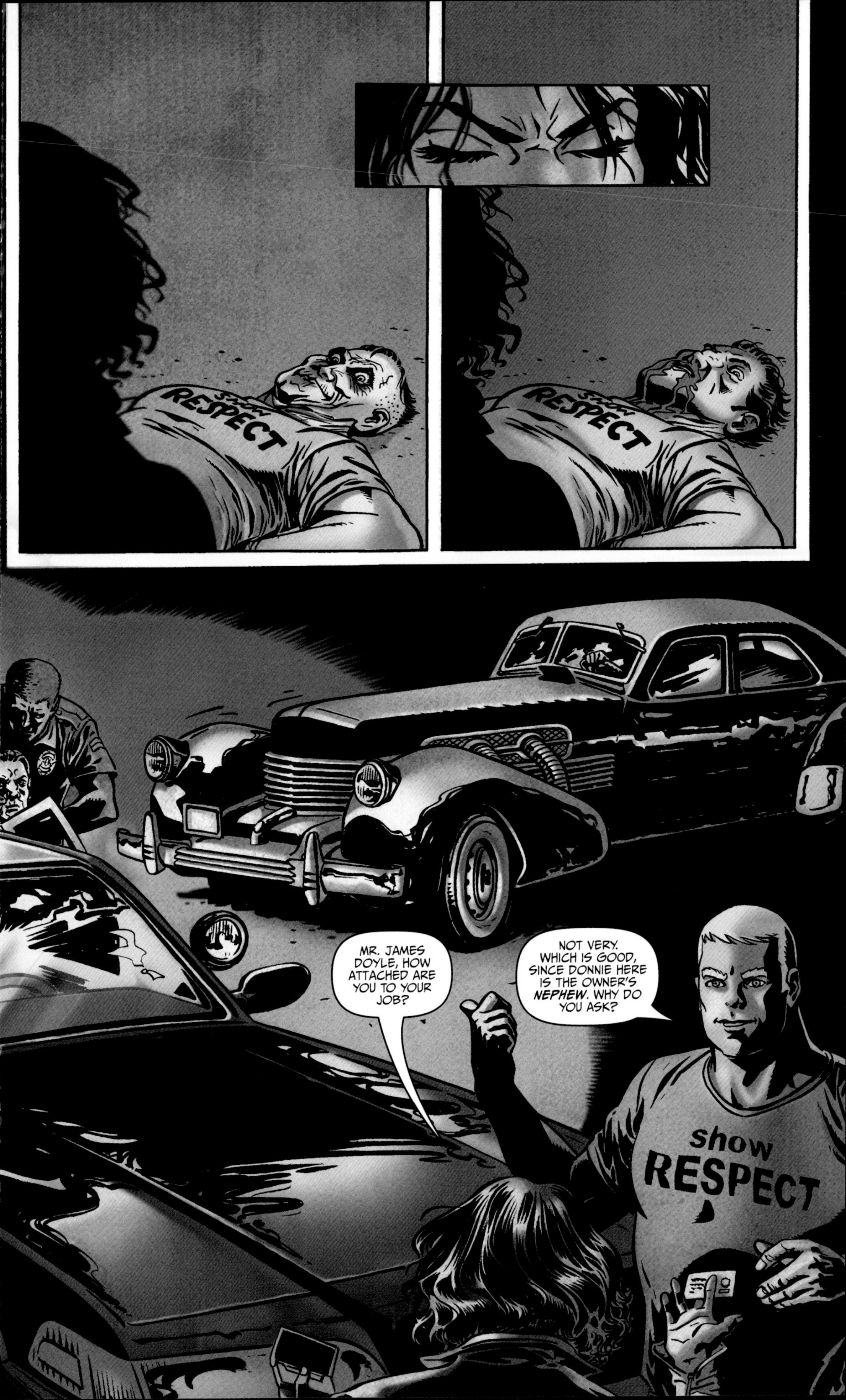
show RESPECT
show RESPECT
MR. JAMES DOYLE, HOW ATTACHED ARE YOU TO YOUR JOB?
NOT VERY. WHICH IS GOOD, SINCE DONNIE HERE IS THE OWNER'S NEPHEW. WHY DO YOU ASK?
show RESPECT

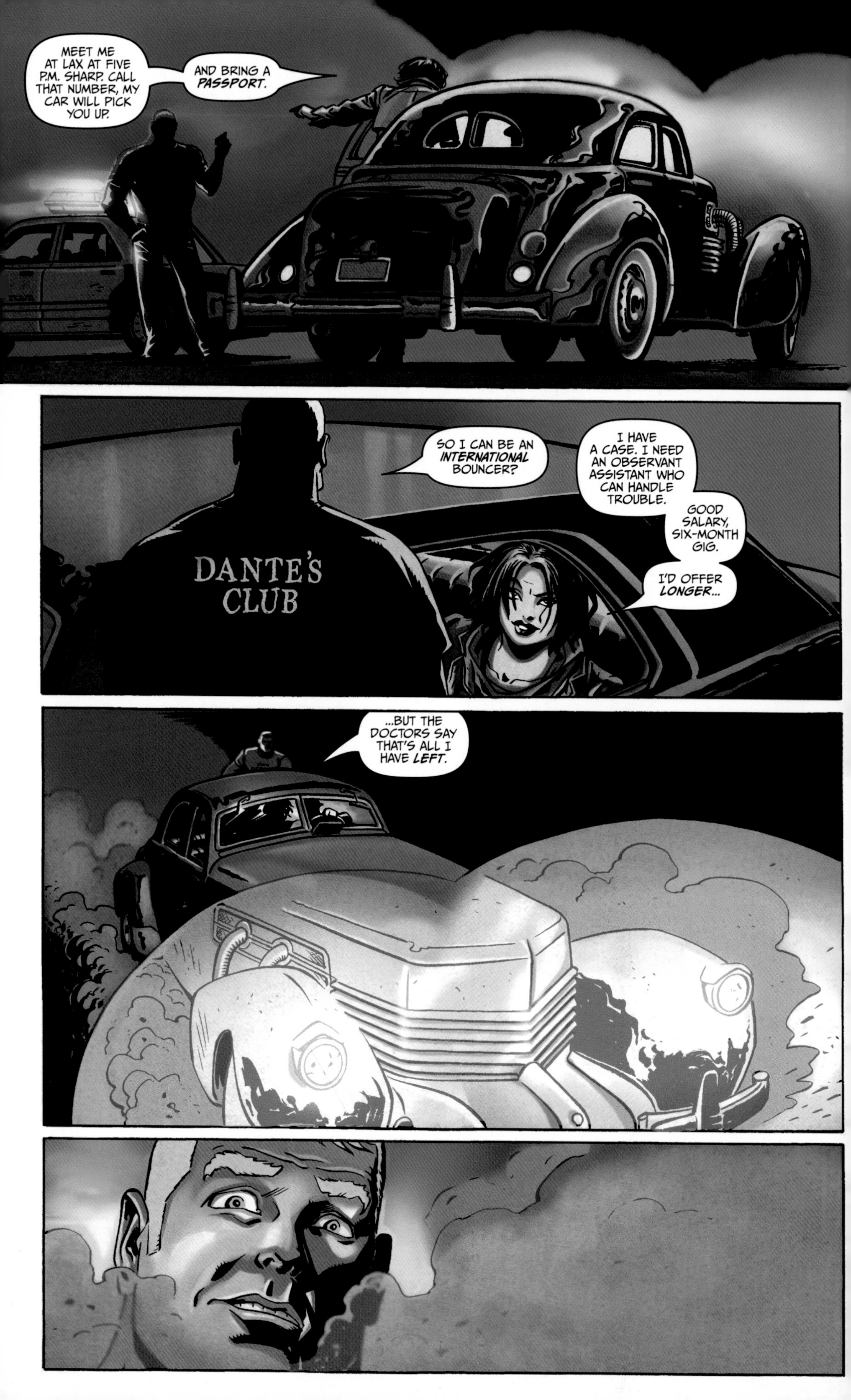
MEET ME AT LAX AT FIVE P.M. SHARP. CALL THAT NUMBER, MY CAR WILL PICK YOU UP.
AND BRING A *PASSPORT*.
SO I CAN BE AN *INTERNATIONAL* BOUNCER?
DANTE'S CLUB
I HAVE A CASE. I NEED AN OBSERVANT ASSISTANT WHO CAN HANDLE TROUBLE.
GOOD SALARY, SIX-MONTH GIG.
I'D OFFER *LONGER*...
...BUT THE DOCTORS SAY THAT'S ALL I HAVE *LEFT*.

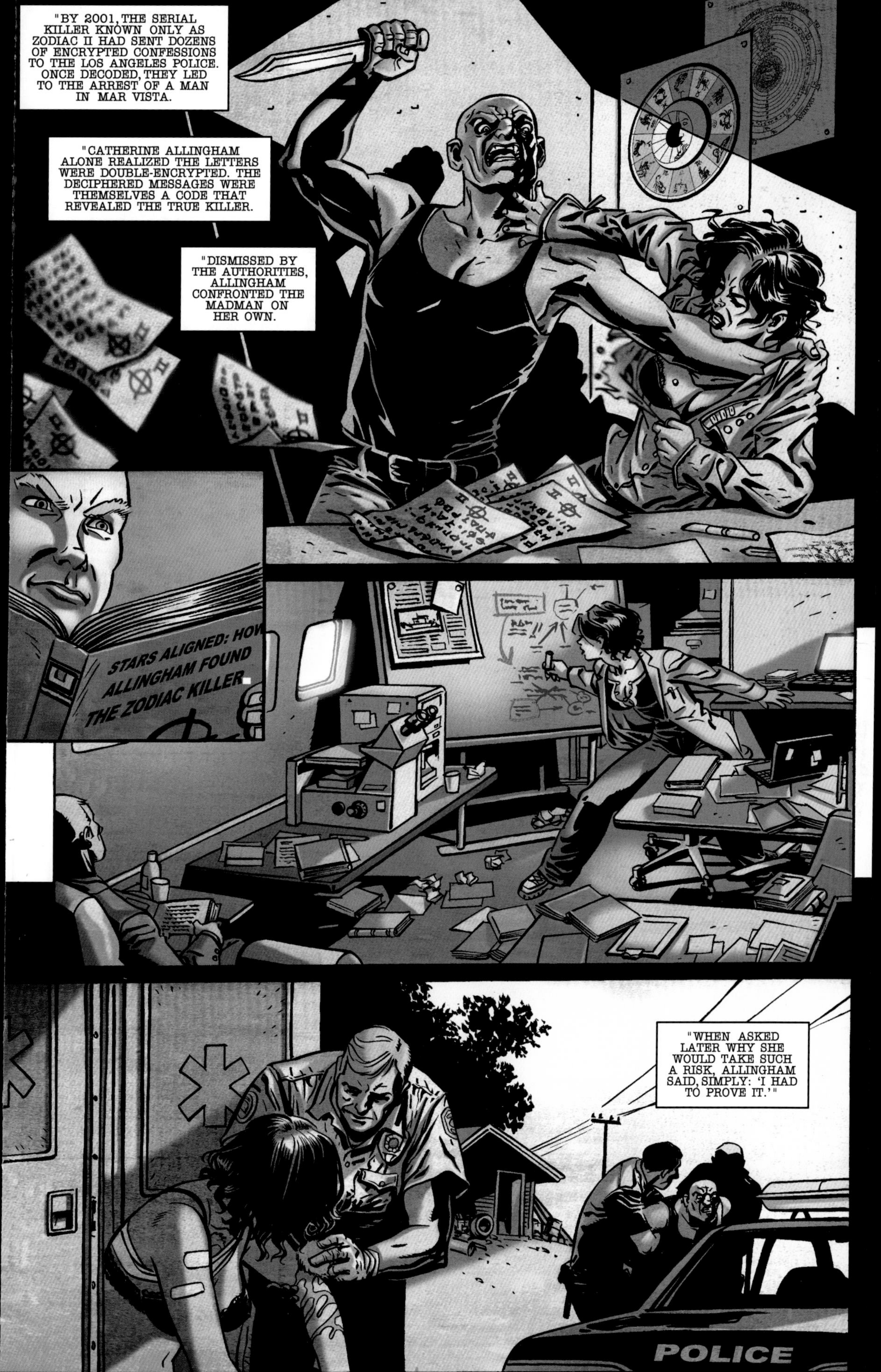
"BY 2001, THE SERIAL KILLER KNOWN ONLY AS ZODIAC II HAD SENT DOZENS OF ENCRYPTED CONFESSIONS TO THE LOS ANGELES POLICE. ONCE DECODED, THEY LED TO THE ARREST OF A MAN IN MAR VISTA.
"CATHERINE ALLINGHAM ALONE REALIZED THE LETTERS WERE DOUBLE-ENCRYPTED. THE DECIPHERED MESSAGES WERE THEMSELVES A CODE THAT REVEALED THE TRUE KILLER.
"DISMISSED BY THE AUTHORITIES, ALLINGHAM CONFRONTED THE MADMAN ON HER OWN.
STARS ALIGNED: HOW ALLINGHAM FOUND THE ZODIAC KILLER
"WHEN ASKED LATER WHY SHE WOULD TAKE SUCH A RISK, ALLINGHAM SAID, SIMPLY: 'I HAD TO PROVE IT.'"
POLICE

ARE YOU *BORED?* IF YOU DON'T WANT TO *READ,* DO SOMETHING *ELSE.*

USE TIME *EFFICIENTLY.* WHAT WOULD YOU NORMALLY DO ON A LONG FLIGHT?

CROSSWORDS, BUT THAT SEEMS KIND OF *UNAMBITIOUS* BY COMPARISON.

CAN I ASK WHAT YOU'RE WORKING ON SO FEVERISHLY?

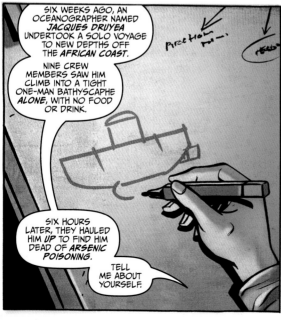

SIX WEEKS AGO, AN OCEANOGRAPHER NAMED *JACQUES DRUYEA* UNDERTOOK A SOLO VOYAGE TO NEW DEPTHS OFF THE *AFRICAN COAST.*

NINE CREW MEMBERS SAW HIM CLIMB INTO A TIGHT ONE-MAN BATHYSCAPHE *ALONE,* WITH NO FOOD OR DRINK.

SIX HOURS LATER, THEY HAULED HIM *UP* TO FIND HIM DEAD OF *ARSENIC POISONING.*

TELL ME ABOUT YOURSELF.

I DON'T WANT TO DISTRACT YOU.

I CAN WORK WHILE YOU TALK. HOW OLD ARE YOU?

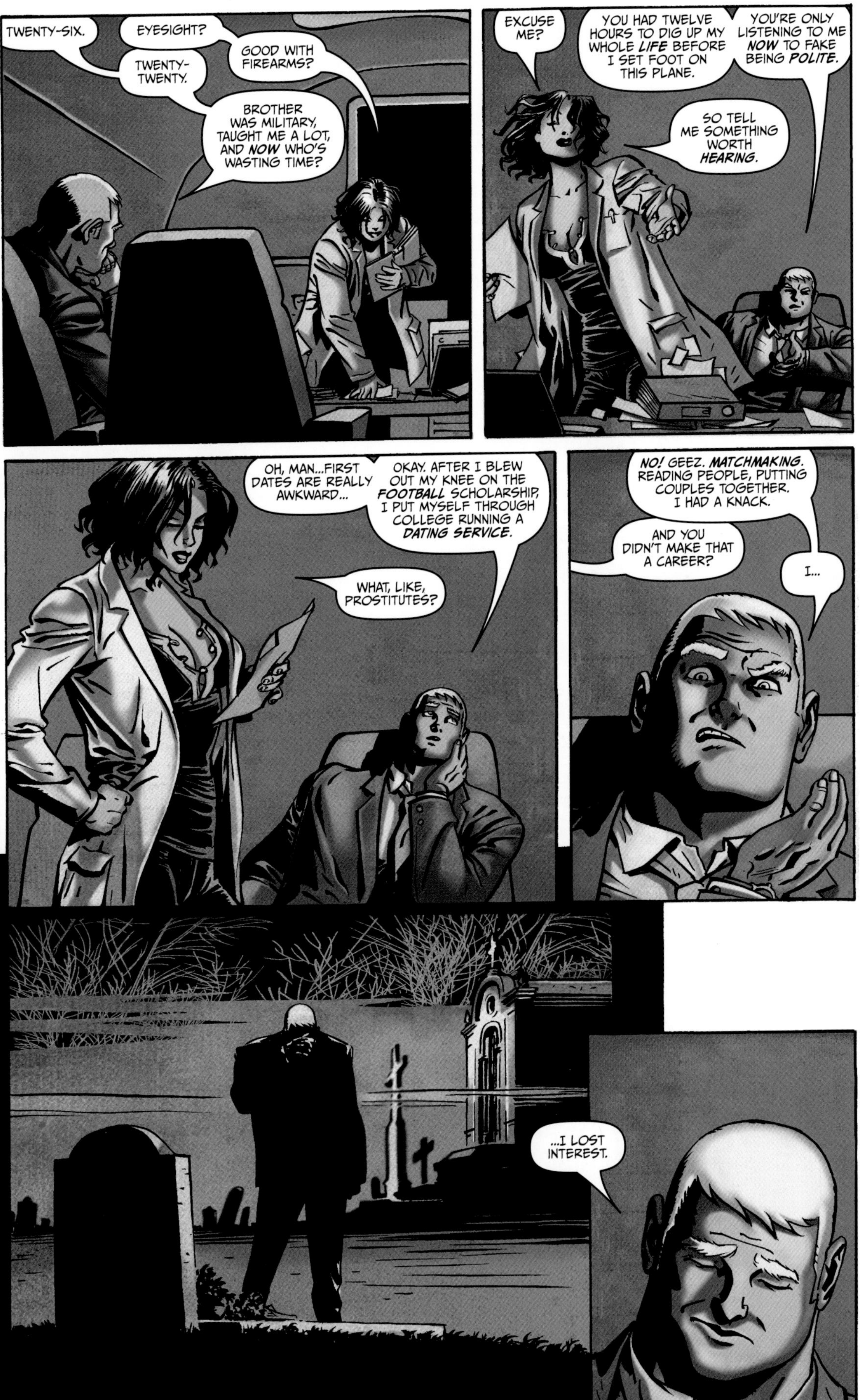
TWENTY-SIX.
EYESIGHT?
TWENTY-TWENTY.
GOOD WITH FIREARMS?
BROTHER WAS MILITARY, TAUGHT ME A LOT, AND NOW WHO'S WASTING TIME?
EXCUSE ME?
YOU HAD TWELVE HOURS TO DIG UP MY WHOLE LIFE BEFORE I SET FOOT ON THIS PLANE.
YOU'RE ONLY LISTENING TO ME NOW TO FAKE BEING POLITE.
SO TELL ME SOMETHING WORTH HEARING.
OH, MAN...FIRST DATES ARE REALLY AWKWARD...
OKAY. AFTER I BLEW OUT MY KNEE ON THE FOOTBALL SCHOLARSHIP, I PUT MYSELF THROUGH COLLEGE RUNNING A DATING SERVICE.
WHAT, LIKE, PROSTITUTES?
NO! GEEZ. MATCHMAKING. READING PEOPLE, PUTTING COUPLES TOGETHER. I HAD A KNACK.
AND YOU DIDN'T MAKE THAT A CAREER?
I...
...I LOST INTEREST.

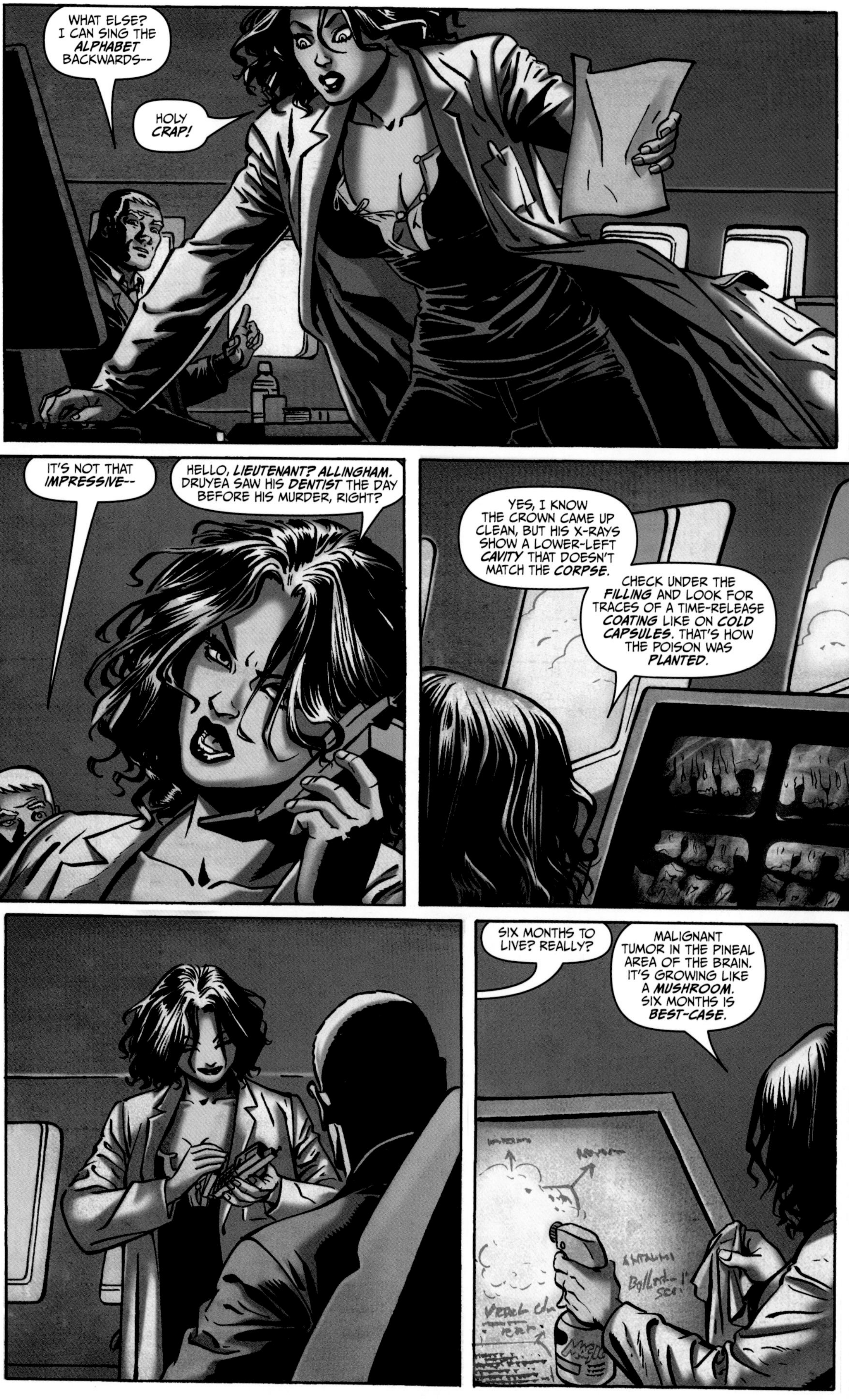
WHAT ELSE? I CAN SING THE ALPHABET BACKWARDS--
HOLY CRAP!
IT'S NOT THAT IMPRESSIVE--
HELLO, LIEUTENANT? ALLINGHAM. DRUYEA SAW HIS DENTIST THE DAY BEFORE HIS MURDER, RIGHT?
YES, I KNOW THE CROWN CAME UP CLEAN, BUT HIS X-RAYS SHOW A LOWER-LEFT CAVITY THAT DOESN'T MATCH THE CORPSE.
CHECK UNDER THE FILLING AND LOOK FOR TRACES OF A TIME-RELEASE COATING LIKE ON COLD CAPSULES. THAT'S HOW THE POISON WAS PLANTED.
SIX MONTHS TO LIVE? REALLY?
MALIGNANT TUMOR IN THE PINEAL AREA OF THE BRAIN. IT'S GROWING LIKE A MUSHROOM. SIX MONTHS IS BEST-CASE.

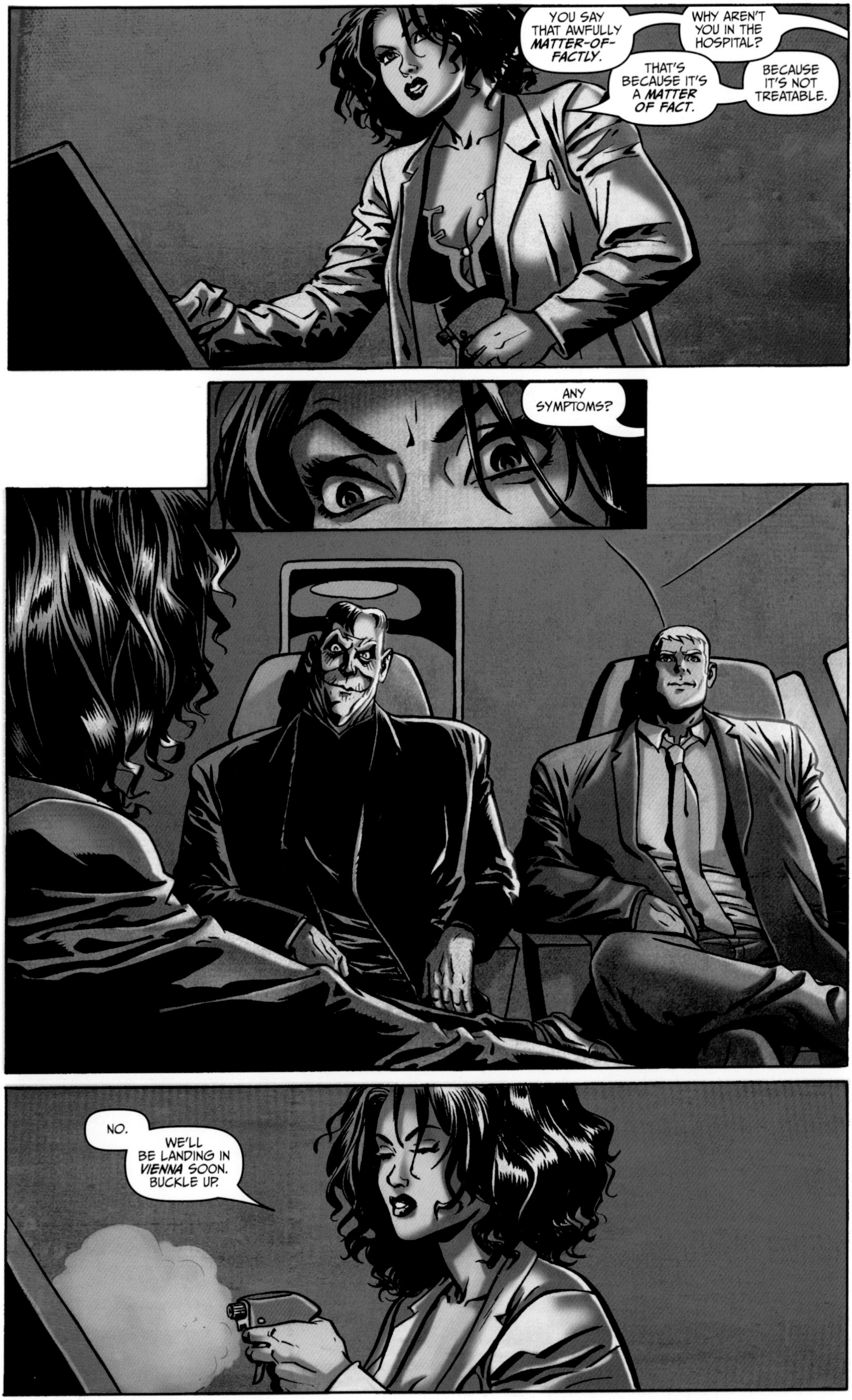
YOU SAY THAT AWFULLY MATTER-OF-FACTLY.
THAT'S BECAUSE IT'S A MATTER OF FACT.
WHY AREN'T YOU IN THE HOSPITAL?
BECAUSE IT'S NOT TREATABLE.
ANY SYMPTOMS?
NO.
WE'LL BE LANDING IN VIENNA SOON. BUCKLE UP.

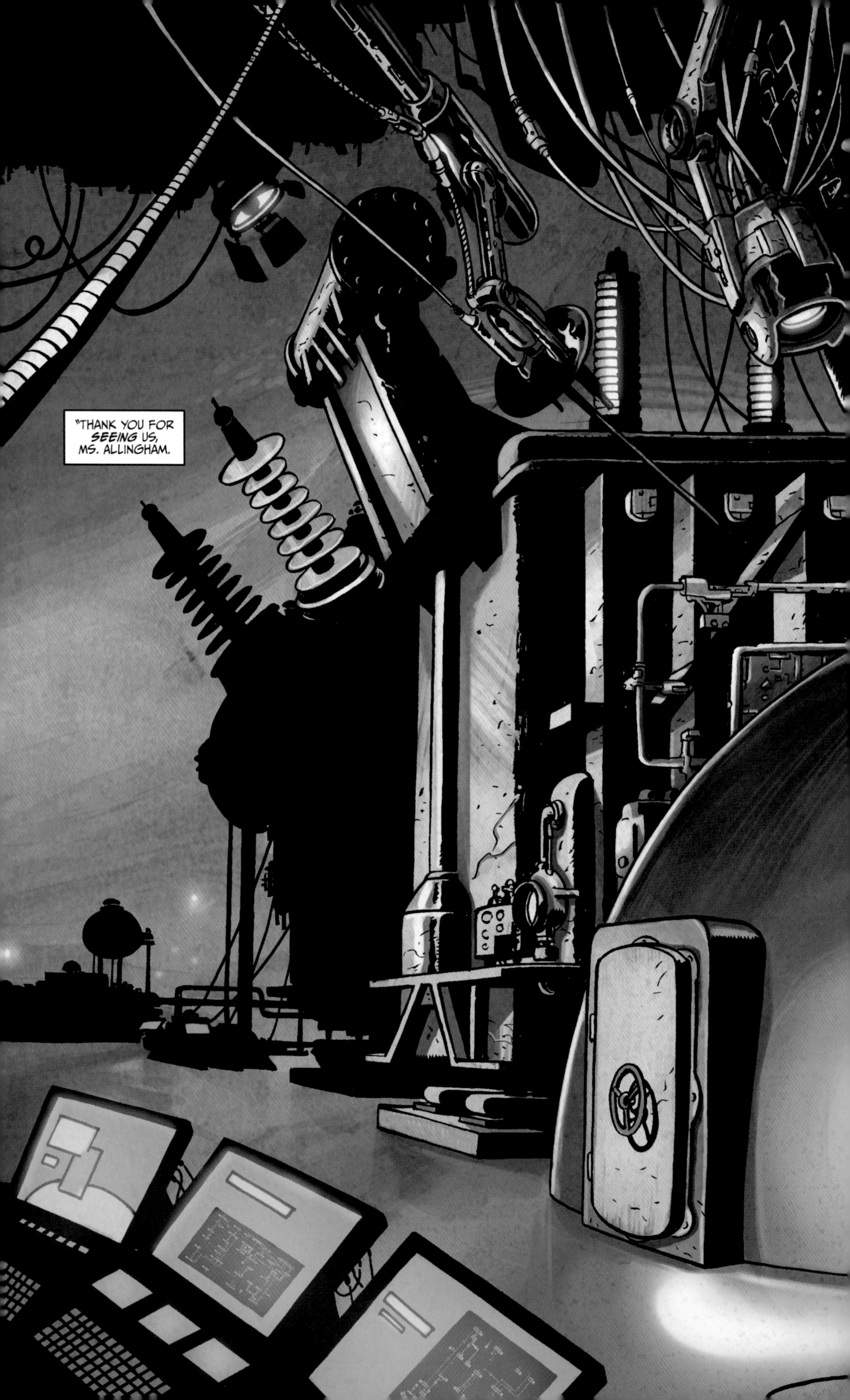
"THANK YOU FOR *SEEING* US, MS. ALLINGHAM.

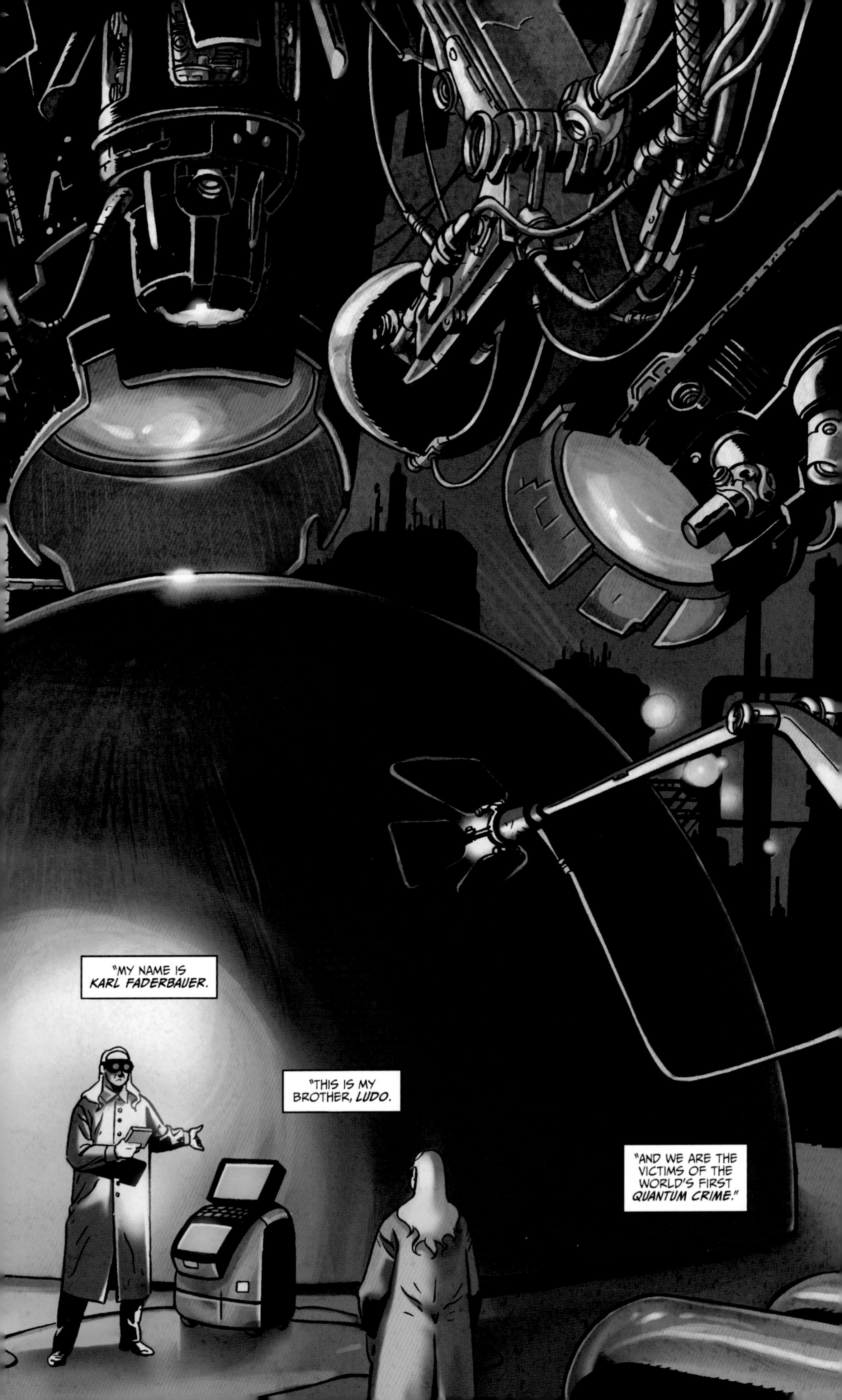
"MY NAME IS KARL FADERBAUER.
"THIS IS MY BROTHER, LUDO.
"AND WE ARE THE VICTIMS OF THE WORLD'S FIRST QUANTUM CRIME."

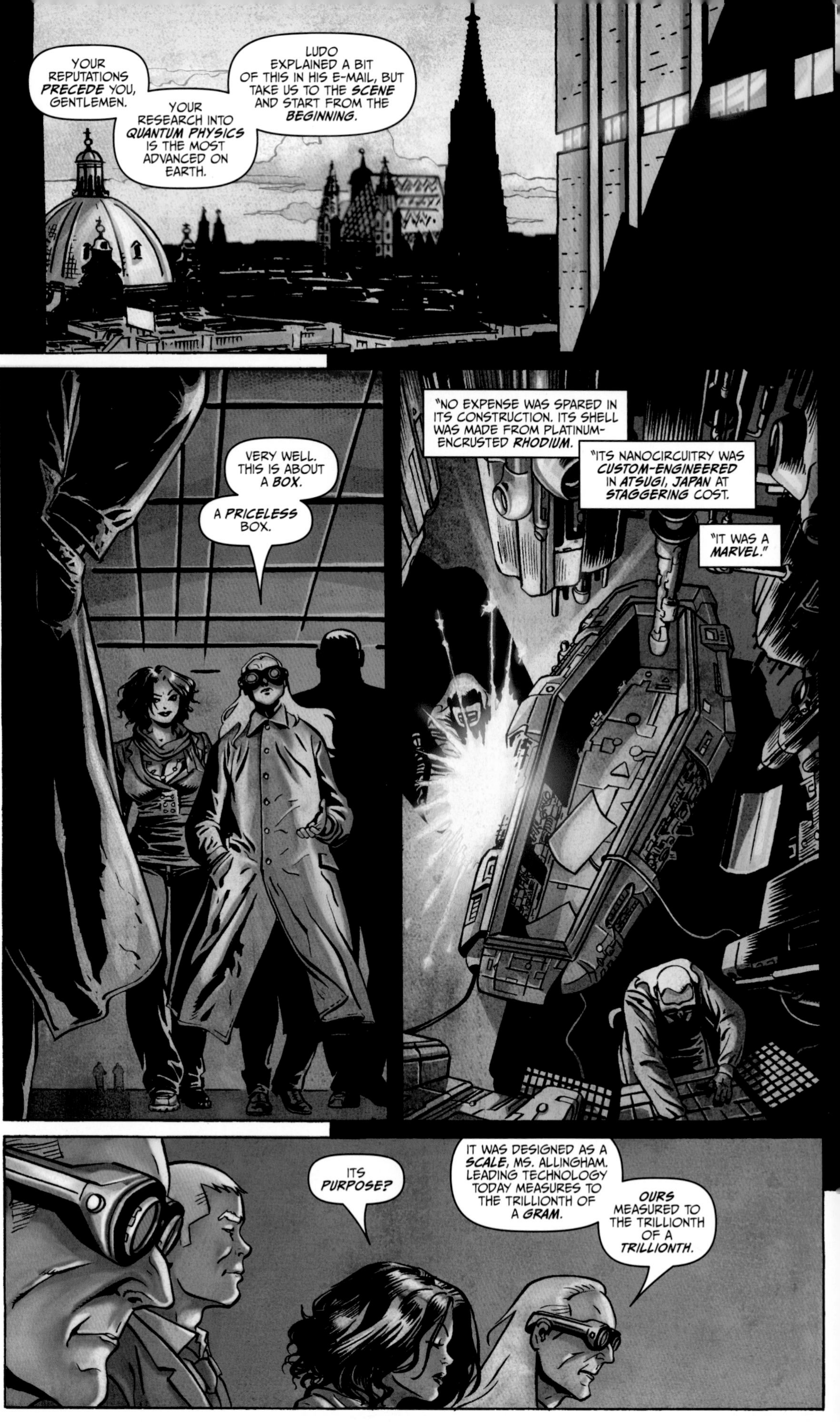
YOUR REPUTATIONS *PRECEDE* YOU, GENTLEMEN.
YOUR RESEARCH INTO *QUANTUM PHYSICS* IS THE MOST ADVANCED ON EARTH.
LUDO EXPLAINED A BIT OF THIS IN HIS E-MAIL, BUT TAKE US TO THE *SCENE* AND START FROM THE *BEGINNING*.
VERY WELL. THIS IS ABOUT A *BOX*.
A *PRICELESS* BOX.
"NO EXPENSE WAS SPARED IN ITS CONSTRUCTION. ITS SHELL WAS MADE FROM PLATINUM-ENCRUSTED *RHODIUM*.
"ITS NANOCIRCUITRY WAS *CUSTOM-ENGINEERED* IN *ATSUGI, JAPAN* AT *STAGGERING* COST.
"IT WAS A *MARVEL*."
ITS *PURPOSE?*
IT WAS DESIGNED AS A *SCALE*, MS. ALLINGHAM. LEADING TECHNOLOGY TODAY MEASURES TO THE TRILLIONTH OF A *GRAM*.
OURS MEASURED TO THE TRILLIONTH OF A *TRILLIONTH*.

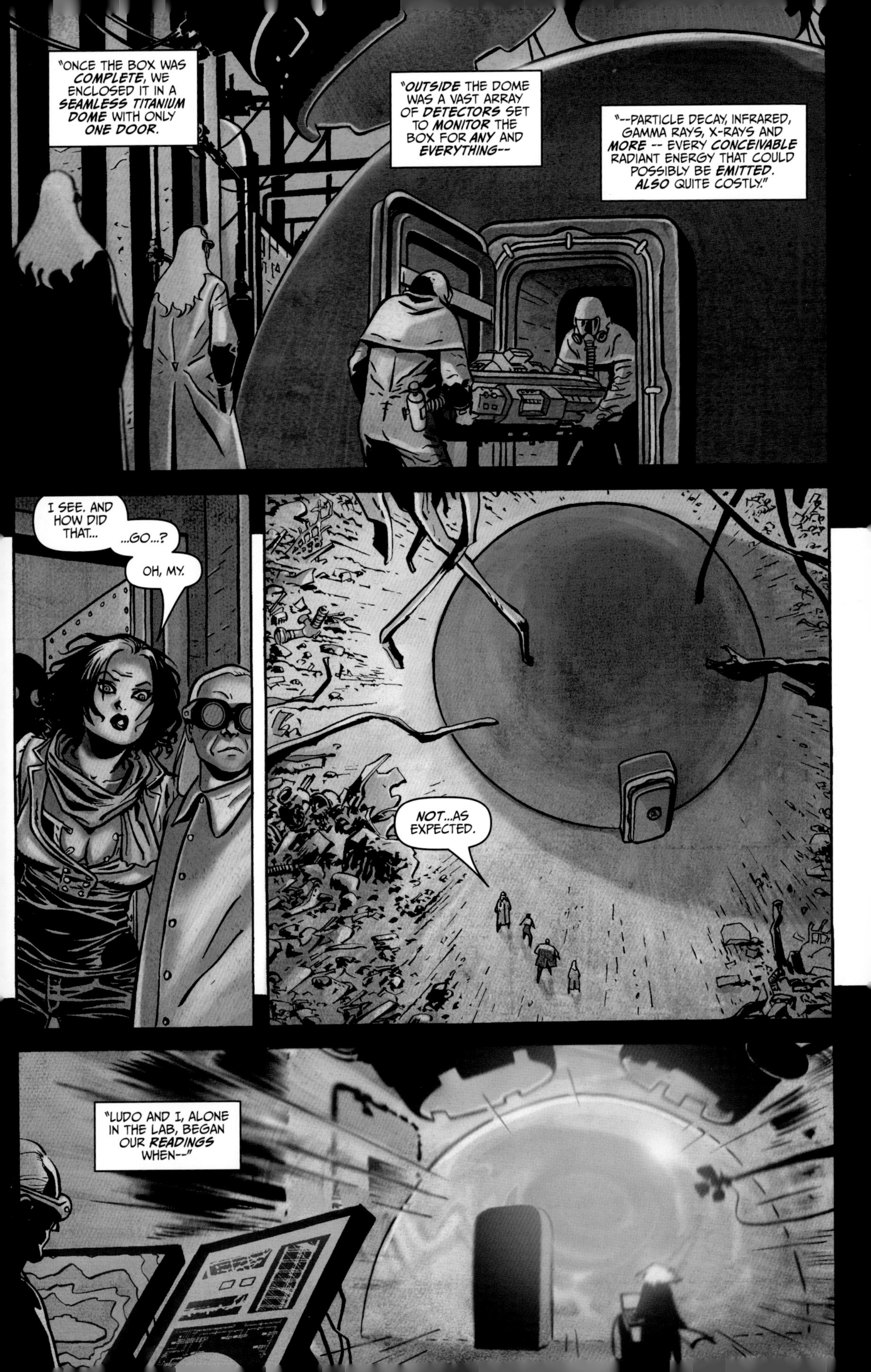
"ONCE THE BOX WAS COMPLETE, WE ENCLOSED IT IN A SEAMLESS TITANIUM DOME WITH ONLY ONE DOOR.
"OUTSIDE THE DOME WAS A VAST ARRAY OF DETECTORS SET TO MONITOR THE BOX FOR ANY AND EVERYTHING--
"--PARTICLE DECAY, INFRARED, GAMMA RAYS, X-RAYS AND MORE -- EVERY CONCEIVABLE RADIANT ENERGY THAT COULD POSSIBLY BE EMITTED. ALSO QUITE COSTLY."
I SEE. AND HOW DID THAT...
...GO...?
OH, MY.
NOT...AS EXPECTED.
"LUDO AND I, ALONE IN THE LAB, BEGAN OUR READINGS WHEN--"

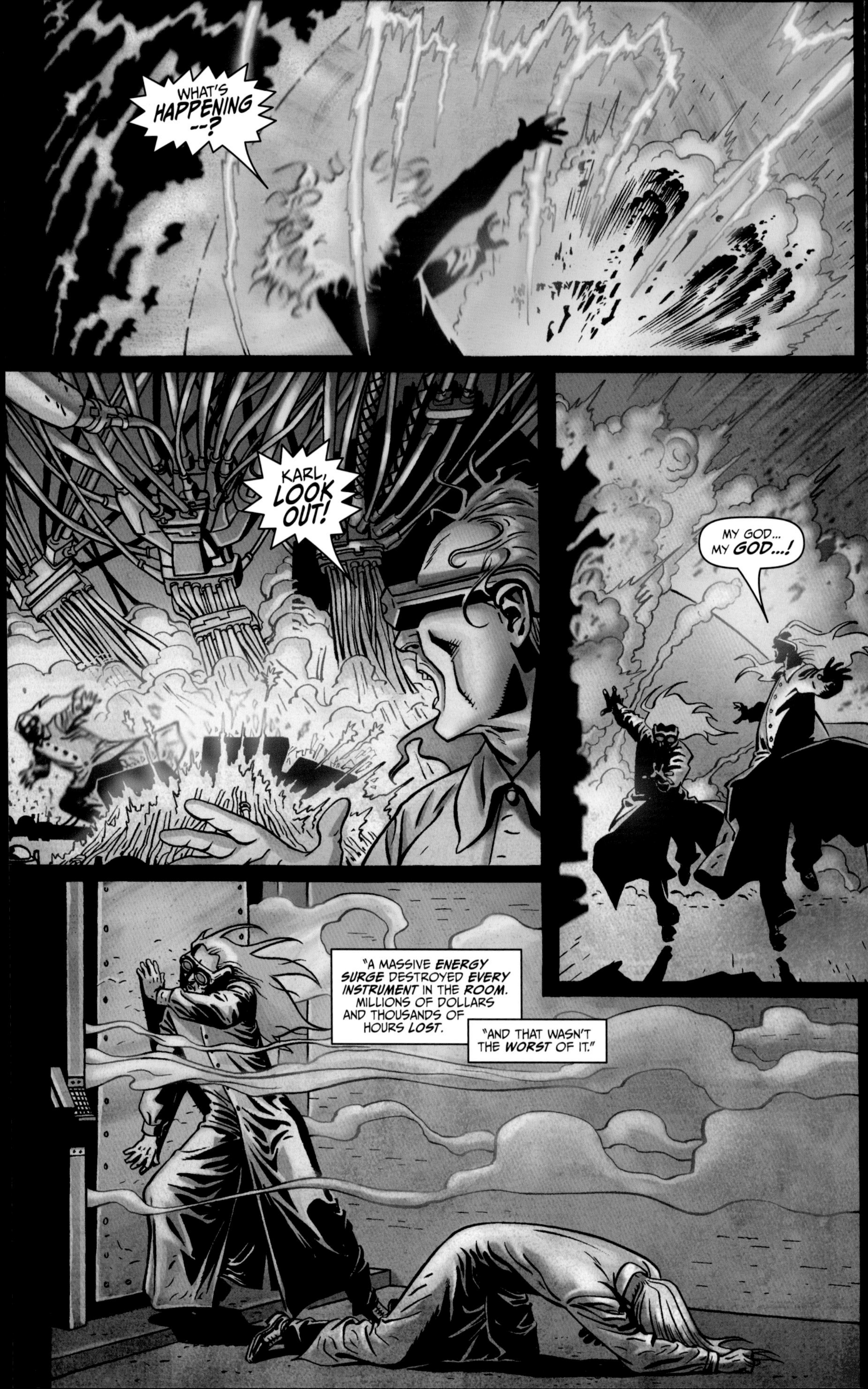
WHAT'S HAPPENING --?
KARL, LOOK OUT!
MY GOD... MY GOD...!
"A MASSIVE ENERGY SURGE DESTROYED EVERY INSTRUMENT IN THE ROOM. MILLIONS OF DOLLARS AND THOUSANDS OF HOURS LOST.
"AND THAT WASN'T THE WORST OF IT."

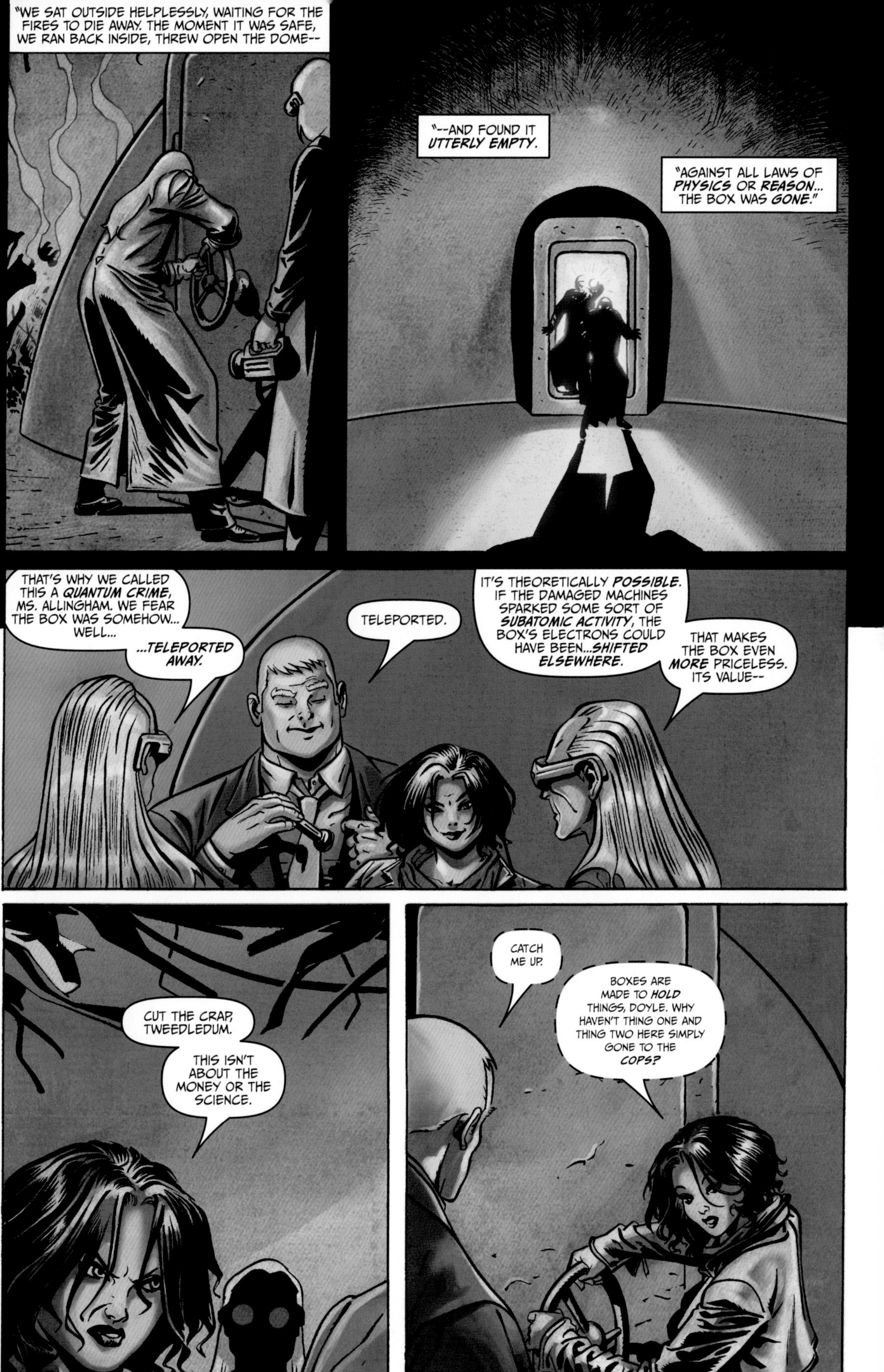
"WE SAT OUTSIDE HELPLESSLY, WAITING FOR THE FIRES TO DIE AWAY. THE MOMENT IT WAS SAFE, WE RAN BACK INSIDE, THREW OPEN THE DOME--
"--AND FOUND IT UTTERLY EMPTY.
"AGAINST ALL LAWS OF PHYSICS OR REASON... THE BOX WAS GONE."
THAT'S WHY WE CALLED THIS A QUANTUM CRIME, MS. ALLINGHAM. WE FEAR THE BOX WAS SOMEHOW... WELL...
...TELEPORTED AWAY.
TELEPORTED.
IT'S THEORETICALLY POSSIBLE. IF THE DAMAGED MACHINES SPARKED SOME SORT OF SUBATOMIC ACTIVITY, THE BOX'S ELECTRONS COULD HAVE BEEN...SHIFTED ELSEWHERE.
THAT MAKES THE BOX EVEN MORE PRICELESS. ITS VALUE--
CUT THE CRAP, TWEEDLEDUM.
THIS ISN'T ABOUT THE MONEY OR THE SCIENCE.
CATCH ME UP.
BOXES ARE MADE TO HOLD THINGS, DOYLE. WHY HAVEN'T THING ONE AND THING TWO HERE SIMPLY GONE TO THE COPS?

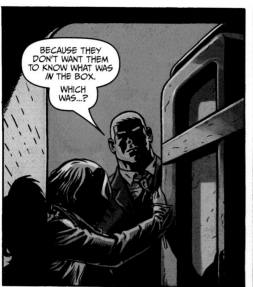

BECAUSE THEY DON'T WANT THEM TO KNOW WHAT WAS *IN THE BOX.*

WHICH WAS...?

A HUMAN BEING.

THIS IS WHY I TOOK THE *CASE,* DOYLE. I'VE READ UP QUITE A BIT MYSELF ON THIS SUBJECT. WHAT WERE THEY TESTING *FOR?*

COMBING THE ENTIRE ELECTROMAGNETIC SPECTRUM? DESIGNING SCALES THAT CAN WEIGH A *SINGLE ATOM?*

THERE'S ONLY ONE IMAGINABLE APPLICATION FOR THAT LEVEL OF PRECISION, DOYLE.

THE FADERBAUERS HAVE BUILT A MACHINE TO MEASURE THE *HUMAN SOUL.*

CHAPTER TWO

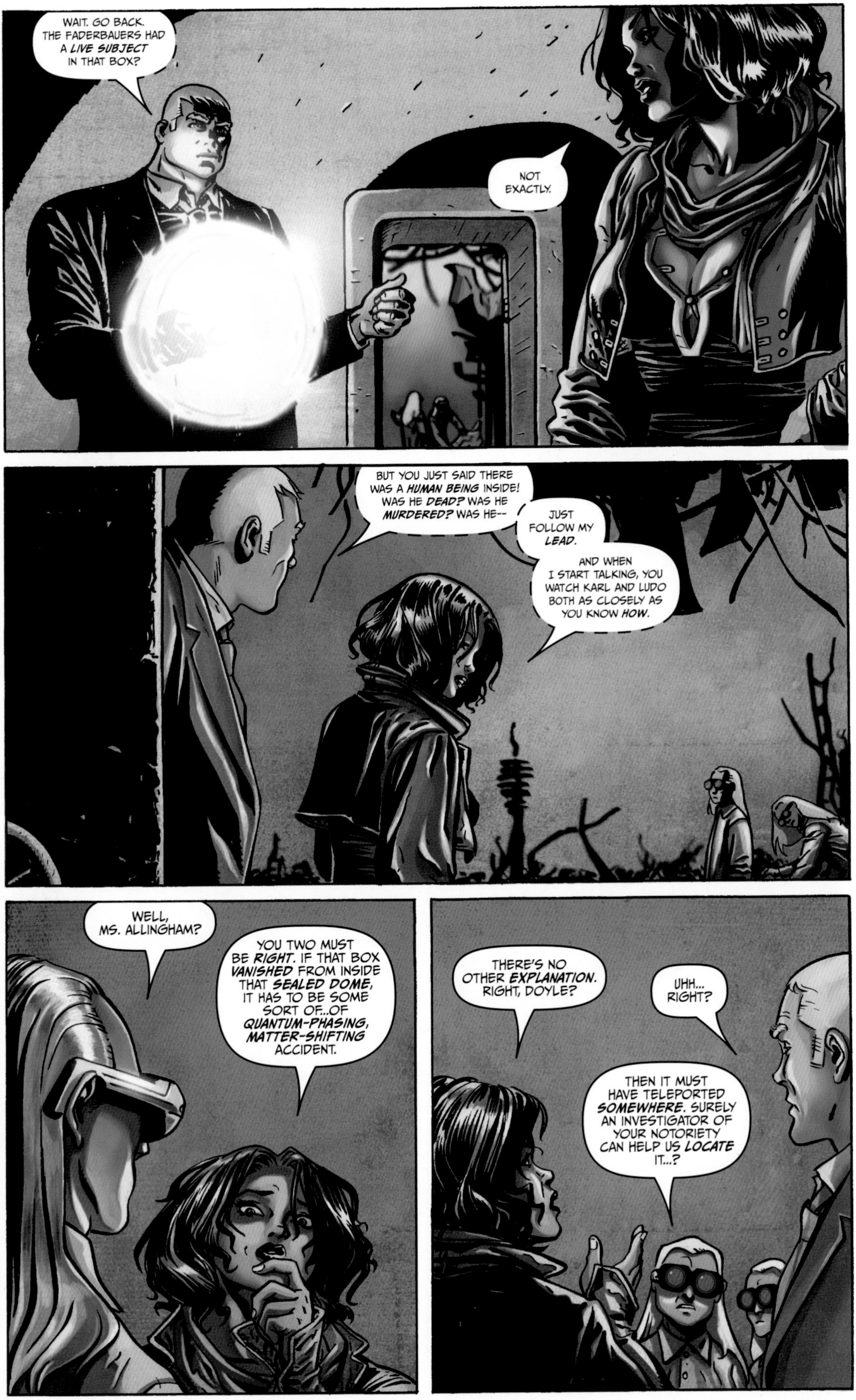

WAIT. GO BACK. THE FADERBAUERS HAD A LIVE SUBJECT IN THAT BOX?
NOT EXACTLY.
BUT YOU JUST SAID THERE WAS A HUMAN BEING INSIDE! WAS HE DEAD? WAS HE MURDERED? WAS HE--
JUST FOLLOW MY LEAD.
AND WHEN I START TALKING, YOU WATCH KARL AND LUDO BOTH AS CLOSELY AS YOU KNOW HOW.
WELL, MS. ALLINGHAM?
YOU TWO MUST BE RIGHT. IF THAT BOX VANISHED FROM INSIDE THAT SEALED DOME, IT HAS TO BE SOME SORT OF...OF QUANTUM-PHASING, MATTER-SHIFTING ACCIDENT.
THERE'S NO OTHER EXPLANATION. RIGHT, DOYLE?
UHH... RIGHT?
THEN IT MUST HAVE TELEPORTED SOMEWHERE. SURELY AN INVESTIGATOR OF YOUR NOTORIETY CAN HELP US LOCATE IT...?

WHO, *ME?* OH, WOW, *NO.* ALL THIS *SUBATOMIC WHAMMERY-FLAMMERY...* WELL...

...WHOO! THAT STUFF'S JUST BEYOND *ME,* Y'KNOW? MESONS, BOSONS...I'M REALLY OUT OF MY *ELEMENT* HERE. SORRY, GENTLEMEN.

BUT--

GOOD LUCK IN YOUR *HUNT.* NO CHARGE FOR THE *HOUSE CALL.*

C'MON, DOYLE.

FADERBAUER TECHNIK AG

"WHAMMERY-FLAMMERY"?

YOU READ PEOPLE. HOW DID THEY *REACT* TO THAT? WERE THEY GENUINELY *DISAPPOINTED,* OR...?

LUDO WAS. KARL, ON THE OTHER HAND, WAS *FEIGNING.* I'D SWEAR HE WAS FIGHTING NOT TO *SMILE.*

YOU'RE CERTAIN?

I'D SAY.

BEAUTIFUL.

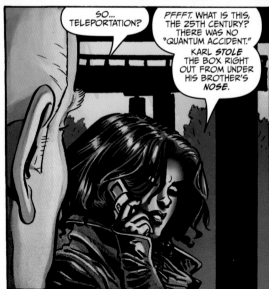

SO... TELEPORTATION?

PFFFT. WHAT IS THIS, THE 25TH CENTURY? THERE WAS NO "QUANTUM ACCIDENT." KARL *STOLE* THE BOX RIGHT OUT FROM UNDER HIS BROTHER'S *NOSE.*

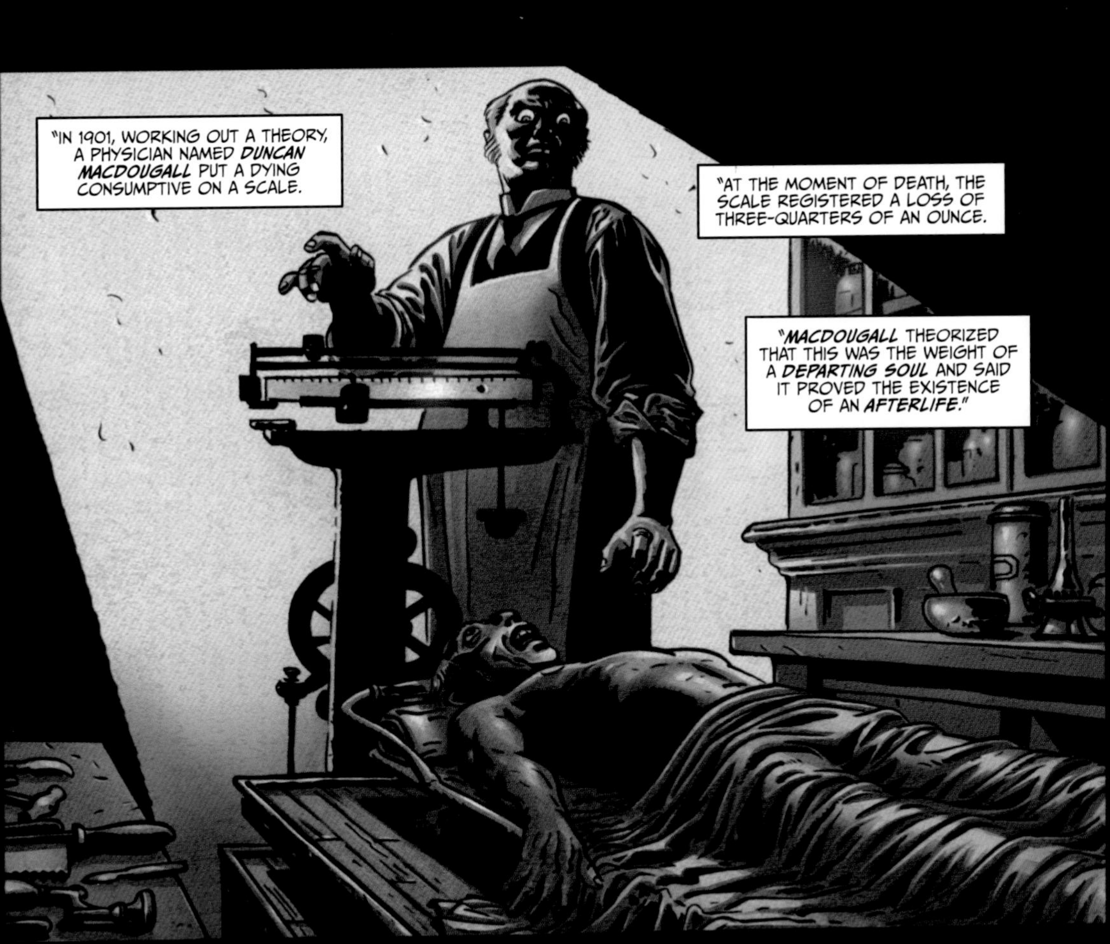
"IN 1901, WORKING OUT A THEORY, A PHYSICIAN NAMED DUNCAN MACDOUGALL PUT A DYING CONSUMPTIVE ON A SCALE.
"AT THE MOMENT OF DEATH, THE SCALE REGISTERED A LOSS OF THREE-QUARTERS OF AN OUNCE.
"MACDOUGALL THEORIZED THAT THIS WAS THE WEIGHT OF A DEPARTING SOUL AND SAID IT PROVED THE EXISTENCE OF AN AFTERLIFE."

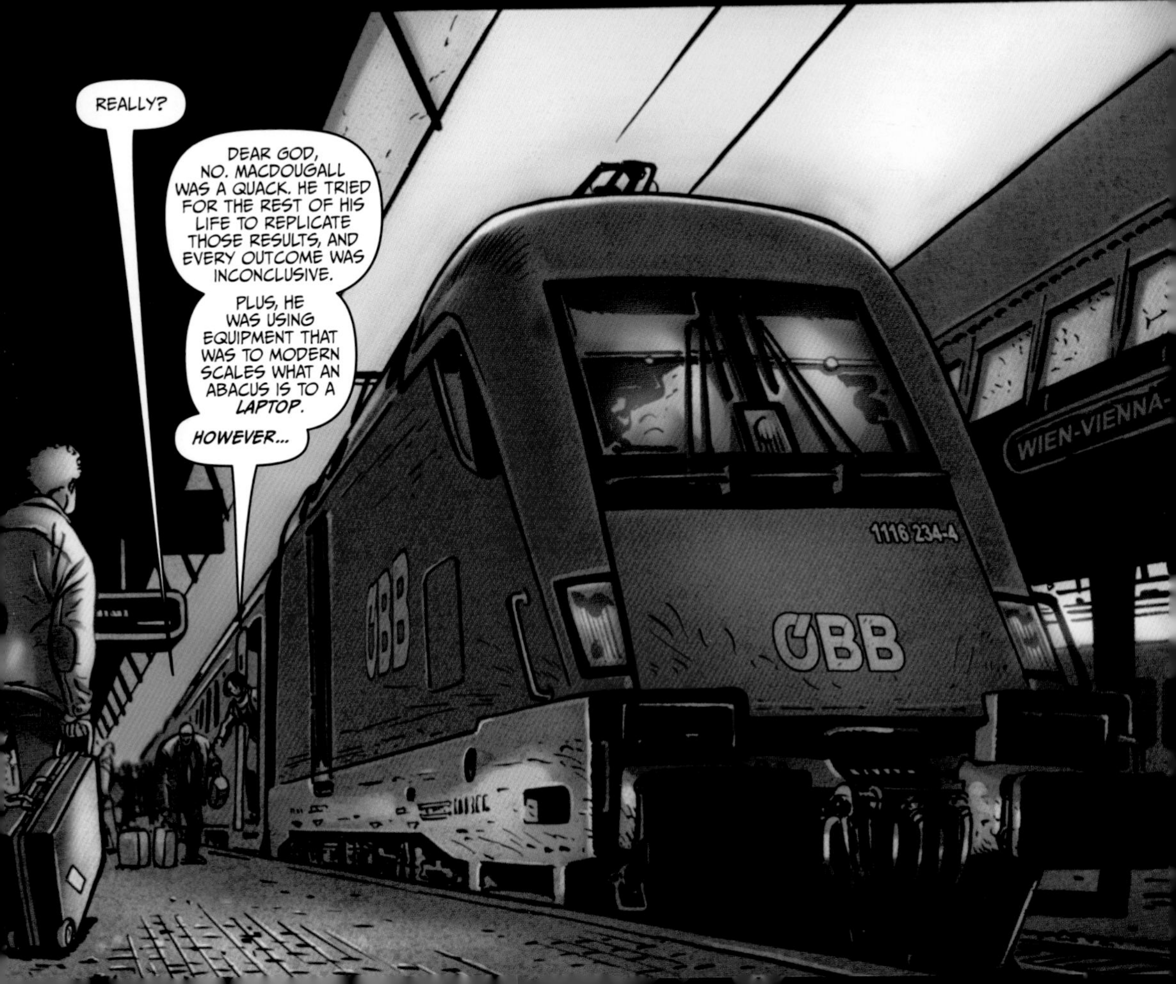
REALLY?
DEAR GOD, NO. MACDOUGALL WAS A QUACK. HE TRIED FOR THE REST OF HIS LIFE TO REPLICATE THOSE RESULTS, AND EVERY OUTCOME WAS INCONCLUSIVE.
PLUS, HE WAS USING EQUIPMENT THAT WAS TO MODERN SCALES WHAT AN ABACUS IS TO A LAPTOP.
HOWEVER...
WIEN-VIENNA-
1116 234-4
ÖBB
ÖBB

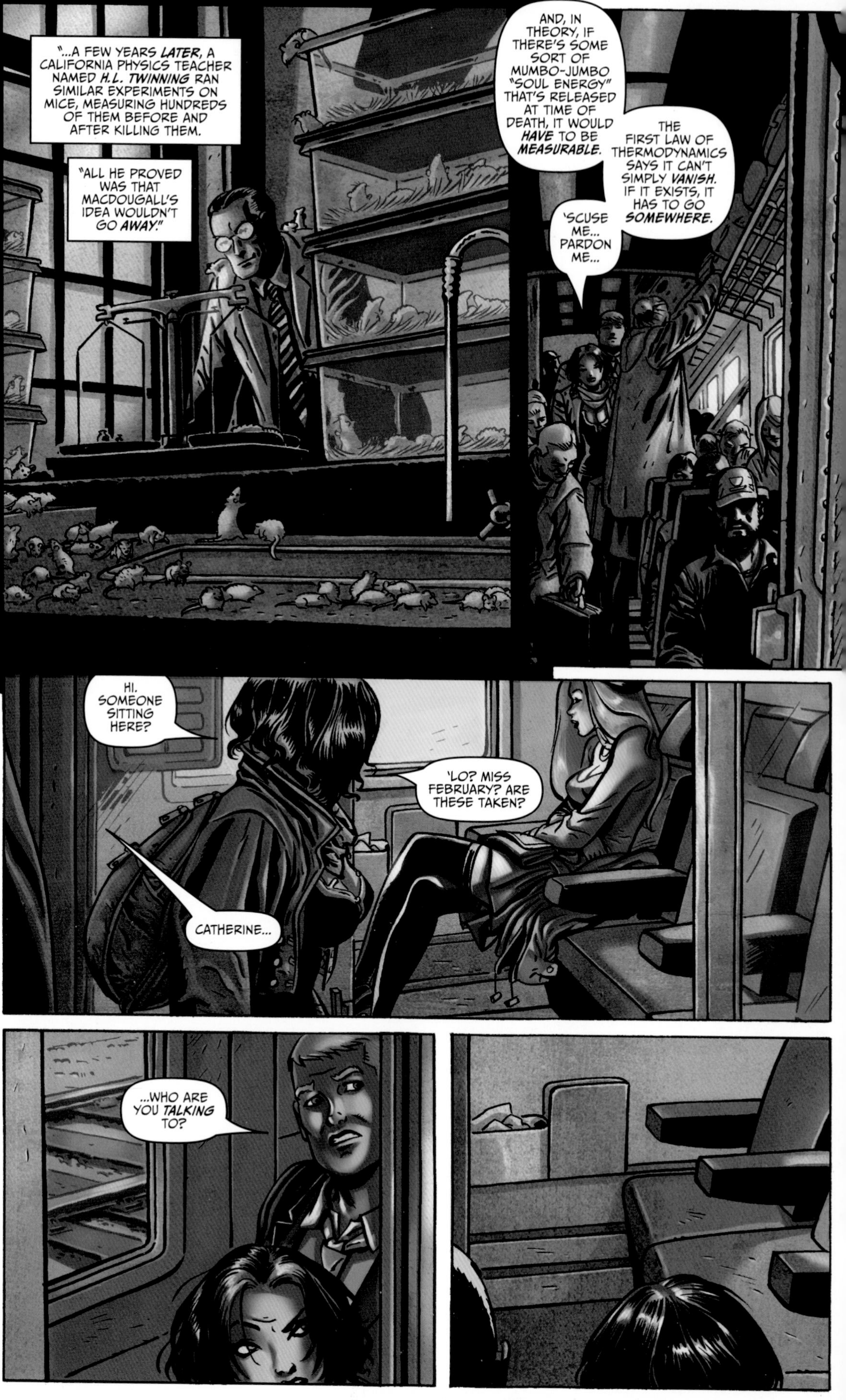
"...A FEW YEARS LATER, A CALIFORNIA PHYSICS TEACHER NAMED H.L. TWINNING RAN SIMILAR EXPERIMENTS ON MICE, MEASURING HUNDREDS OF THEM BEFORE AND AFTER KILLING THEM.
"ALL HE PROVED WAS THAT MACDOUGALL'S IDEA WOULDN'T GO AWAY."
AND, IN THEORY, IF THERE'S SOME SORT OF MUMBO-JUMBO "SOUL ENERGY" THAT'S RELEASED AT TIME OF DEATH, IT WOULD HAVE TO BE MEASURABLE.
THE FIRST LAW OF THERMODYNAMICS SAYS IT CAN'T SIMPLY VANISH. IF IT EXISTS, IT HAS TO GO SOMEWHERE.
'SCUSE ME... PARDON ME...
HI. SOMEONE SITTING HERE?
'LO? MISS FEBRUARY? ARE THESE TAKEN?
CATHERINE...
...WHO ARE YOU TALKING TO?

I WAS JUST...

NEVER MIND. ANYWAY. SOULS. EXISTENCE.

UNTIL RECENTLY, SCIENCE COULDN'T EVEN COME *CLOSE* TO SETTLING THIS HIGHLY IMPROBABLE HYPOTHESIS. BUT QUANTUM PHYSICS GETS MORE EXACTING EVERY DAY.

SCIENTISTS AT *DUKE UNIVERSITY* ARE EXPLORING THIS "WEIGHT OF A SOUL" THING EVEN *NOW.*

BUT WHILE DUKE DOESN'T HAVE THE FUNDING TO INVENT A DEVICE THAT MEASURES THAT *MINUTELY* OR TO SURROUND IT WITH COSTLY APPARATI THAT CAN DETECT *EVERYTHING* ON THE *ELECTROMAGNETIC SPECTRUM...*

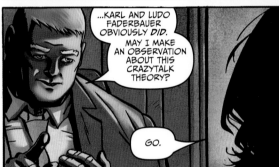

...KARL AND LUDO FADERBAUER OBVIOUSLY *DID.*

MAY I MAKE AN OBSERVATION ABOUT THIS CRAZYTALK THEORY?

GO.

YOU SOUND LIKE YOU *WANT* IT TO BE TRUE.

LET ME TELL YOU SOMETHING.

I DON'T REALLY CARE WHO STOLE WHAT FROM WHERE ANYMORE. THE MORAL ASPECTS OF THIS CRIME DON'T INTEREST ME IN THE LEAST.

THE FADERBAUERS' BOX IS ON THIS TRAIN. AND ALL THAT MATTERS TO ME...*ALL* THAT MATTERS...

...IS SEEING THAT DAMN THING *WORK.*

SHERLOCK HOLMES WAS WRONG

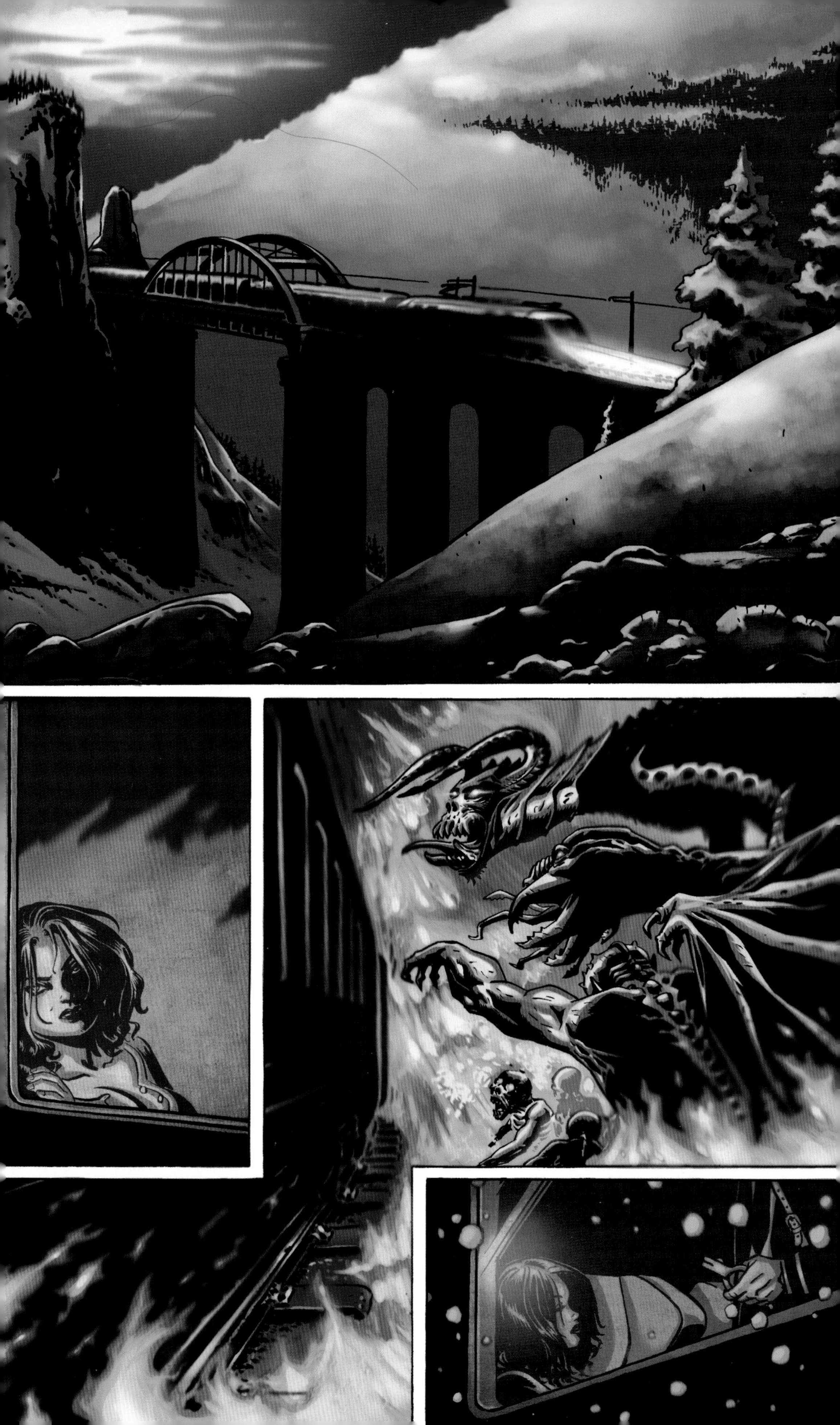

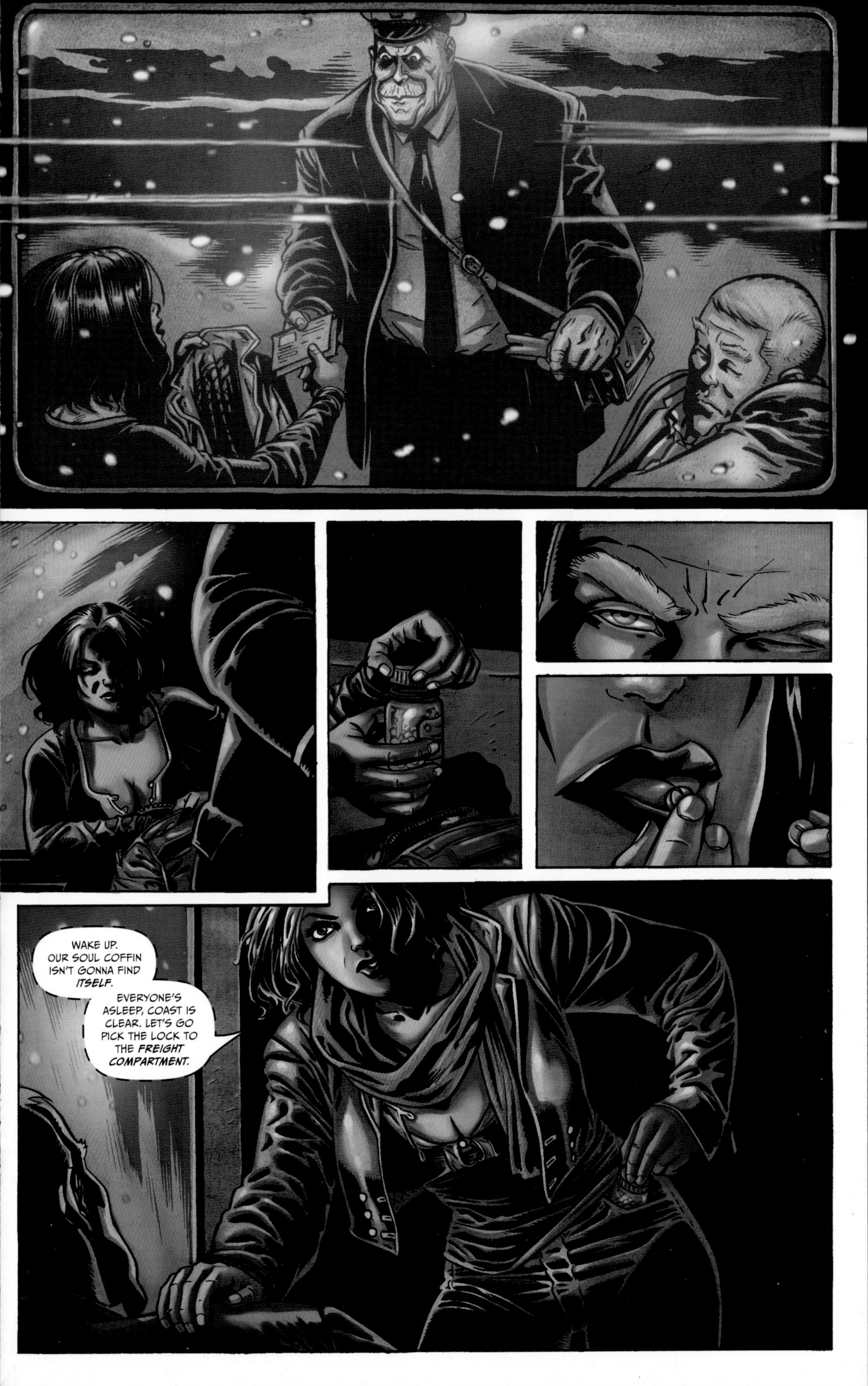
WAKE UP. OUR SOUL COFFIN ISN'T GONNA FIND *ITSELF*.
EVERYONE'S ASLEEP, COAST IS CLEAR. LET'S GO PICK THE LOCK TO THE *FREIGHT COMPARTMENT*.

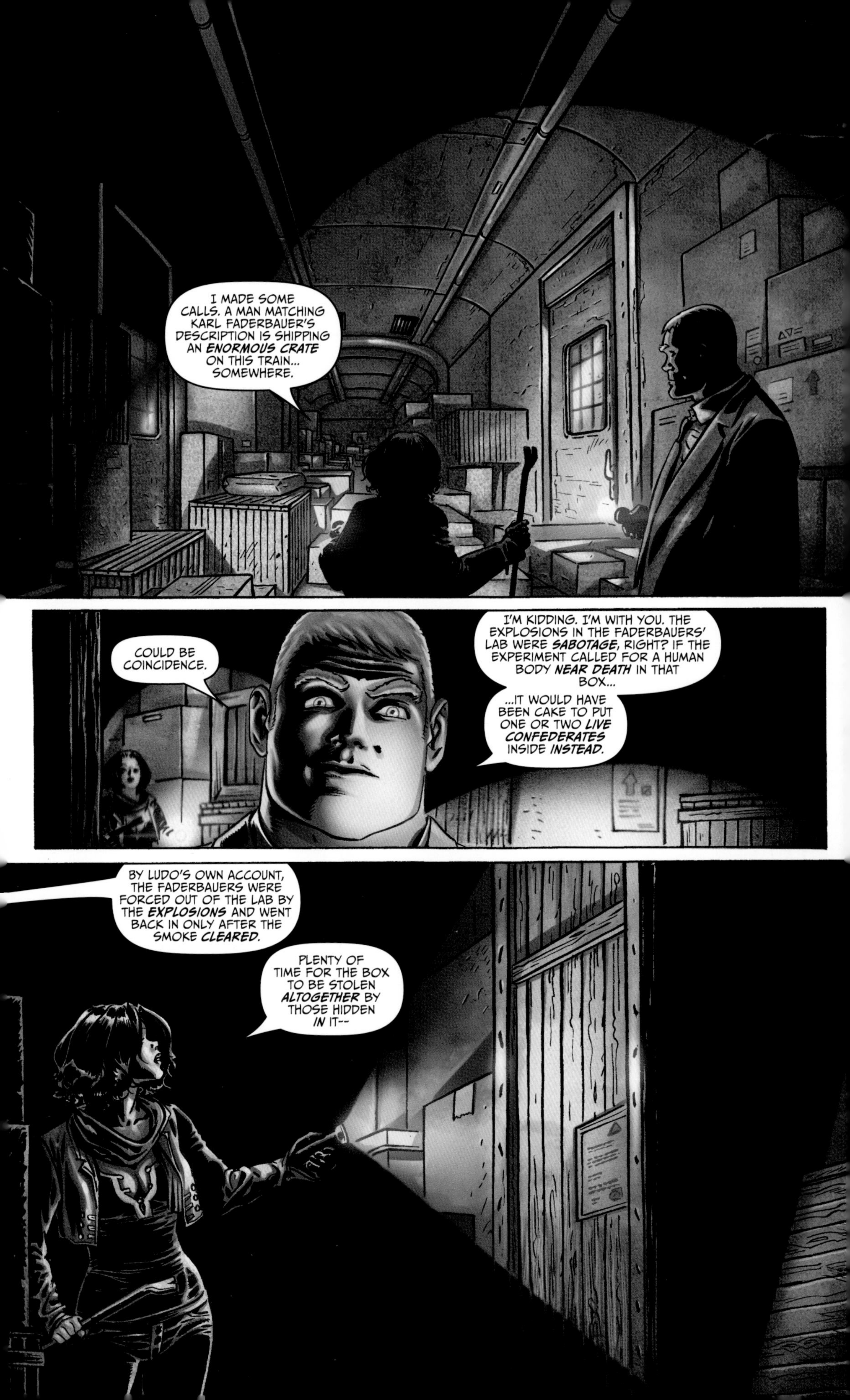

I MADE SOME CALLS. A MAN MATCHING KARL FADERBAUER'S DESCRIPTION IS SHIPPING AN ENORMOUS CRATE ON THIS TRAIN... SOMEWHERE.
COULD BE COINCIDENCE.
I'M KIDDING. I'M WITH YOU. THE EXPLOSIONS IN THE FADERBAUERS' LAB WERE SABOTAGE, RIGHT? IF THE EXPERIMENT CALLED FOR A HUMAN BODY NEAR DEATH IN THAT BOX...
...IT WOULD HAVE BEEN CAKE TO PUT ONE OR TWO LIVE CONFEDERATES INSIDE INSTEAD.
BY LUDO'S OWN ACCOUNT, THE FADERBAUERS WERE FORCED OUT OF THE LAB BY THE EXPLOSIONS AND WENT BACK IN ONLY AFTER THE SMOKE CLEARED.
PLENTY OF TIME FOR THE BOX TO BE STOLEN ALTOGETHER BY THOSE HIDDEN IN IT--

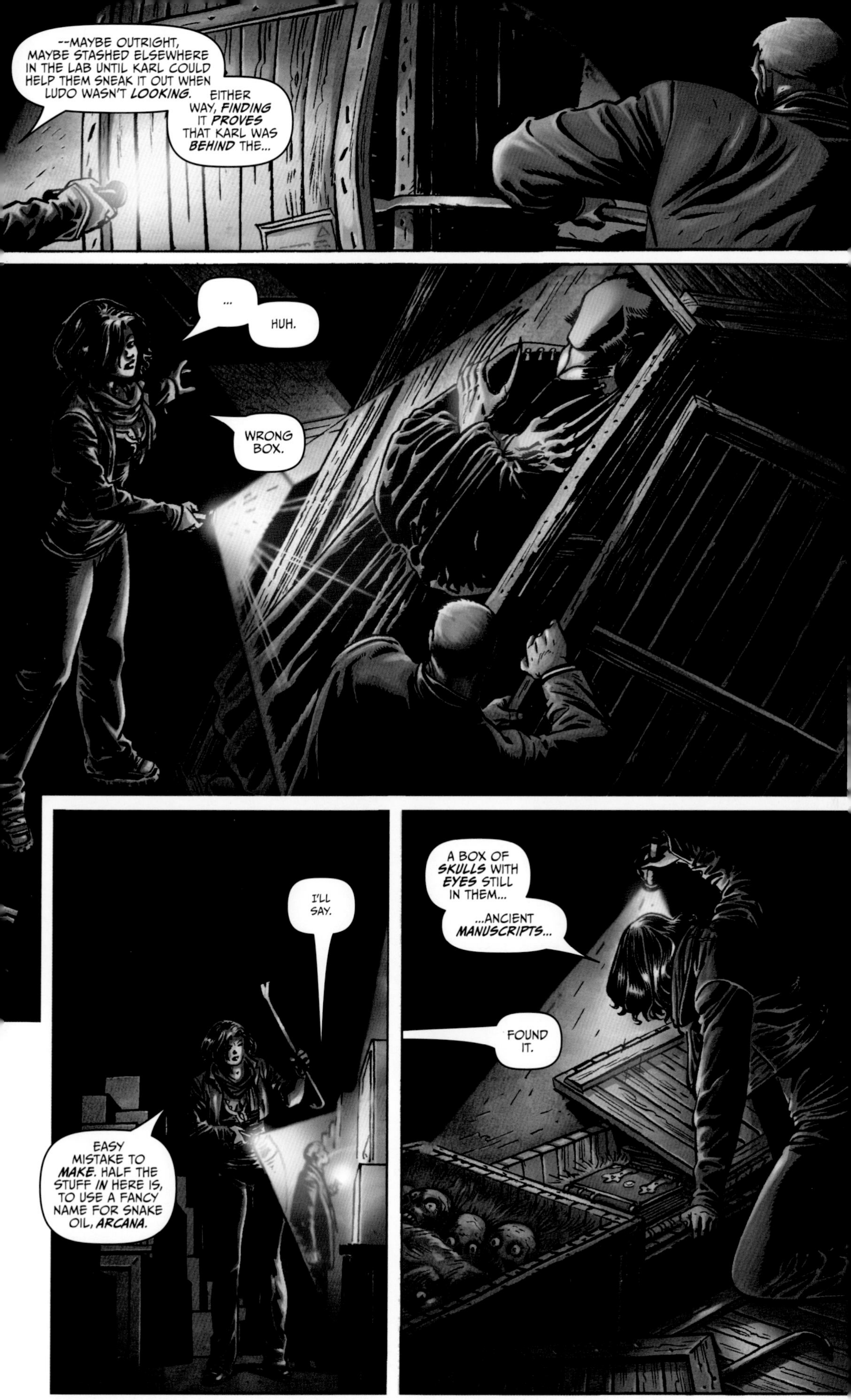
--MAYBE OUTRIGHT, MAYBE STASHED ELSEWHERE IN THE LAB UNTIL KARL COULD HELP THEM SNEAK IT OUT WHEN LUDO WASN'T *LOOKING.*
EITHER WAY, *FINDING* IT *PROVES* THAT KARL WAS *BEHIND* THE...
...
HUH.
WRONG BOX.
I'LL SAY.
EASY MISTAKE TO *MAKE*. HALF THE STUFF *IN* HERE IS, TO USE A FANCY NAME FOR SNAKE OIL, *ARCANA.*
A BOX OF *SKULLS* WITH *EYES* STILL IN THEM...
...ANCIENT *MANUSCRIPTS*...
FOUND IT.

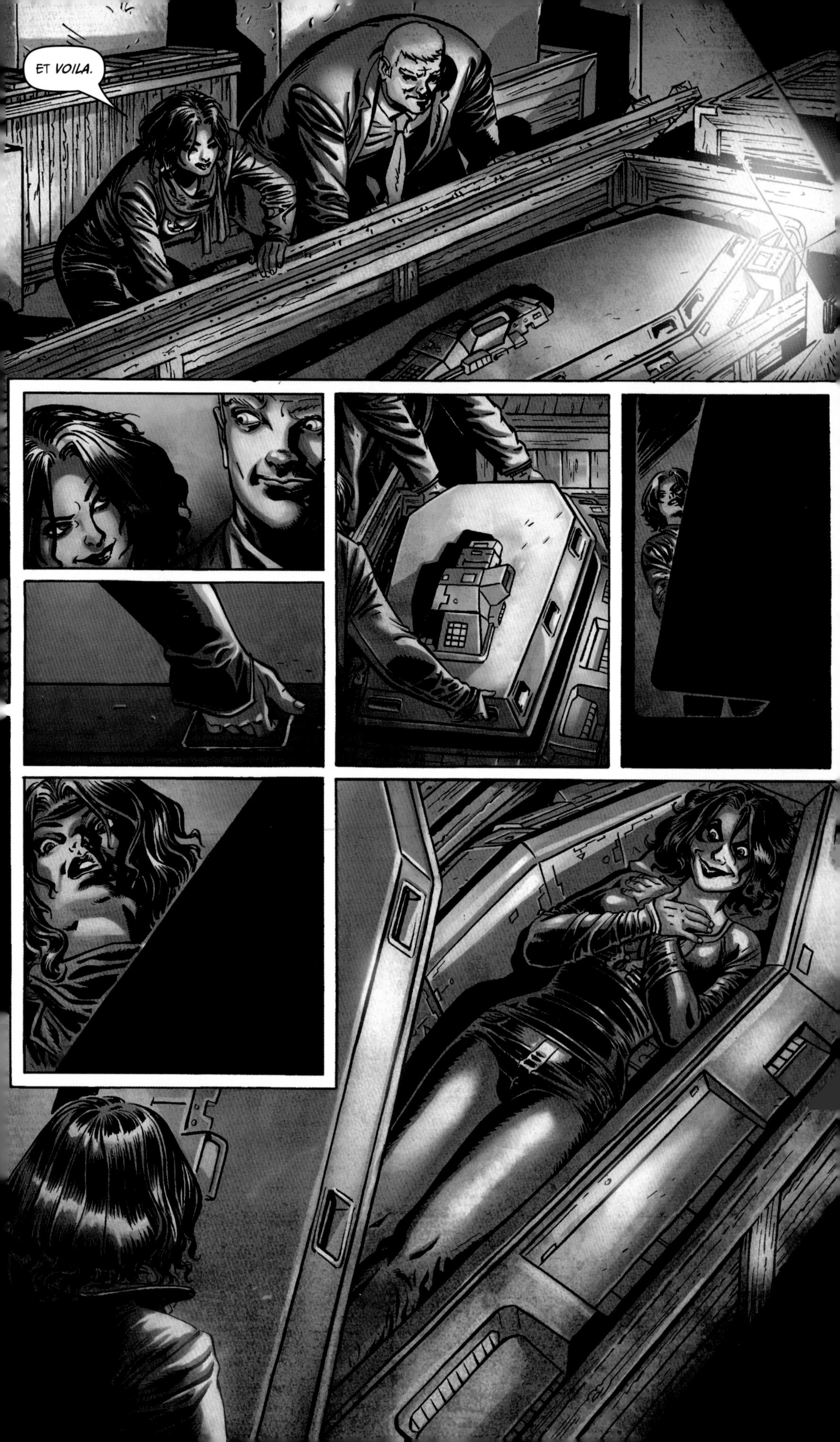
ET VOILA.

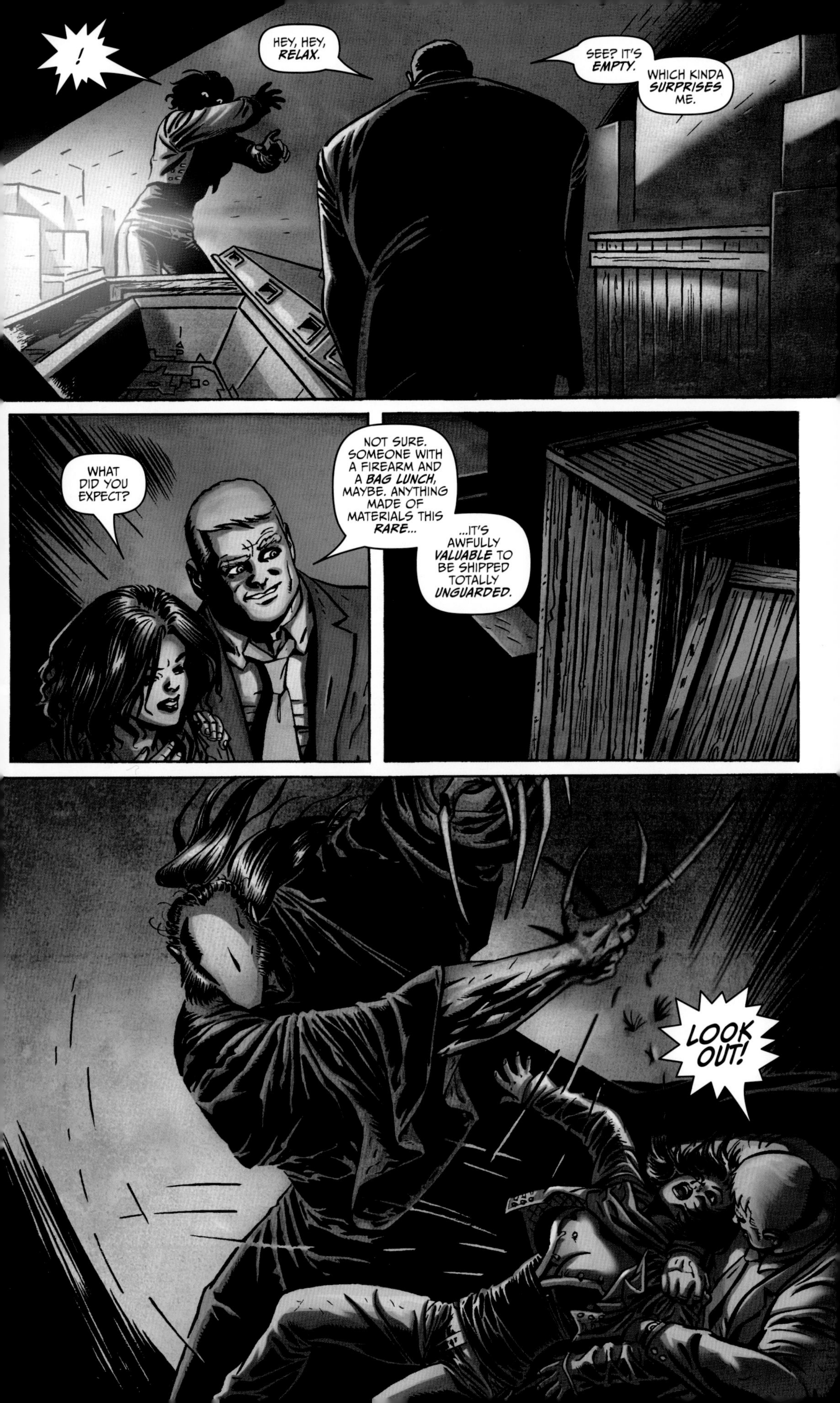

!
HEY, HEY, RELAX.
SEE? IT'S EMPTY.
WHICH KINDA SURPRISES ME.
WHAT DID YOU EXPECT?
NOT SURE. SOMEONE WITH A FIREARM AND A BAG LUNCH, MAYBE. ANYTHING MADE OF MATERIALS THIS RARE...
...IT'S AWFULLY VALUABLE TO BE SHIPPED TOTALLY UNGUARDED.
LOOK OUT!

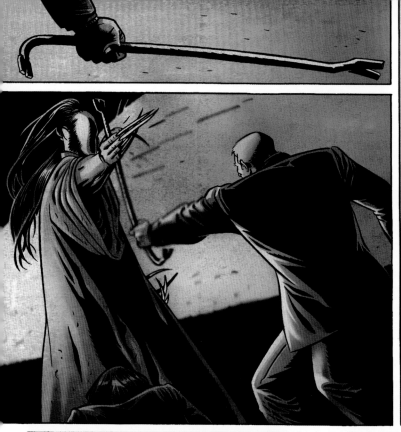

WHAT *ARE* YOU?

WHAT, ARE YOU *KIDDING ME? C'MON!*

THERE'S A *GUN* IN MY CARRY-ON!

YOU'RE NOT CARRYING *NOW?*

FORGIVE ME FOR NOT ANTICIPATING AN *ASIAN GOLEM* WITH NEEDLES FOR FINGERS!

WHAT'S HE-- *DUCK!*

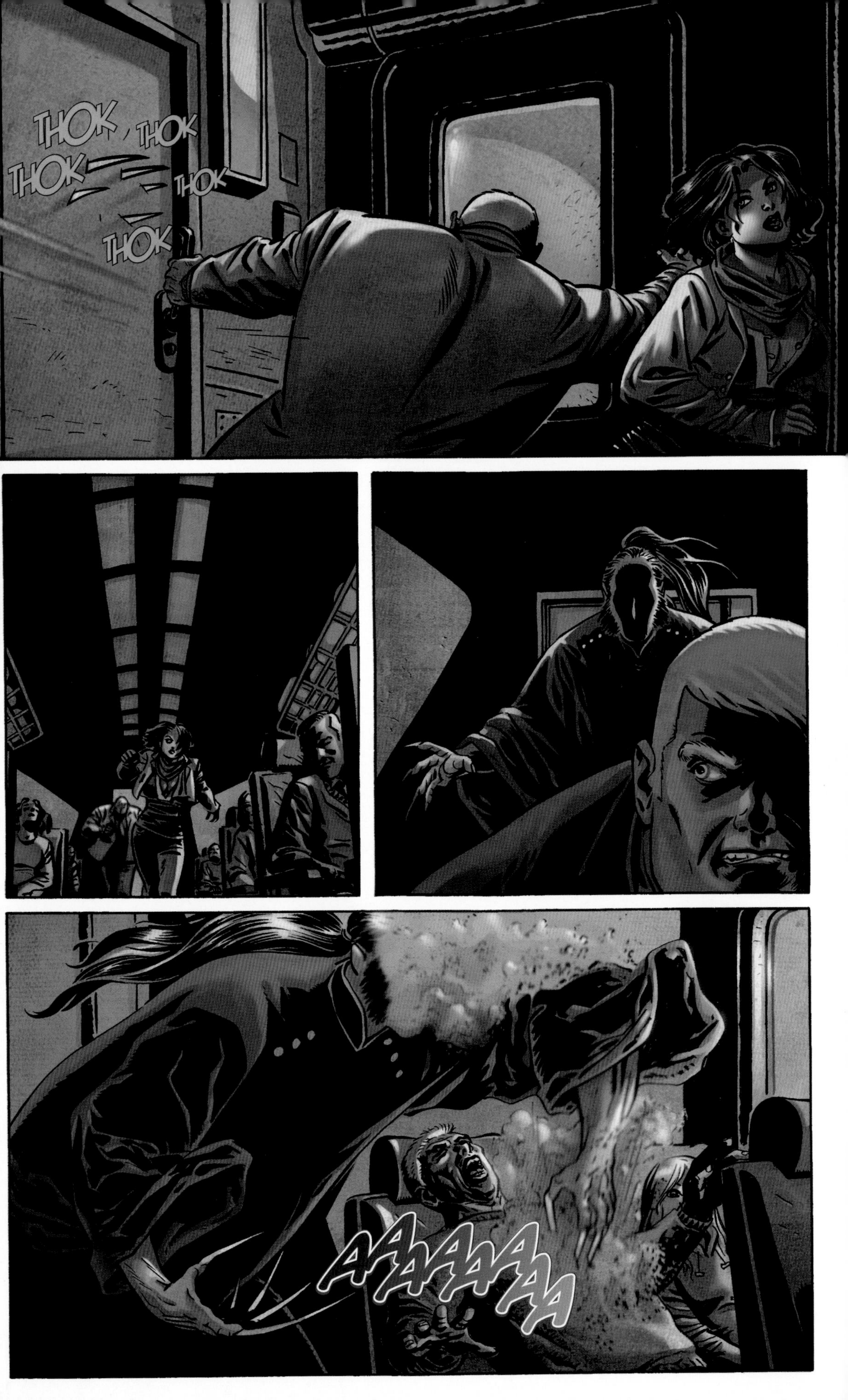
THOK THOK
THOK
THOK
THOK
AAAAAAAA

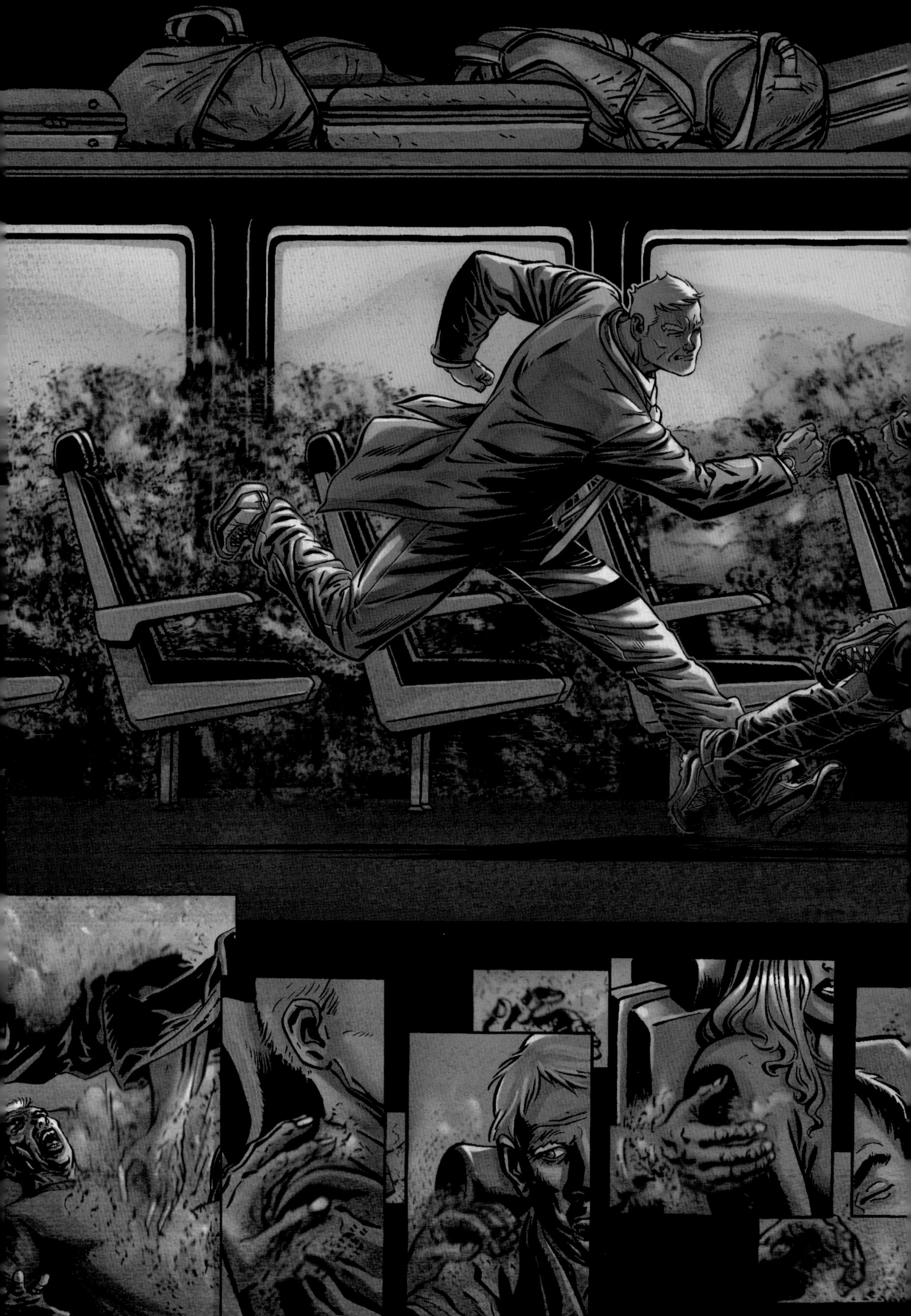

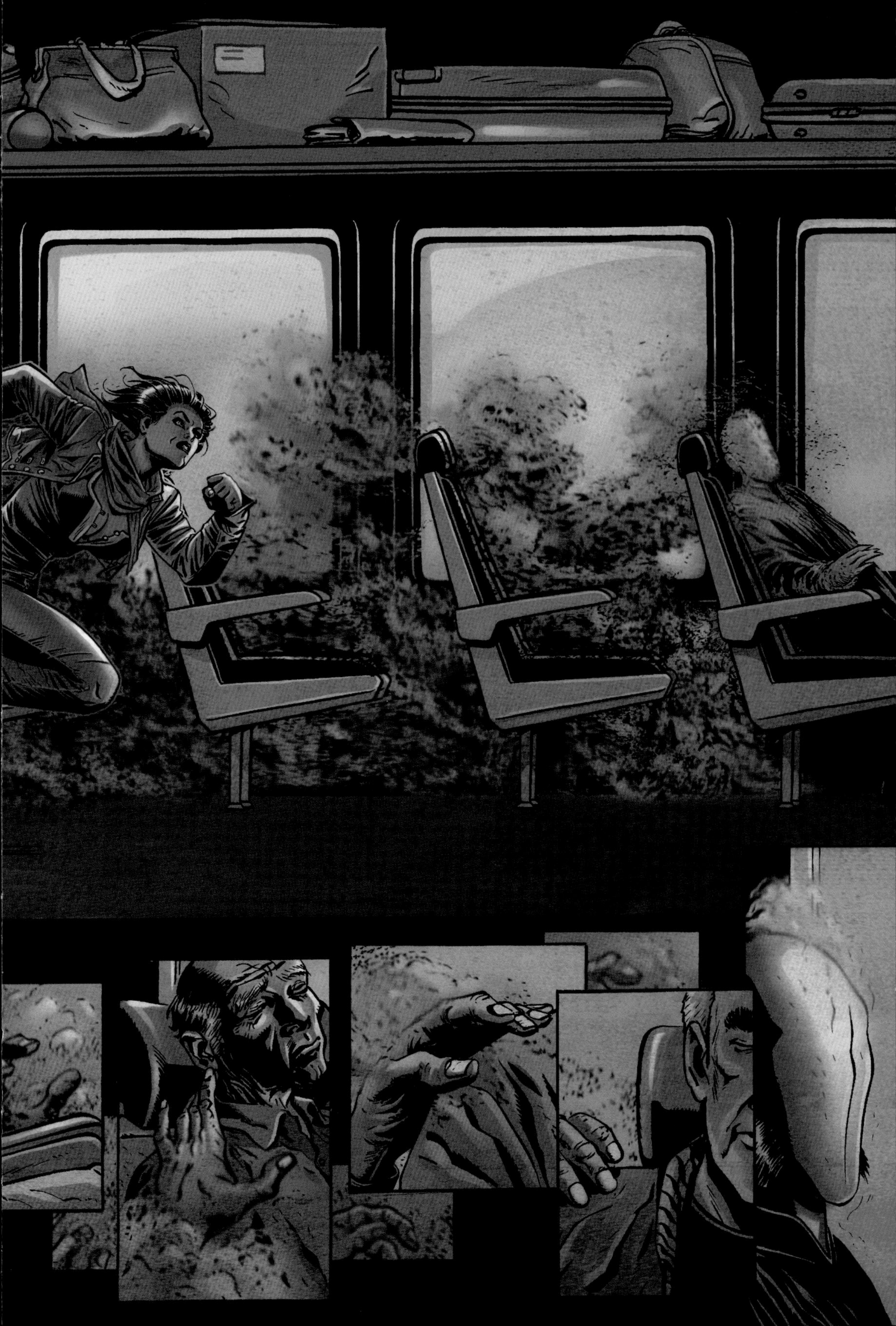

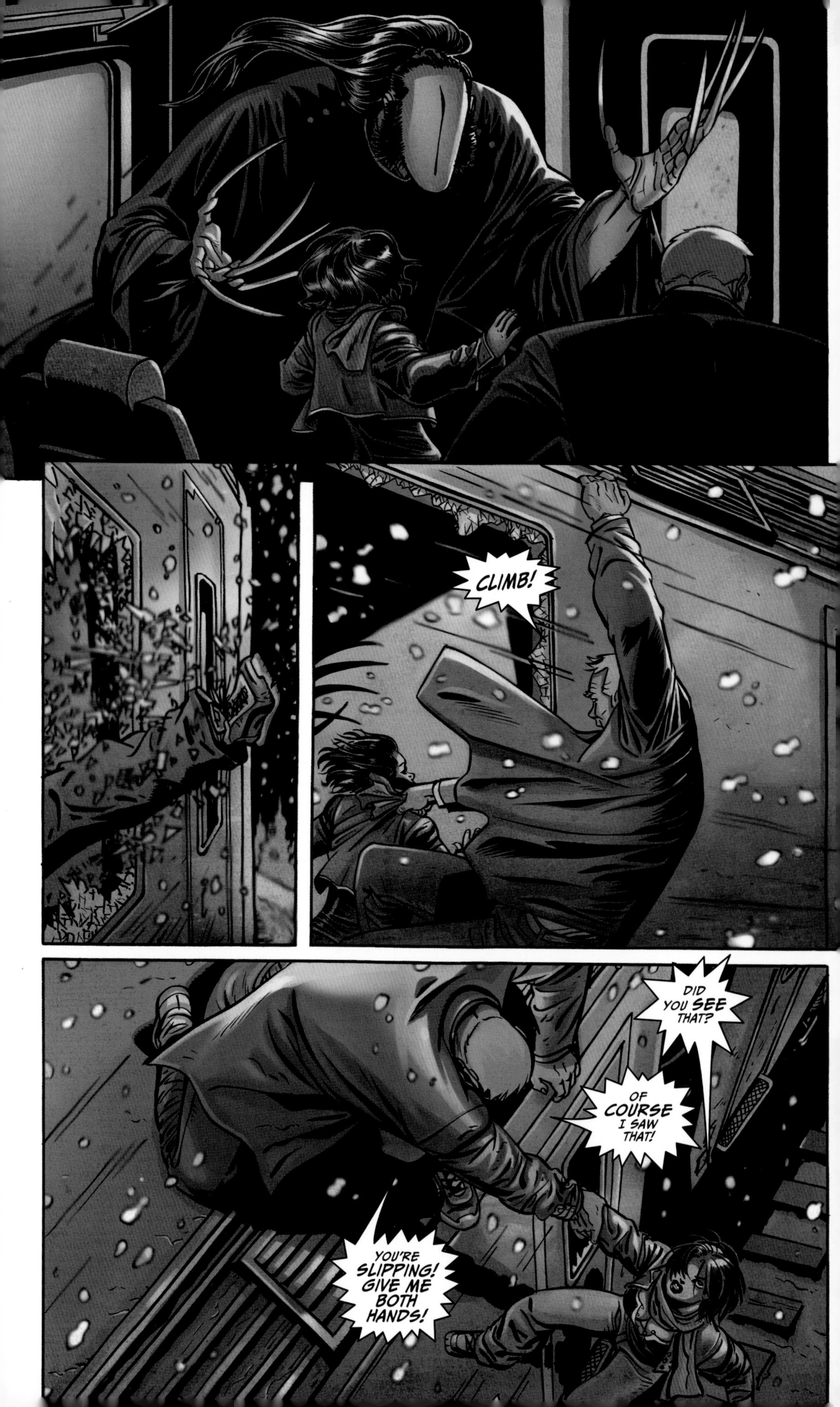
CLIMB!
DID YOU SEE THAT?
OF COURSE I SAW THAT!
YOU'RE SLIPPING! GIVE ME BOTH HANDS!

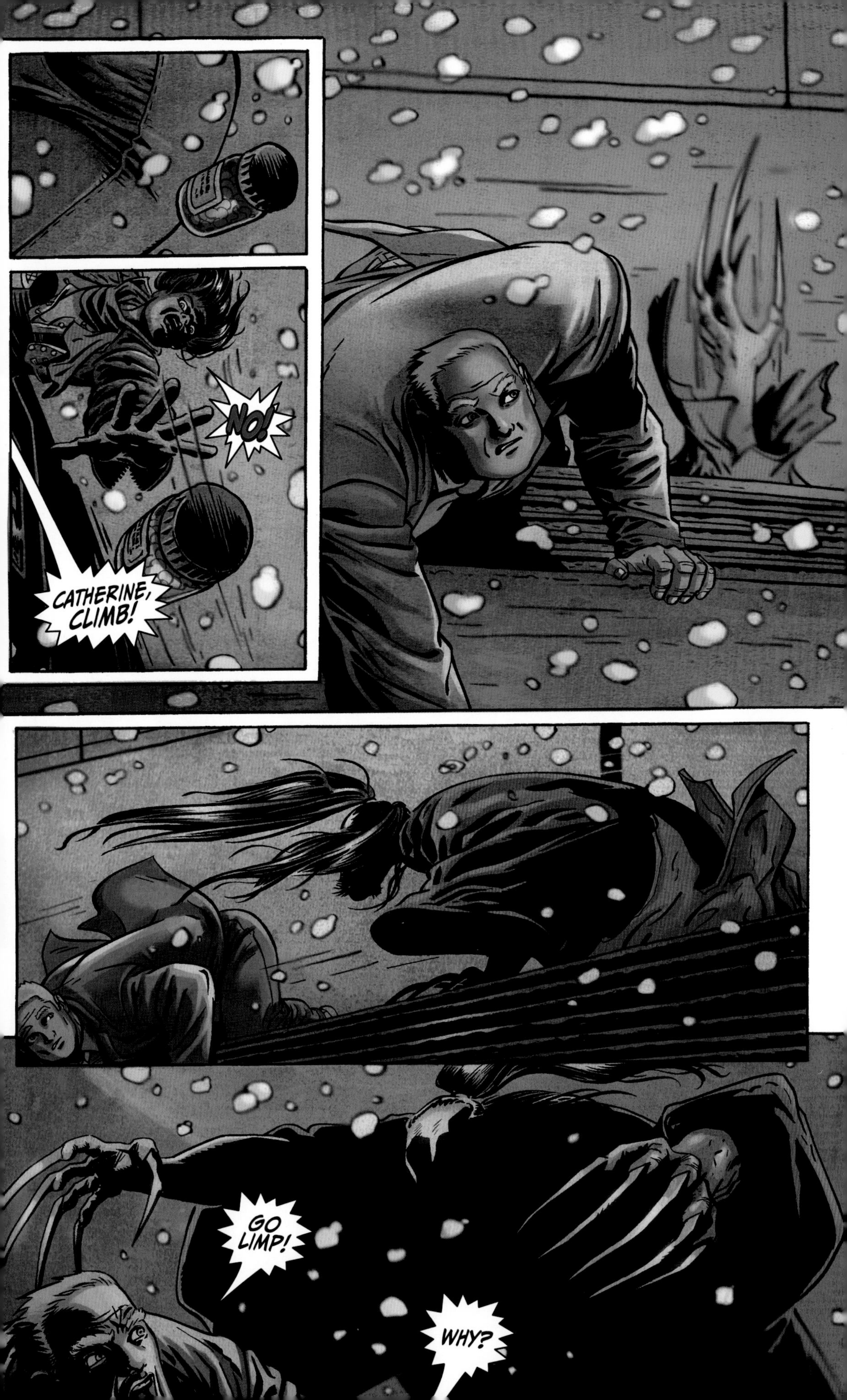
NO!
CATHERINE, CLIMB!
GO LIMP!
WHY?

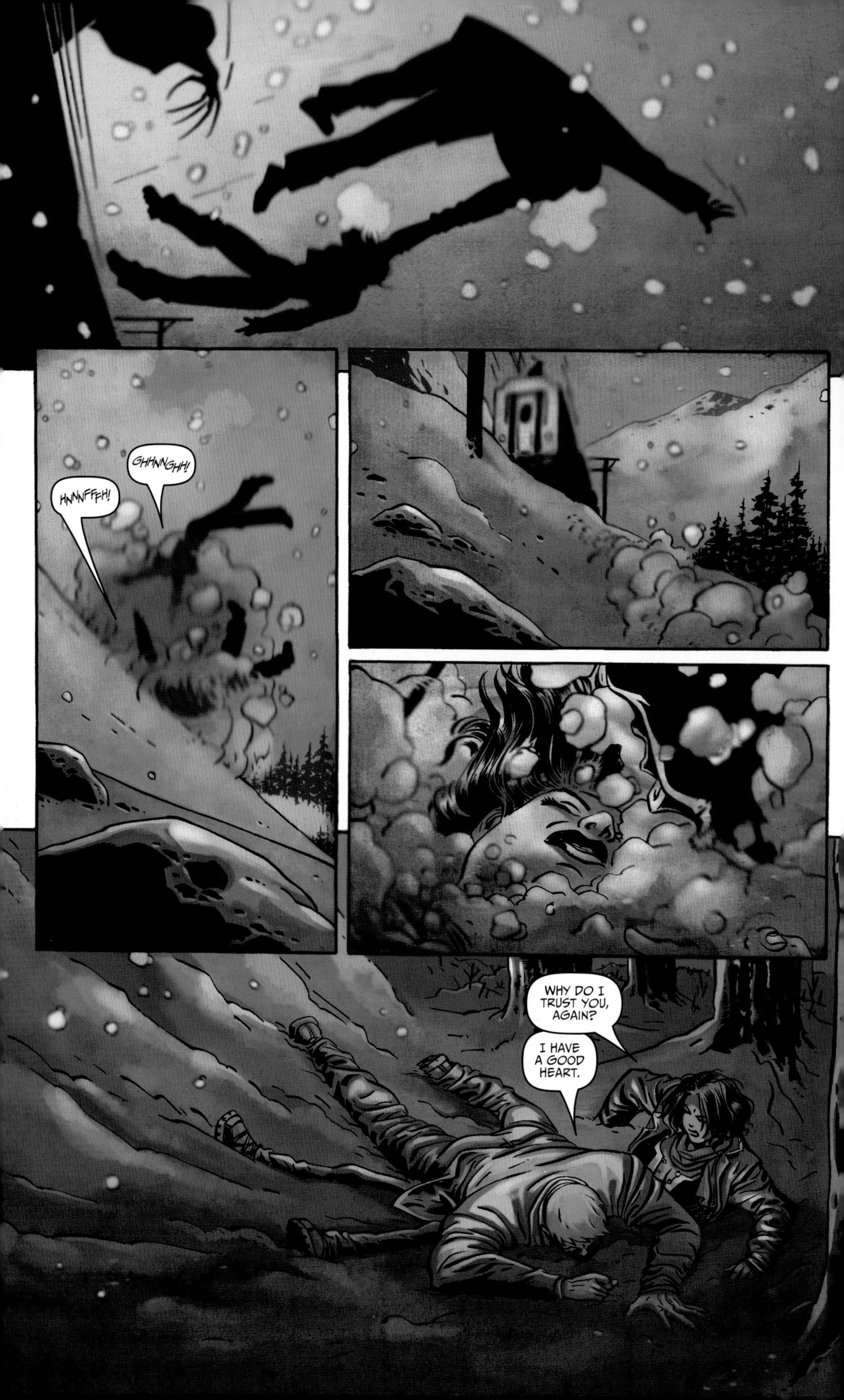
GHHNNGHH!
HNNNFFFH!
WHY DO I TRUST YOU, AGAIN?
I HAVE A GOOD HEART.

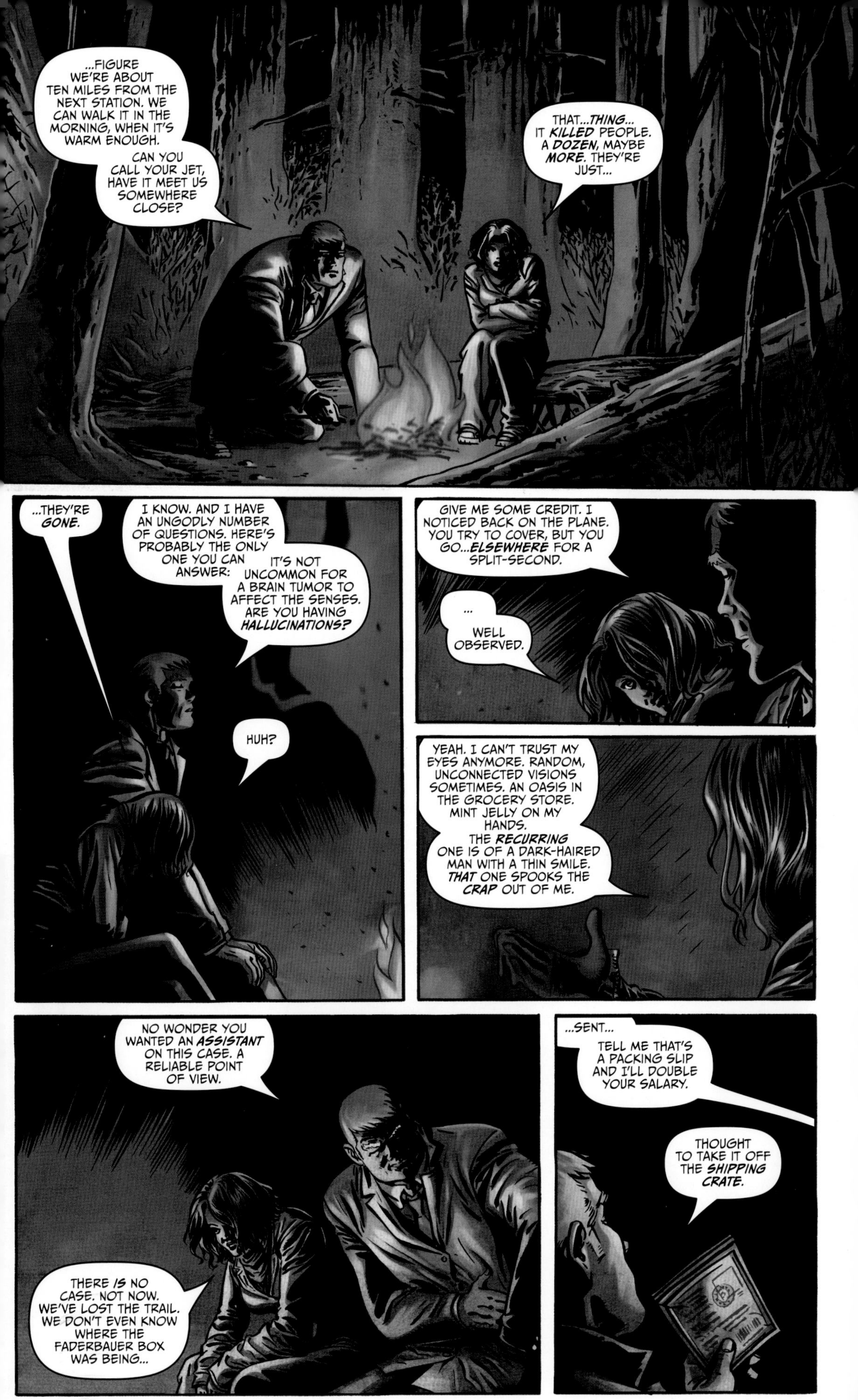

...FIGURE WE'RE ABOUT TEN MILES FROM THE NEXT STATION. WE CAN WALK IT IN THE MORNING, WHEN IT'S WARM ENOUGH.
CAN YOU CALL YOUR JET, HAVE IT MEET US SOMEWHERE CLOSE?
THAT...THING... IT KILLED PEOPLE. A DOZEN, MAYBE MORE. THEY'RE JUST...
...THEY'RE GONE.
I KNOW. AND I HAVE AN UNGODLY NUMBER OF QUESTIONS. HERE'S PROBABLY THE ONLY ONE YOU CAN ANSWER:
IT'S NOT UNCOMMON FOR A BRAIN TUMOR TO AFFECT THE SENSES. ARE YOU HAVING HALLUCINATIONS?
HUH?
GIVE ME SOME CREDIT. I NOTICED BACK ON THE PLANE. YOU TRY TO COVER, BUT YOU GO...ELSEWHERE FOR A SPLIT-SECOND.
...
WELL OBSERVED.
YEAH. I CAN'T TRUST MY EYES ANYMORE. RANDOM, UNCONNECTED VISIONS SOMETIMES. AN OASIS IN THE GROCERY STORE. MINT JELLY ON MY HANDS.
THE RECURRING ONE IS OF A DARK-HAIRED MAN WITH A THIN SMILE. THAT ONE SPOOKS THE CRAP OUT OF ME.
NO WONDER YOU WANTED AN ASSISTANT ON THIS CASE. A RELIABLE POINT OF VIEW.
THERE IS NO CASE. NOT NOW. WE'VE LOST THE TRAIL. WE DON'T EVEN KNOW WHERE THE FADERBAUER BOX WAS BEING...
...SENT...
TELL ME THAT'S A PACKING SLIP AND I'LL DOUBLE YOUR SALARY.
THOUGHT TO TAKE IT OFF THE SHIPPING CRATE.

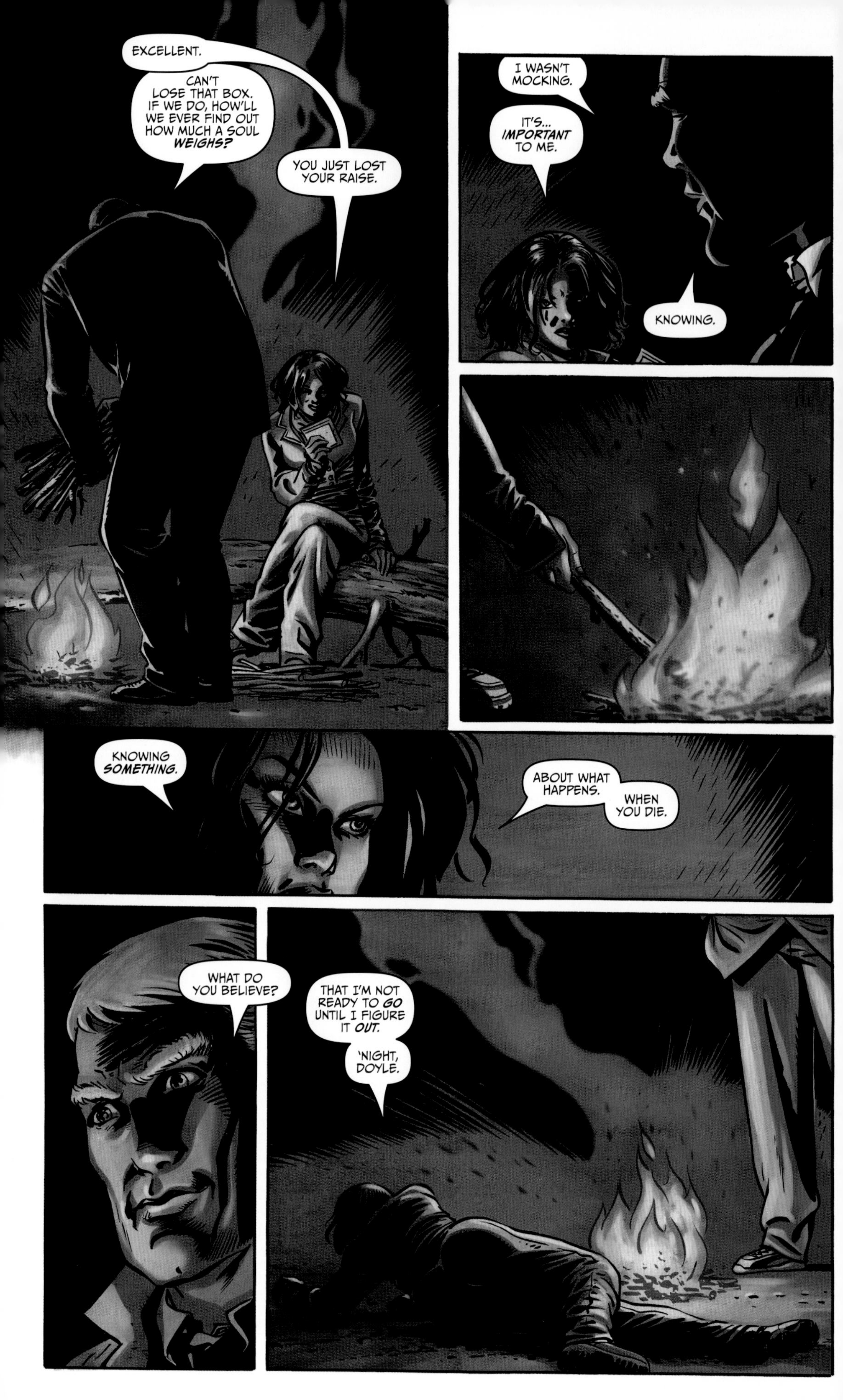

EXCELLENT.
CAN'T LOSE THAT BOX. IF WE DO, HOW'LL WE EVER FIND OUT HOW MUCH A SOUL *WEIGHS?*
YOU JUST LOST YOUR RAISE.
I WASN'T MOCKING.
IT'S... *IMPORTANT* TO ME.
KNOWING.
KNOWING *SOMETHING.*
ABOUT WHAT HAPPENS.
WHEN YOU DIE.
WHAT DO YOU BELIEVE?
THAT I'M NOT READY TO *GO* UNTIL I FIGURE IT *OUT.*
'NIGHT, DOYLE.

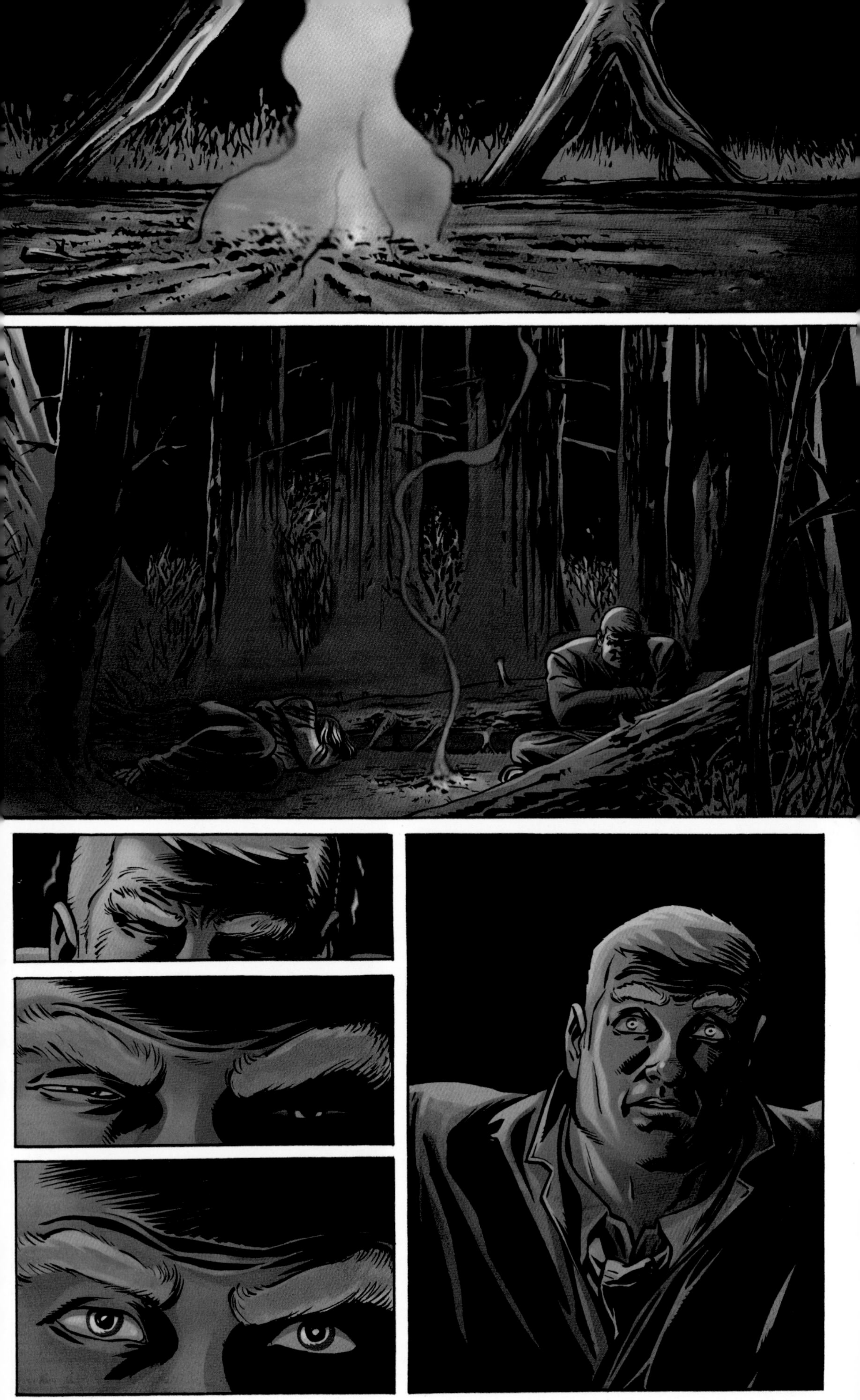

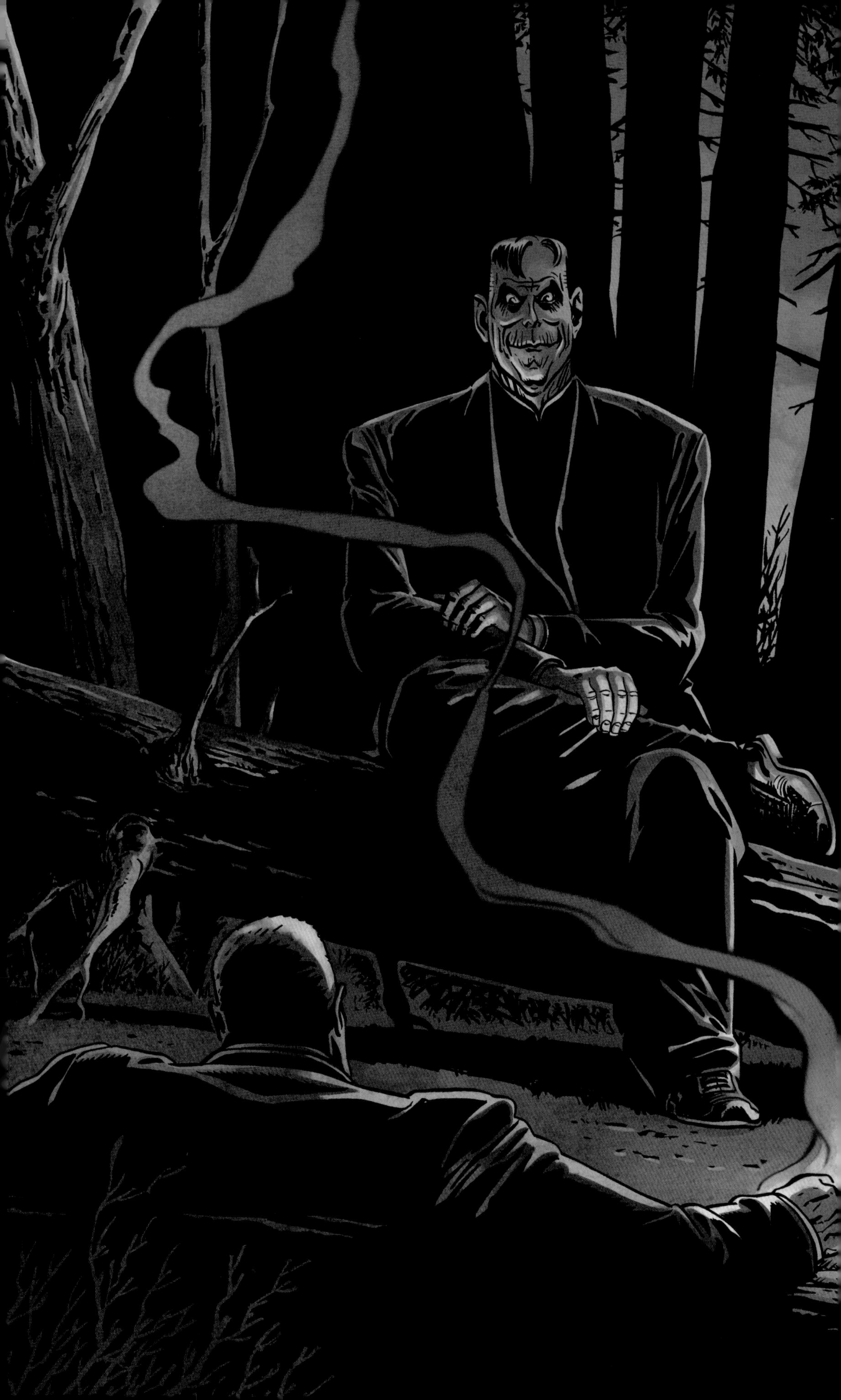

CHAPTER THREE

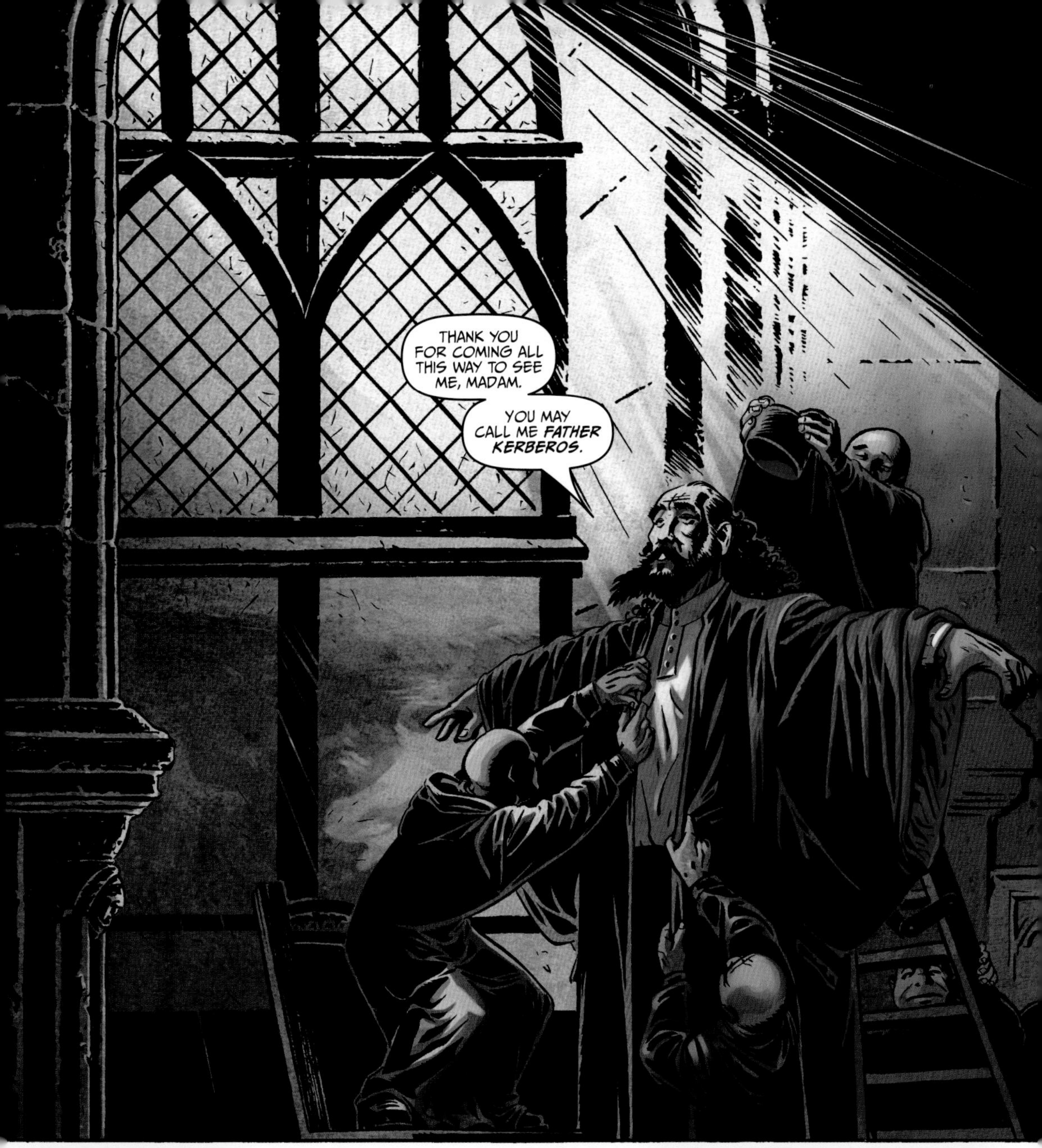
THANK YOU FOR COMING ALL THIS WAY TO SEE ME, MADAM.
YOU MAY CALL ME FATHER KERBEROS.

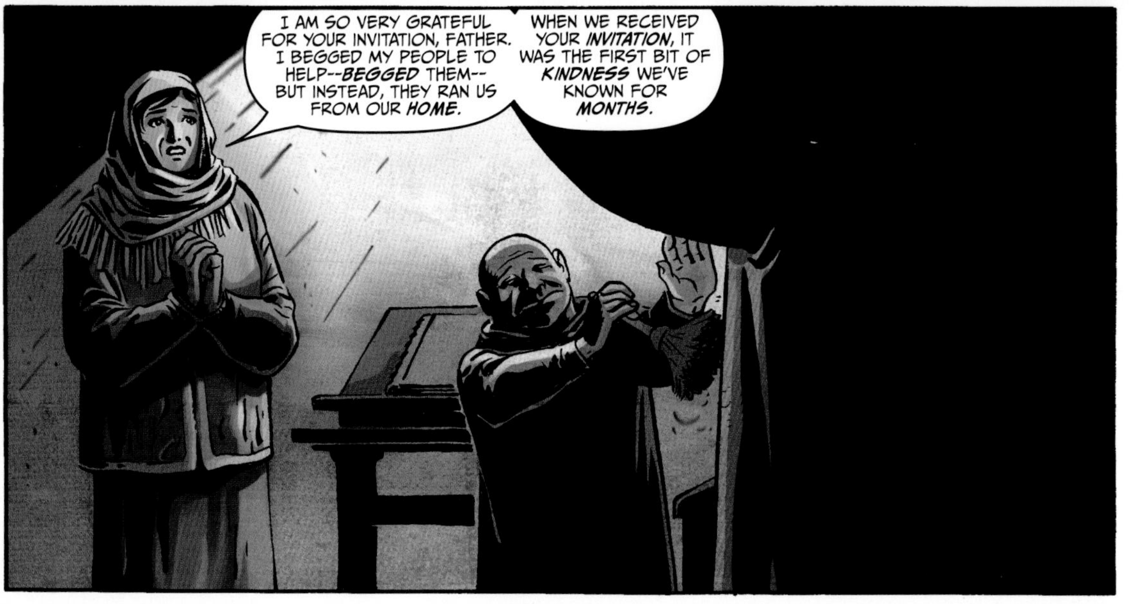
I AM SO VERY GRATEFUL FOR YOUR INVITATION, FATHER. I BEGGED MY PEOPLE TO HELP--BEGGED THEM--BUT INSTEAD, THEY RAN US FROM OUR HOME.
WHEN WE RECEIVED YOUR INVITATION, IT WAS THE FIRST BIT OF KINDNESS WE'VE KNOWN FOR MONTHS.

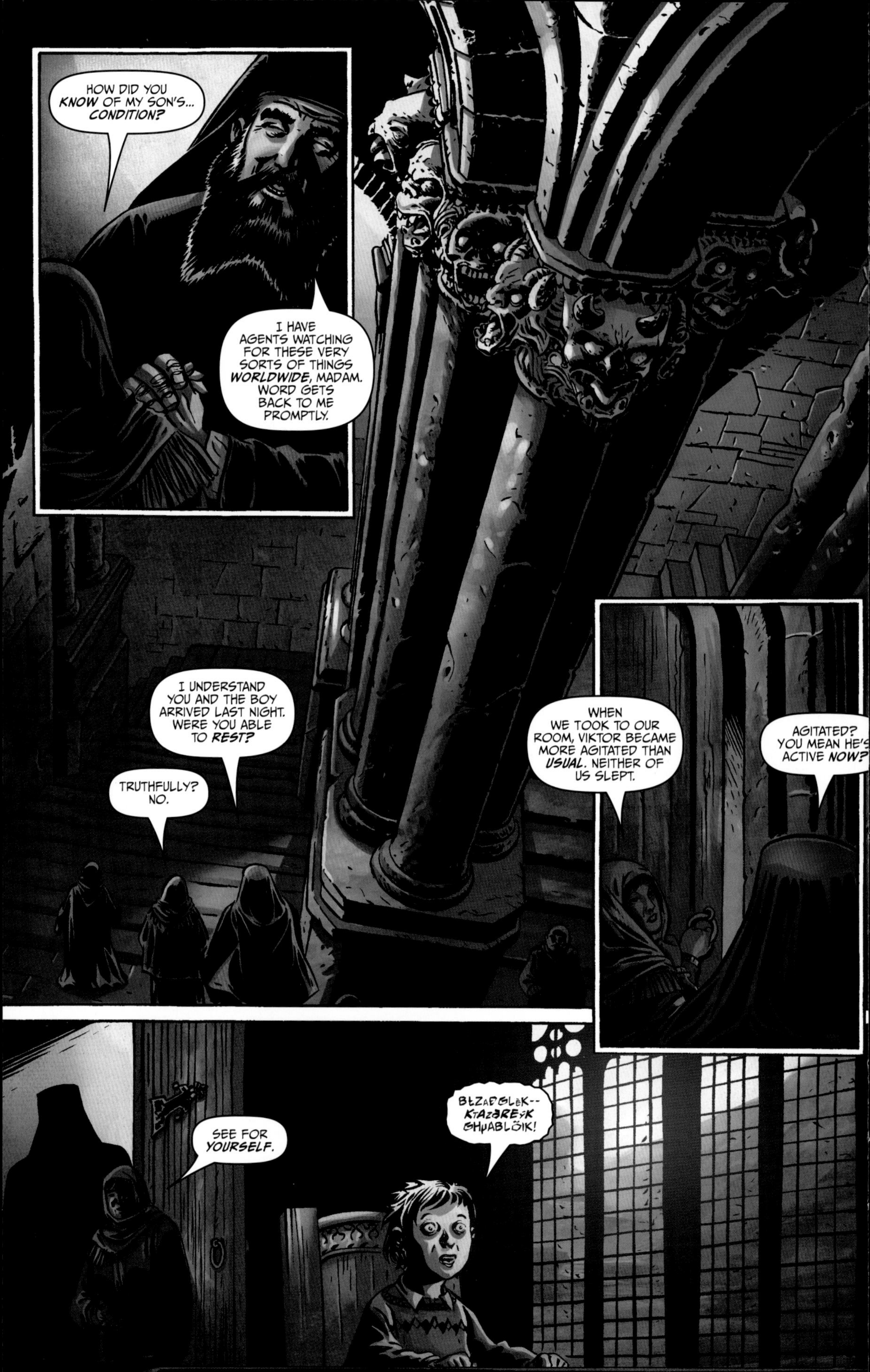
HOW DID YOU KNOW OF MY SON'S... CONDITION?
I HAVE AGENTS WATCHING FOR THESE VERY SORTS OF THINGS WORLDWIDE, MADAM. WORD GETS BACK TO ME PROMPTLY.
I UNDERSTAND YOU AND THE BOY ARRIVED LAST NIGHT. WERE YOU ABLE TO REST?
TRUTHFULLY? NO.
WHEN WE TOOK TO OUR ROOM, VIKTOR BECAME MORE AGITATED THAN USUAL. NEITHER OF US SLEPT.
AGITATED? YOU MEAN HE'S ACTIVE NOW?
SEE FOR YOURSELF.
BŁZAÐGLÈK-- KTAZƏREÿK GHɥABLÖIK!

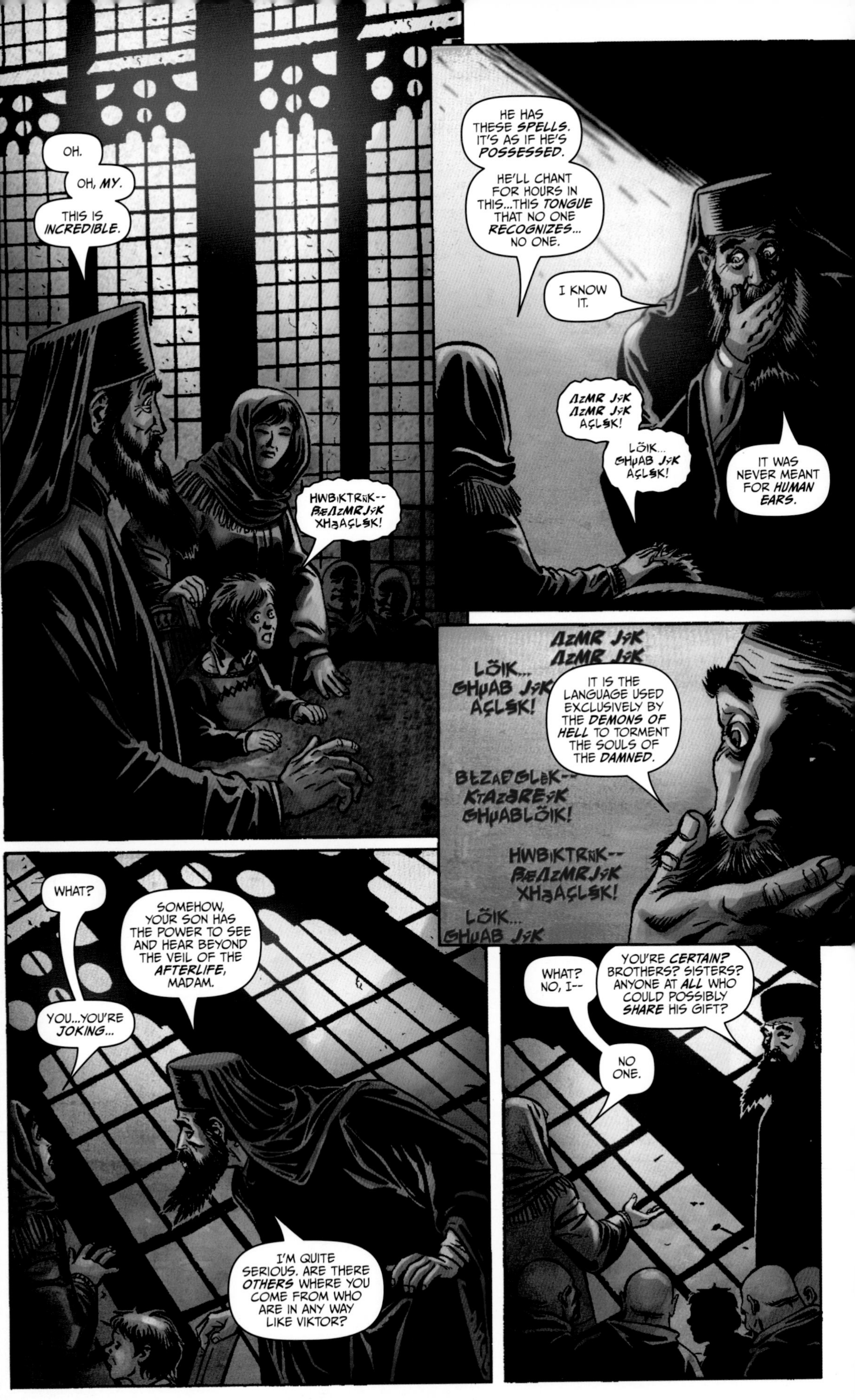
OH.
OH, *MY*.
THIS IS *INCREDIBLE*.
HWBIKTRÑK-- BÆAZMRJЯK XHƏAÇLSK!
HE HAS THESE *SPELLS*. IT'S AS IF HE'S *POSSESSED*.
HE'LL CHANT FOR HOURS IN THIS...THIS *TONGUE* THAT NO ONE *RECOGNIZES*... NO ONE.
I KNOW IT.
AZMR JЯK AZMR JЯK AÇLSK!
LÖIK... GHUAB JЯK AÇLSK!
IT WAS NEVER MEANT FOR *HUMAN EARS*.
AZMR JЯK AZMR JЯK
LÖIK... GHUAB JЯK AÇLSK!
IT IS THE LANGUAGE USED EXCLUSIVELY BY THE *DEMONS OF HELL* TO TORMENT THE SOULS OF THE *DAMNED*.
BLZAEGLEK-- KTAZƏREЯK GHUABLÖIK!
HWBIKTRÑK-- BÆAZMRJЯK XHƏAÇLSK!
LÖIK... GHUAB JЯK
WHAT?
SOMEHOW, YOUR SON HAS THE POWER TO SEE AND HEAR BEYOND THE VEIL OF THE *AFTERLIFE*, MADAM.
YOU...YOU'RE *JOKING*...
I'M QUITE SERIOUS. ARE THERE *OTHERS* WHERE YOU COME FROM WHO ARE IN ANY WAY LIKE VIKTOR?
WHAT? NO, I--
YOU'RE *CERTAIN?* BROTHERS? SISTERS? ANYONE AT *ALL* WHO COULD POSSIBLY *SHARE* HIS GIFT?
NO ONE.

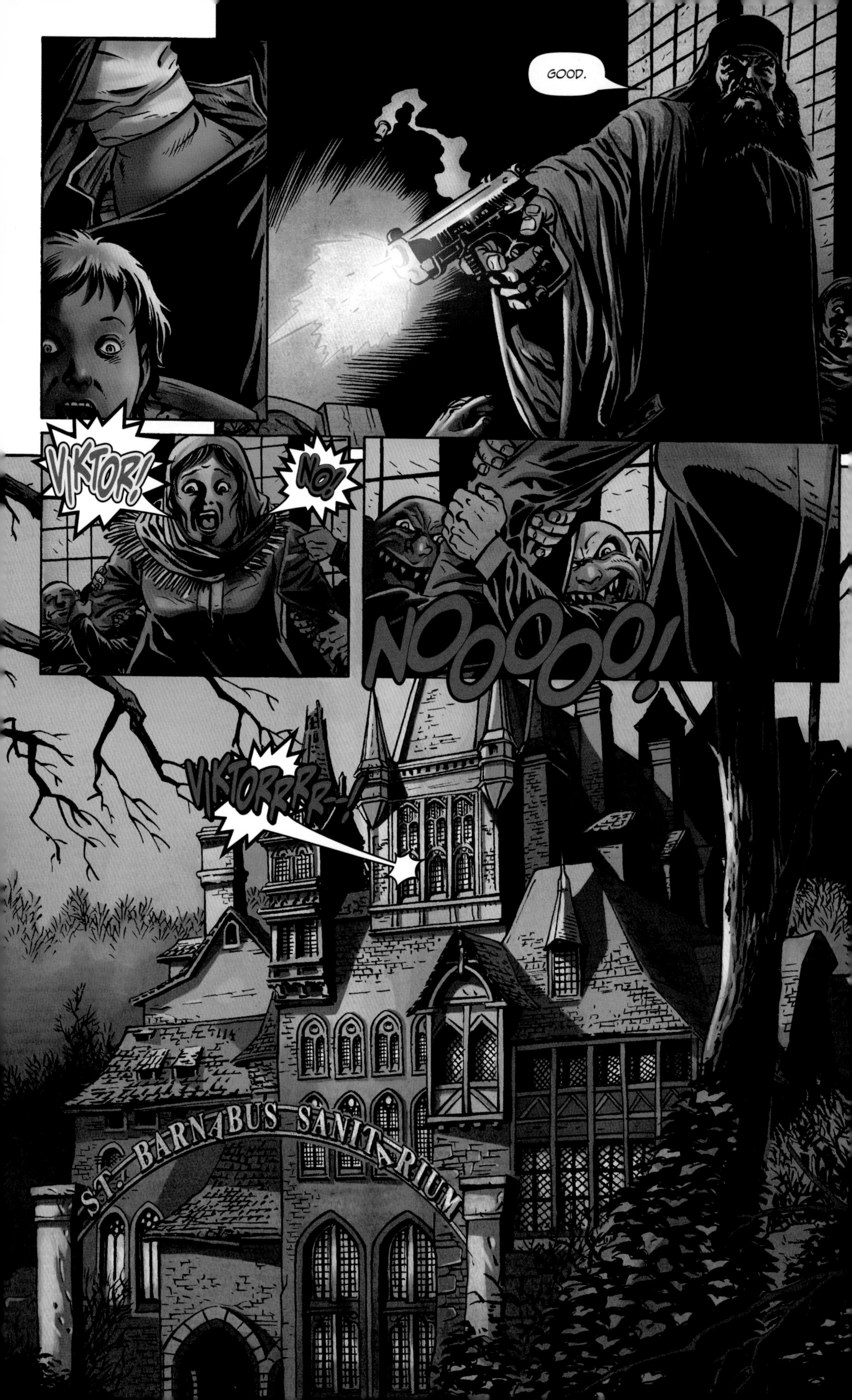
GOOD.
VIKTOR!
NO!
NOOOOO!
VIKTORRRR--!
ST. BARNABUS SANITARIUM

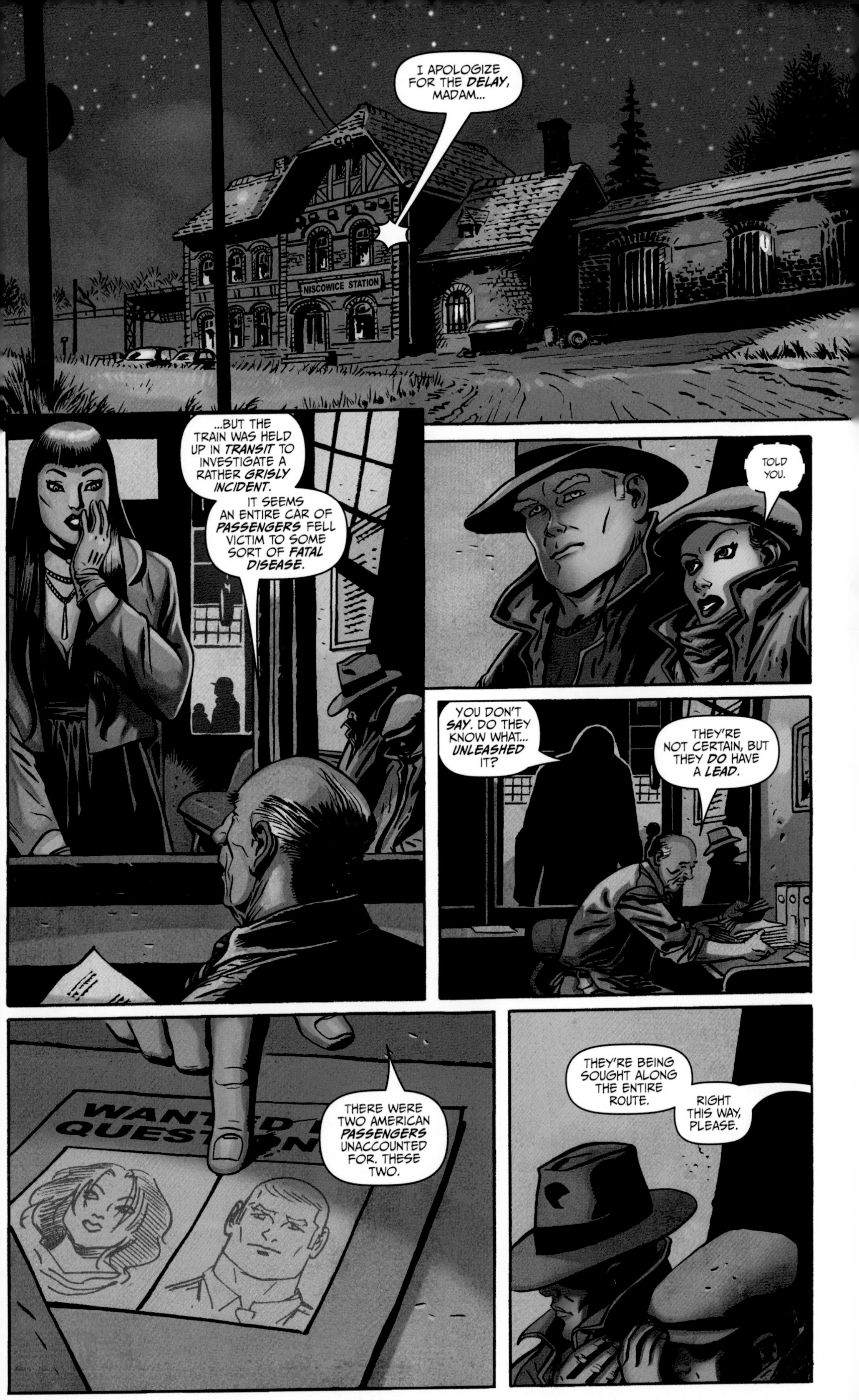
I APOLOGIZE FOR THE DELAY, MADAM...
NISCOWICE STATION
...BUT THE TRAIN WAS HELD UP IN TRANSIT TO INVESTIGATE A RATHER GRISLY INCIDENT.
IT SEEMS AN ENTIRE CAR OF PASSENGERS FELL VICTIM TO SOME SORT OF FATAL DISEASE.
TOLD YOU.
YOU DON'T SAY. DO THEY KNOW WHAT... UNLEASHED IT?
THEY'RE NOT CERTAIN, BUT THEY DO HAVE A LEAD.
THERE WERE TWO AMERICAN PASSENGERS UNACCOUNTED FOR. THESE TWO.
THEY'RE BEING SOUGHT ALONG THE ENTIRE ROUTE.
RIGHT THIS WAY, PLEASE.

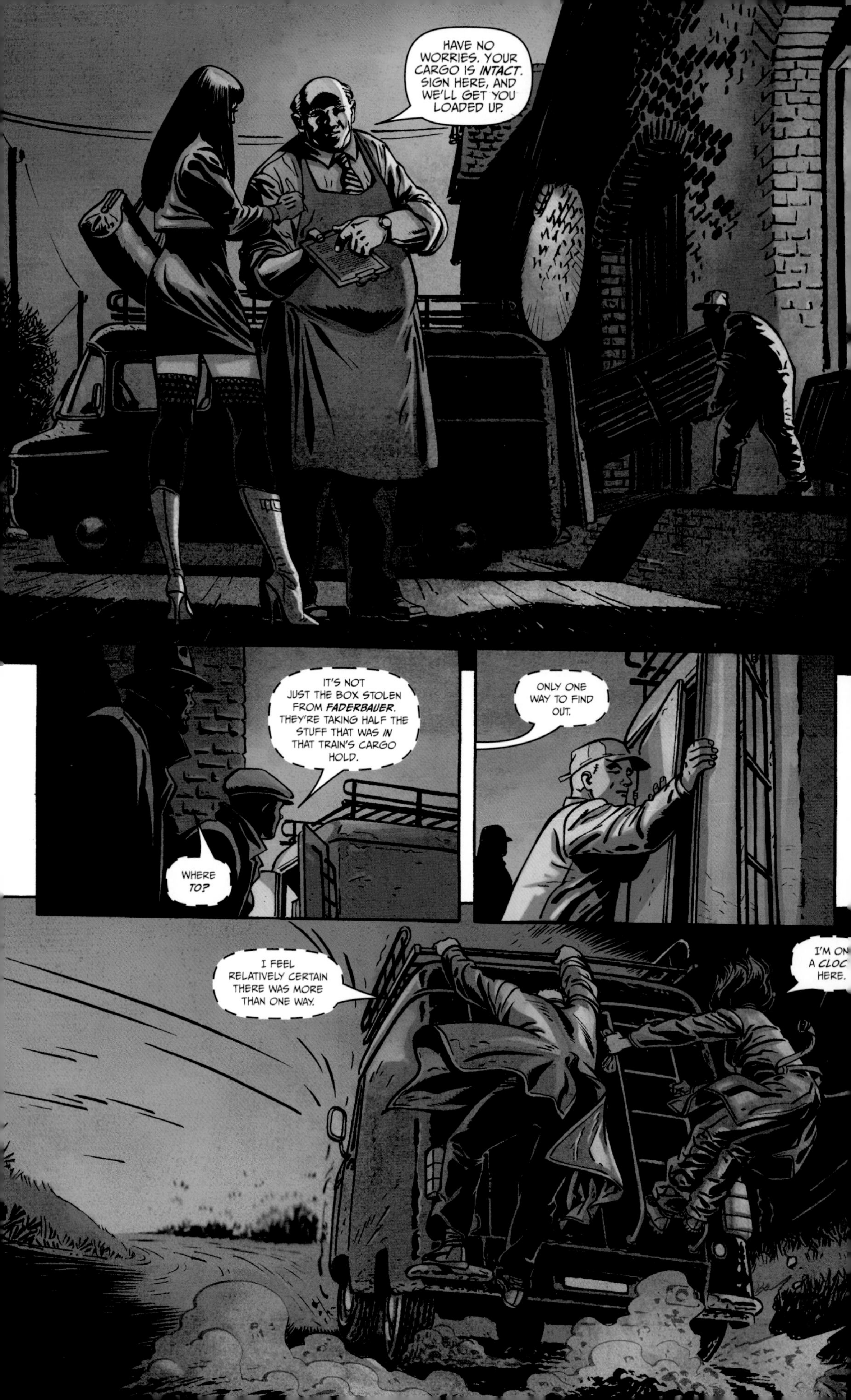
HAVE NO WORRIES. YOUR CARGO IS INTACT. SIGN HERE, AND WE'LL GET YOU LOADED UP.
IT'S NOT JUST THE BOX STOLEN FROM FADERBAUER. THEY'RE TAKING HALF THE STUFF THAT WAS IN THAT TRAIN'S CARGO HOLD.
WHERE TO?
ONLY ONE WAY TO FIND OUT.
I FEEL RELATIVELY CERTAIN THERE WAS MORE THAN ONE WAY.
I'M ON A CLOC HERE.

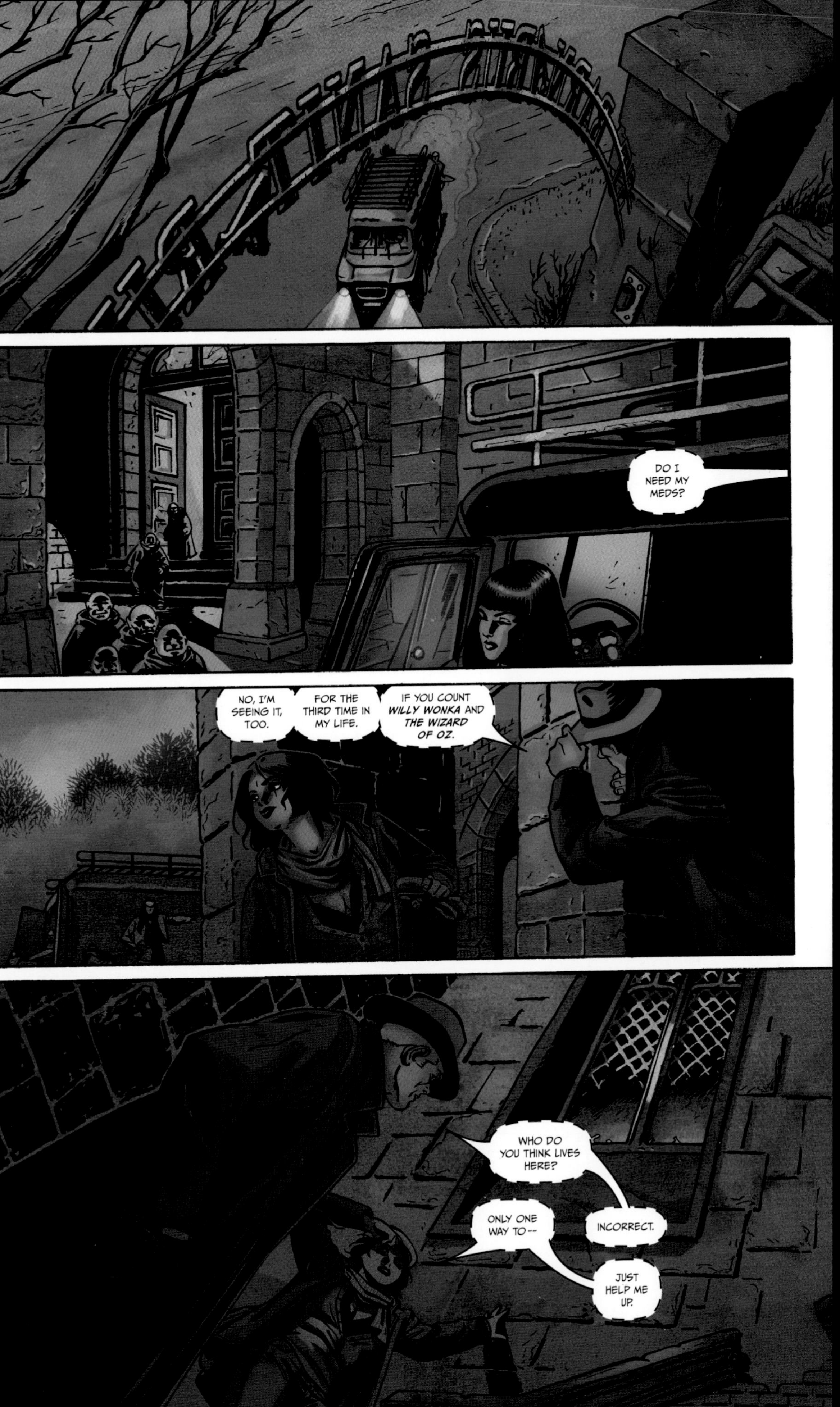
DO I NEED MY MEDS?
NO, I'M SEEING IT, TOO.
FOR THE THIRD TIME IN MY LIFE.
IF YOU COUNT *WILLY WONKA* AND *THE WIZARD OF OZ*.
WHO DO YOU THINK LIVES HERE?
ONLY ONE WAY TO--
INCORRECT.
JUST HELP ME UP.

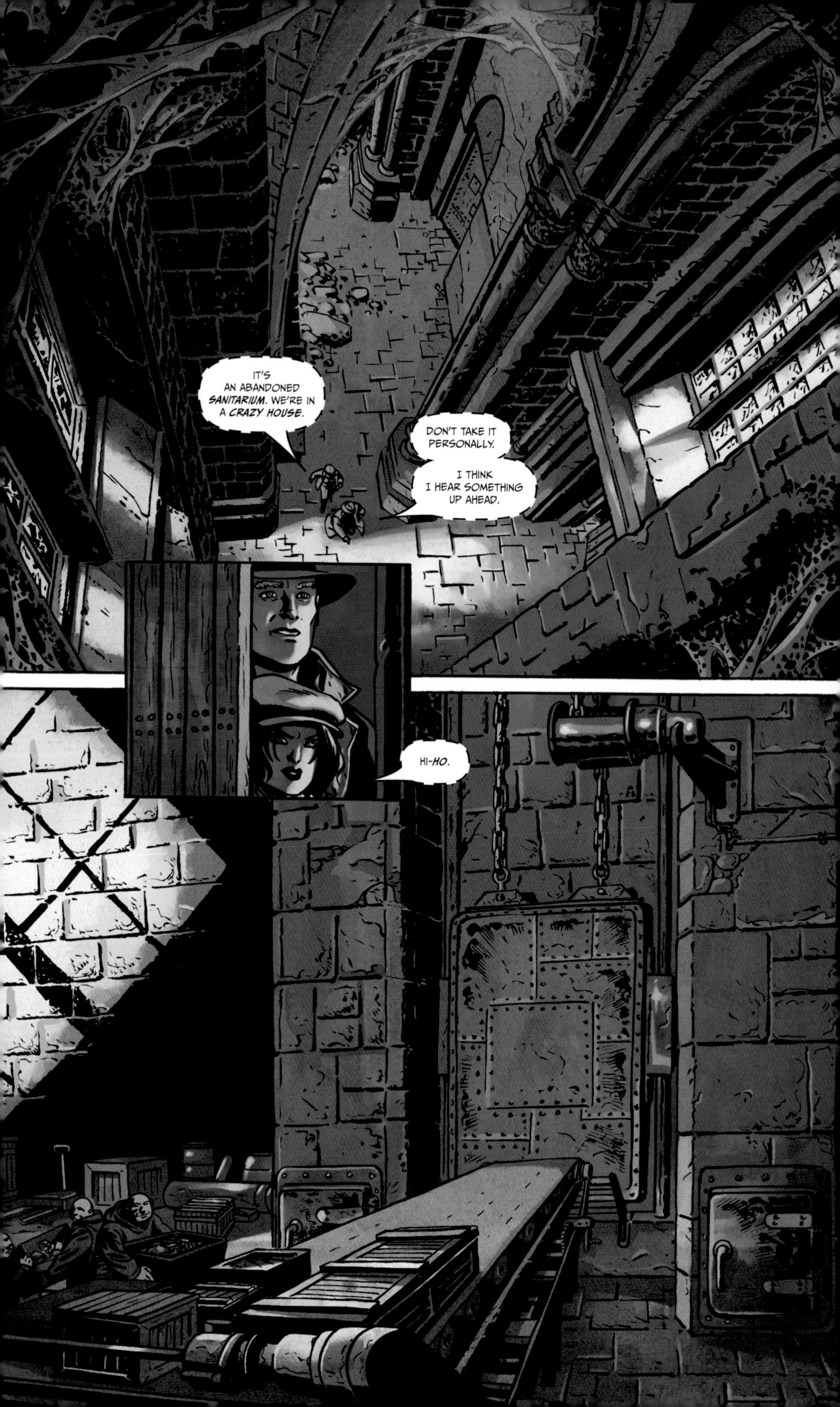

IT'S AN ABANDONED SANITARIUM. WE'RE IN A CRAZY HOUSE.
DON'T TAKE IT PERSONALLY.
I THINK I HEAR SOMETHING UP AHEAD.
HI-HO.

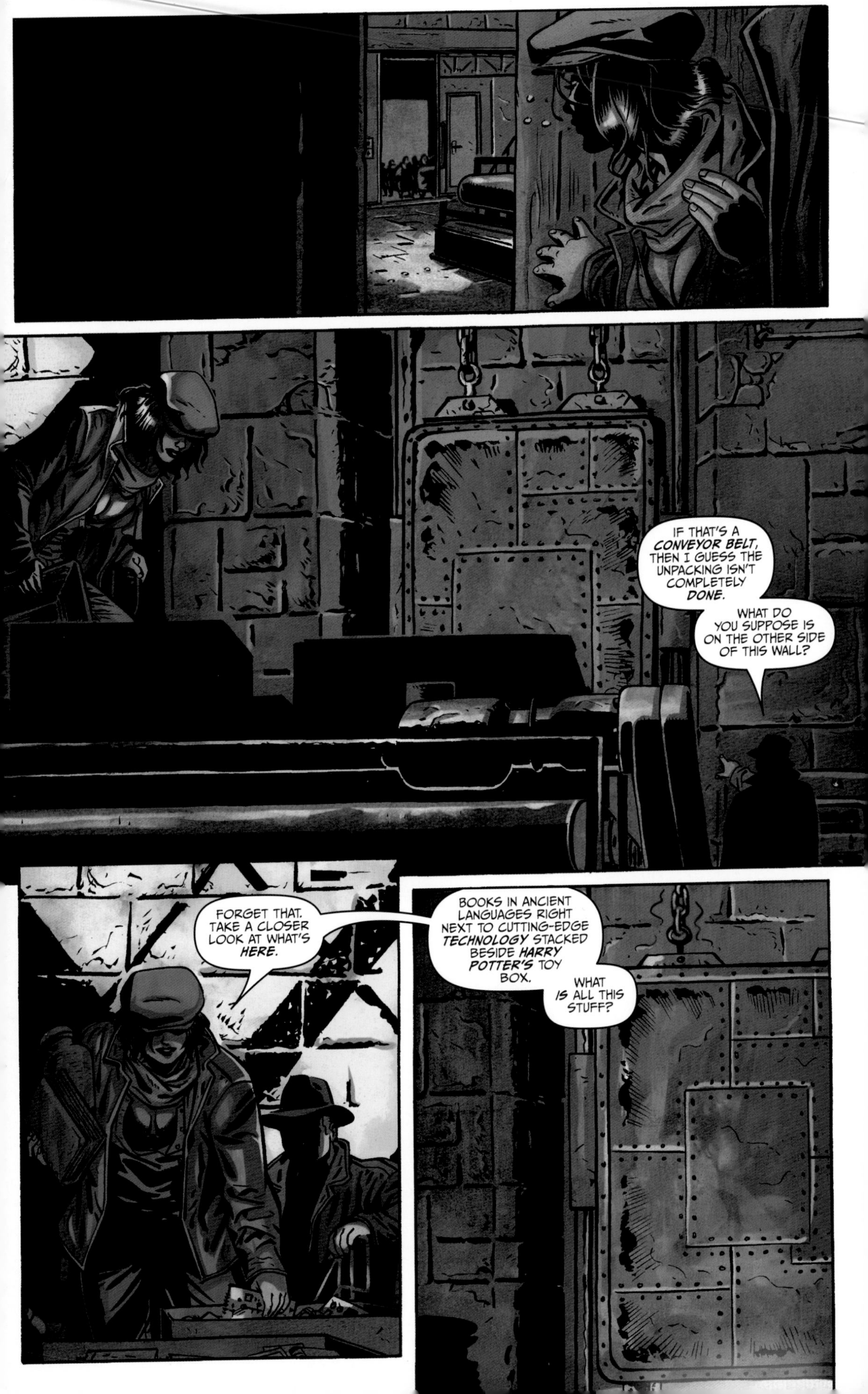
IF THAT'S A *CONVEYOR BELT*, THEN I GUESS THE UNPACKING ISN'T COMPLETELY *DONE*.
WHAT DO YOU SUPPOSE IS ON THE OTHER SIDE OF THIS WALL?
FORGET THAT. TAKE A CLOSER LOOK AT WHAT'S *HERE*.
BOOKS IN ANCIENT LANGUAGES RIGHT NEXT TO CUTTING-EDGE *TECHNOLOGY* STACKED BESIDE *HARRY POTTER'S* TOY BOX.
WHAT *IS* ALL THIS STUFF?

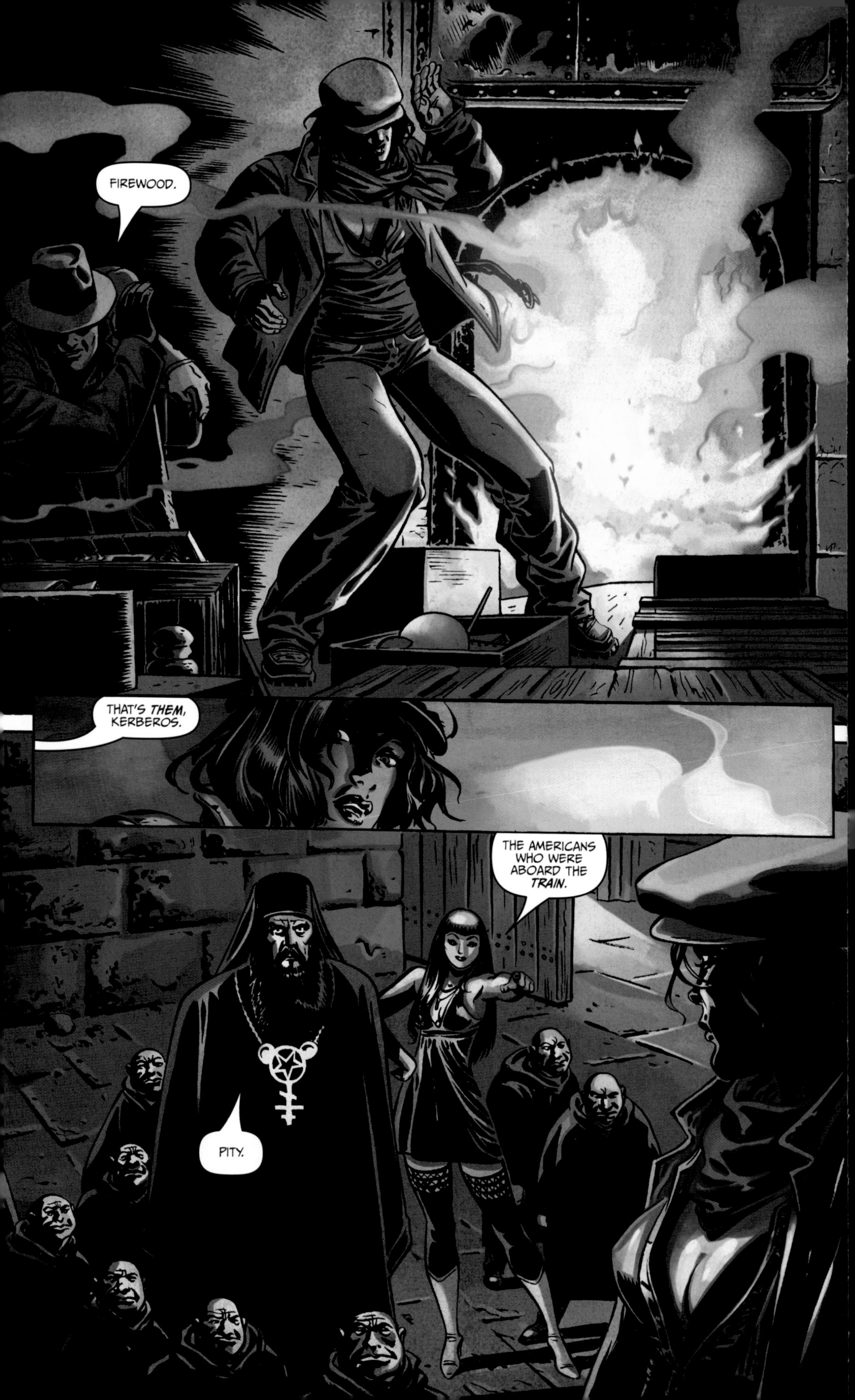
FIREWOOD.
THAT'S *THEM*, KERBEROS.
THE AMERICANS WHO WERE ABOARD THE *TRAIN*.
PITY.

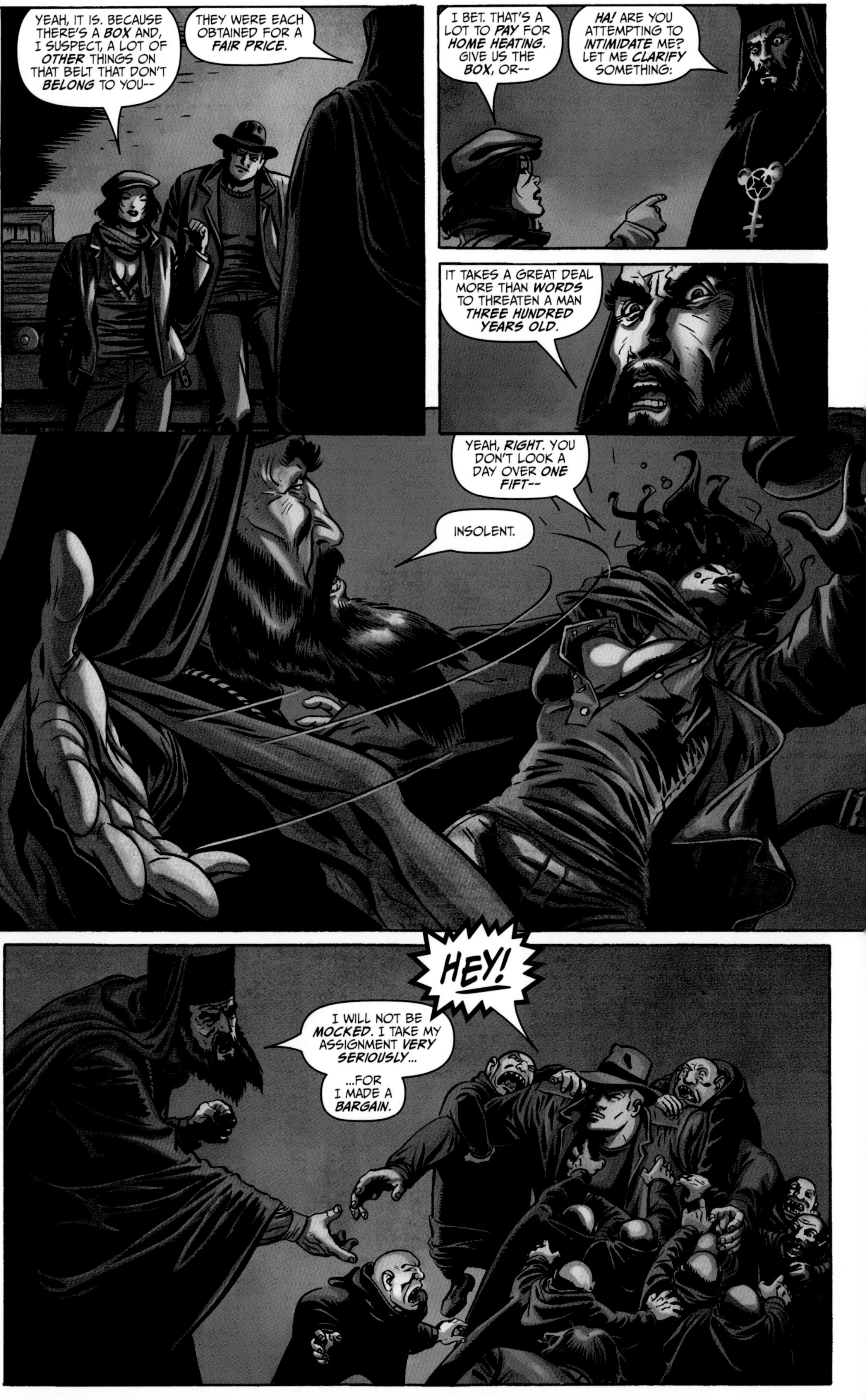
YEAH, IT IS. BECAUSE THERE'S A BOX AND, I SUSPECT, A LOT OF OTHER THINGS ON THAT BELT THAT DON'T BELONG TO YOU--
THEY WERE EACH OBTAINED FOR A FAIR PRICE.
I BET. THAT'S A LOT TO PAY FOR HOME HEATING. GIVE US THE BOX, OR--
HA! ARE YOU ATTEMPTING TO INTIMIDATE ME? LET ME CLARIFY SOMETHING:
IT TAKES A GREAT DEAL MORE THAN WORDS TO THREATEN A MAN THREE HUNDRED YEARS OLD.
YEAH, RIGHT. YOU DON'T LOOK A DAY OVER ONE FIFT--
INSOLENT.
HEY!
I WILL NOT BE MOCKED. I TAKE MY ASSIGNMENT VERY SERIOUSLY...
...FOR I MADE A BARGAIN.

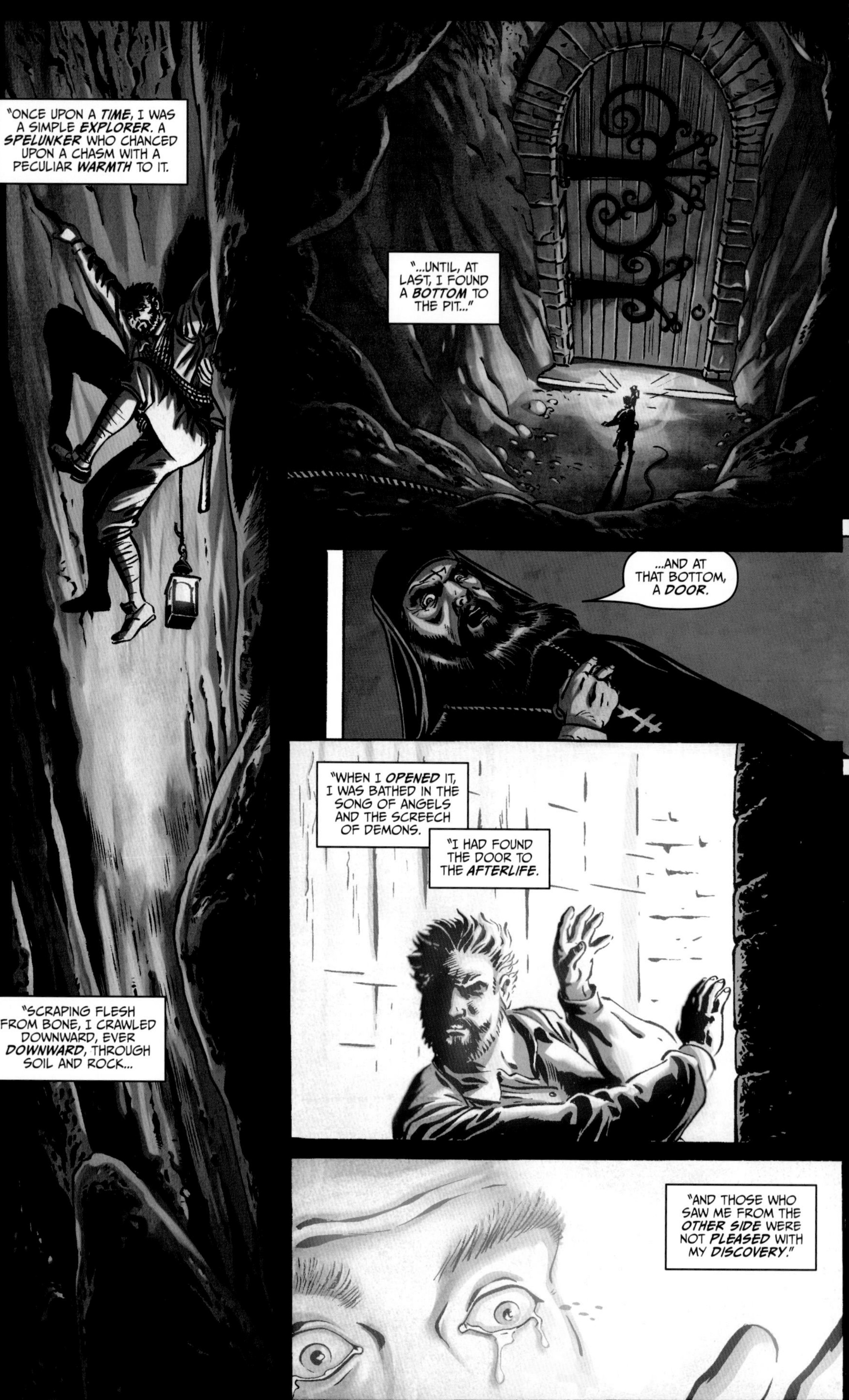
"ONCE UPON A TIME, I WAS A SIMPLE EXPLORER. A SPELUNKER WHO CHANCED UPON A CHASM WITH A PECULIAR WARMTH TO IT.
"SCRAPING FLESH FROM BONE, I CRAWLED DOWNWARD, EVER DOWNWARD, THROUGH SOIL AND ROCK...
"...UNTIL, AT LAST, I FOUND A BOTTOM TO THE PIT..."
...AND AT THAT BOTTOM, A DOOR.
"WHEN I OPENED IT, I WAS BATHED IN THE SONG OF ANGELS AND THE SCREECH OF DEMONS.
"I HAD FOUND THE DOOR TO THE AFTERLIFE.
"AND THOSE WHO SAW ME FROM THE OTHER SIDE WERE NOT PLEASED WITH MY DISCOVERY."

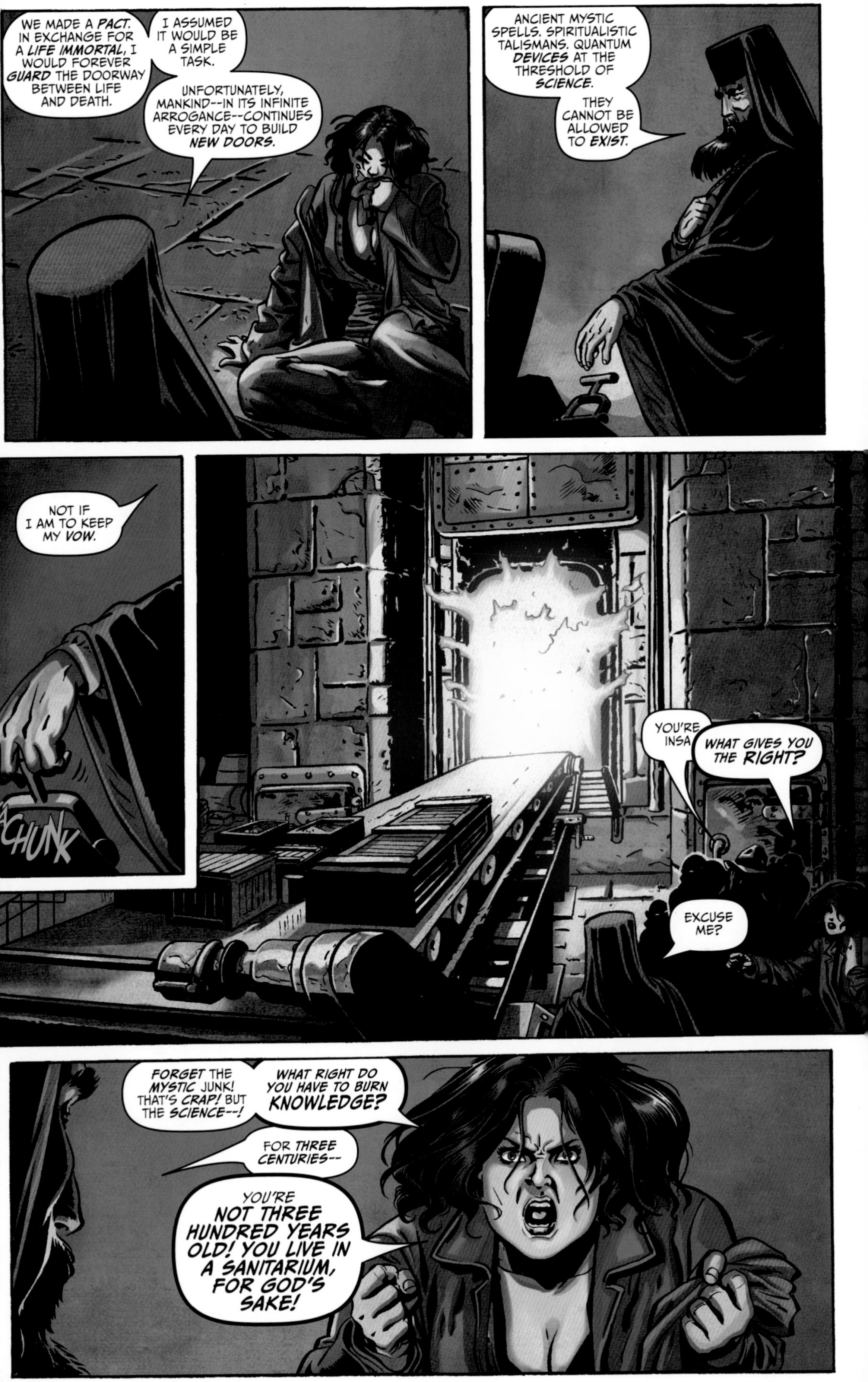
WE MADE A PACT. IN EXCHANGE FOR A LIFE IMMORTAL, I WOULD FOREVER GUARD THE DOORWAY BETWEEN LIFE AND DEATH.
I ASSUMED IT WOULD BE A SIMPLE TASK.
UNFORTUNATELY, MANKIND--IN ITS INFINITE ARROGANCE--CONTINUES EVERY DAY TO BUILD NEW DOORS.
ANCIENT MYSTIC SPELLS. SPIRITUALISTIC TALISMANS. QUANTUM DEVICES AT THE THRESHOLD OF SCIENCE.
THEY CANNOT BE ALLOWED TO EXIST.
NOT IF I AM TO KEEP MY VOW.
CHUNK
YOU'RE INSA
WHAT GIVES YOU THE RIGHT?
EXCUSE ME?
FORGET THE MYSTIC JUNK! THAT'S CRAP! BUT THE SCIENCE--!
WHAT RIGHT DO YOU HAVE TO BURN KNOWLEDGE?
FOR THREE CENTURIES--
YOU'RE NOT THREE HUNDRED YEARS OLD! YOU LIVE IN A SANITARIUM, FOR GOD'S SAKE!

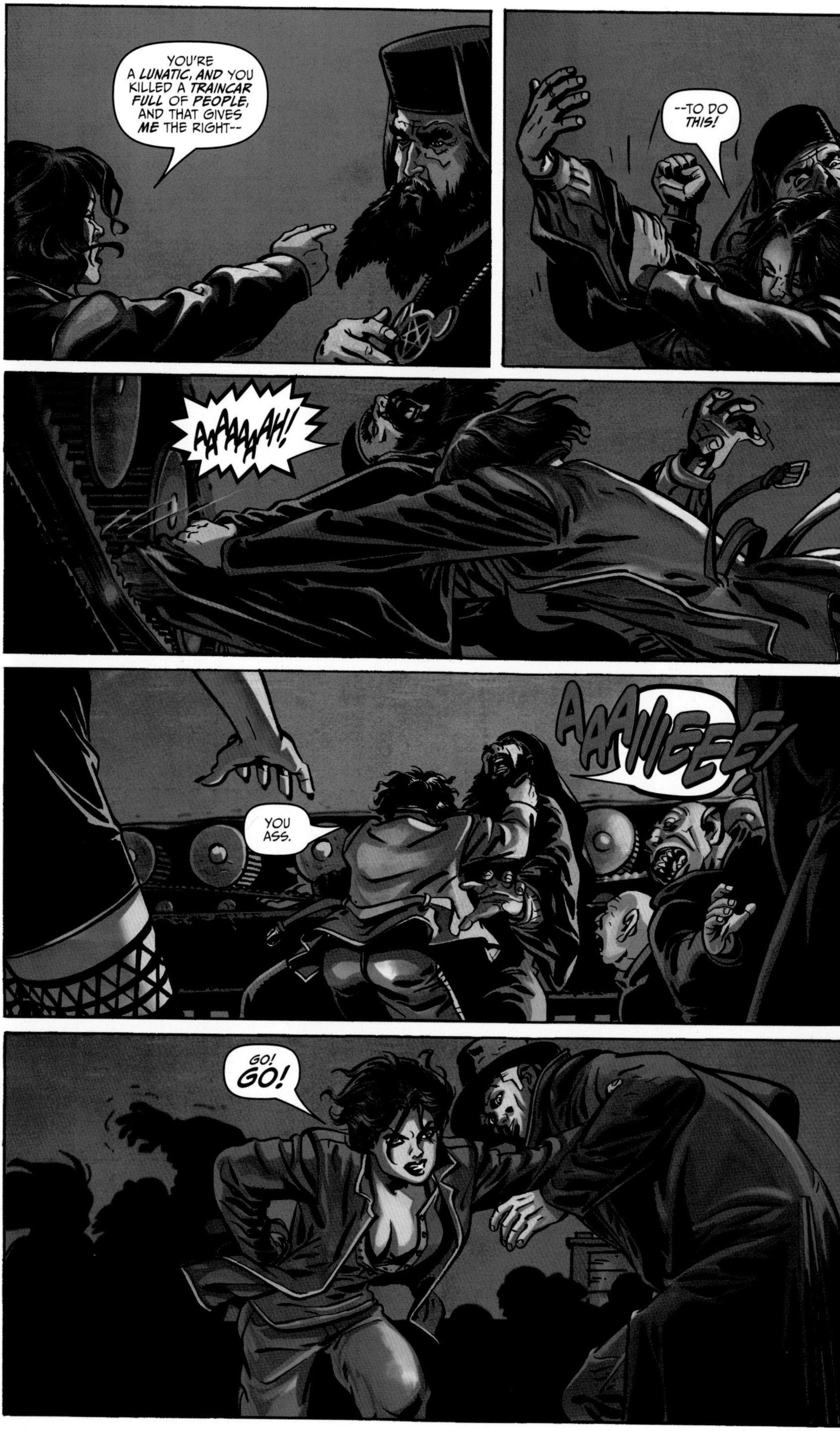

YOU'RE A LUNATIC, AND YOU KILLED A TRAINCAR FULL OF PEOPLE, AND THAT GIVES ME THE RIGHT--
--TO DO THIS!
AAAAAAH!
AAAIIIEEEE!
YOU ASS.
GO! GO!

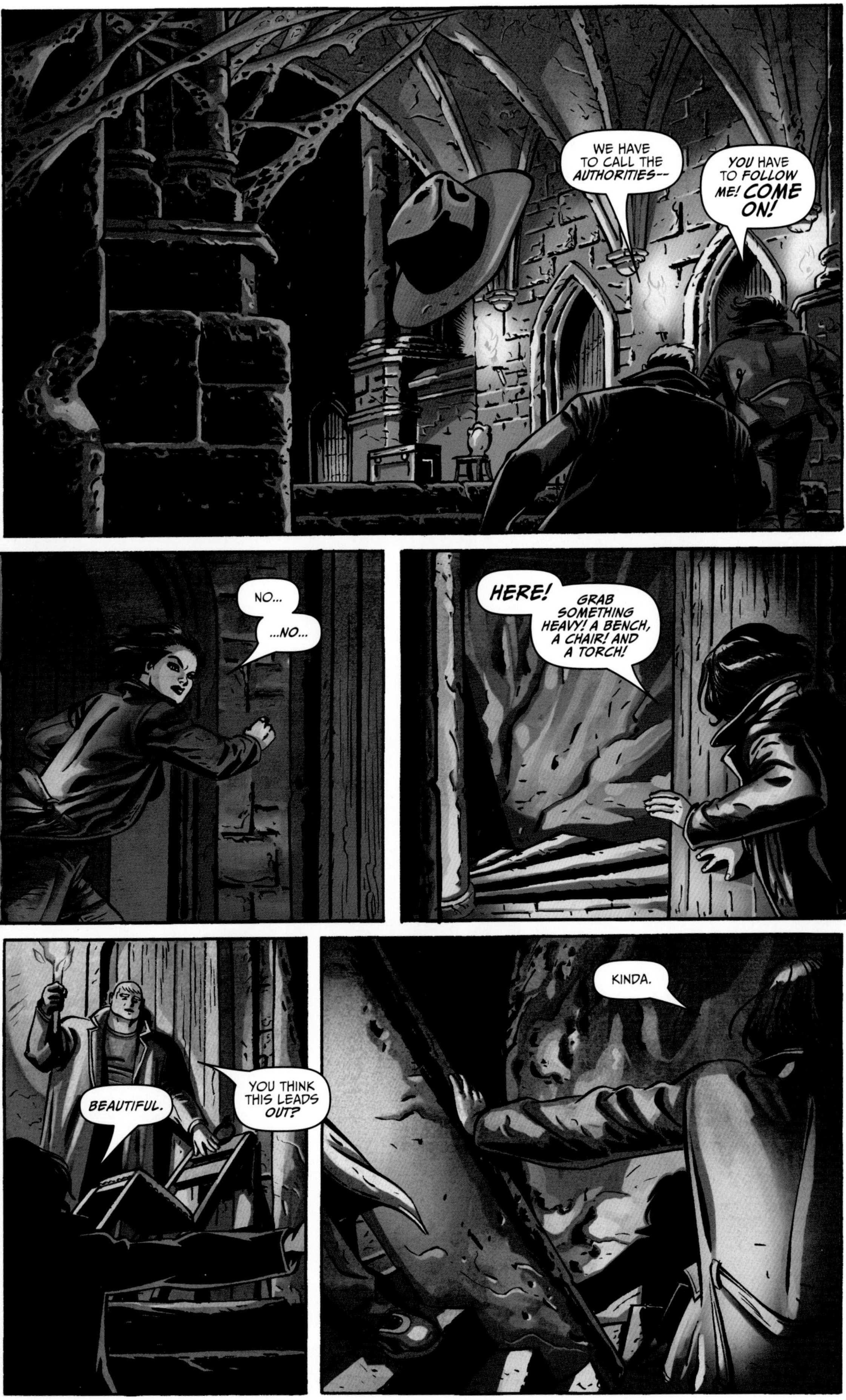
WE HAVE TO CALL THE AUTHORITIES--
YOU HAVE TO FOLLOW ME! COME ON!
NO...
...NO...
HERE!
GRAB SOMETHING HEAVY! A BENCH, A CHAIR! AND A TORCH!
BEAUTIFUL.
YOU THINK THIS LEADS OUT?
KINDA.

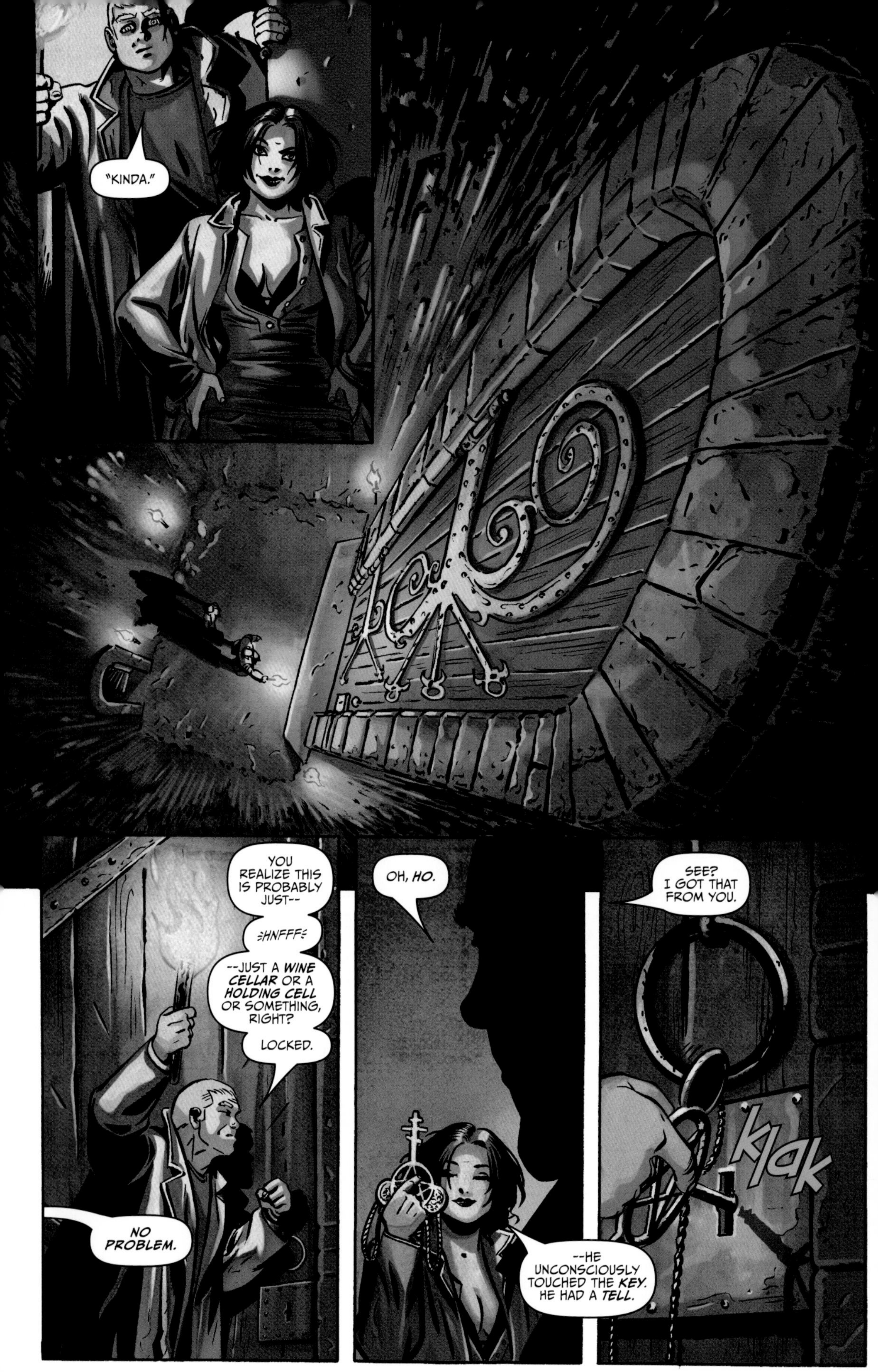
"KINDA."
YOU REALIZE THIS IS PROBABLY JUST--
HNFFF
--JUST A WINE CELLAR OR A HOLDING CELL OR SOMETHING, RIGHT?
LOCKED.
NO PROBLEM.
OH, HO.
--HE UNCONSCIOUSLY TOUCHED THE KEY. HE HAD A TELL.
SEE? I GOT THAT FROM YOU.
klak

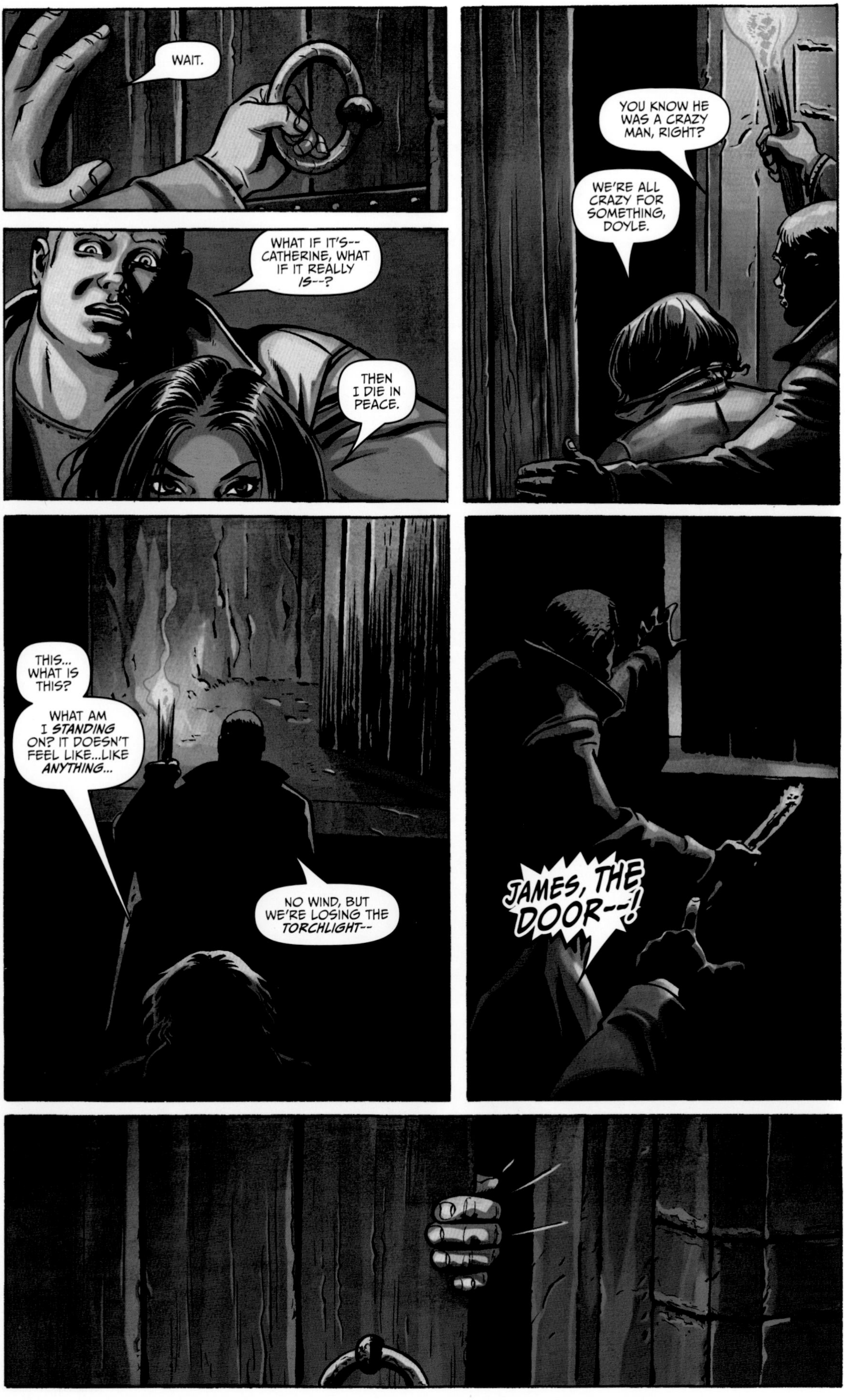
WAIT.
WHAT IF IT'S-- CATHERINE, WHAT IF IT REALLY *IS*--?
THEN I DIE IN PEACE.
YOU KNOW HE WAS A CRAZY MAN, RIGHT?
WE'RE ALL CRAZY FOR SOMETHING, DOYLE.
THIS... WHAT IS THIS?
WHAT AM I *STANDING* ON? IT DOESN'T FEEL LIKE...LIKE *ANYTHING*...
NO WIND, BUT WE'RE LOSING THE *TORCHLIGHT*--
JAMES, THE DOOR--!

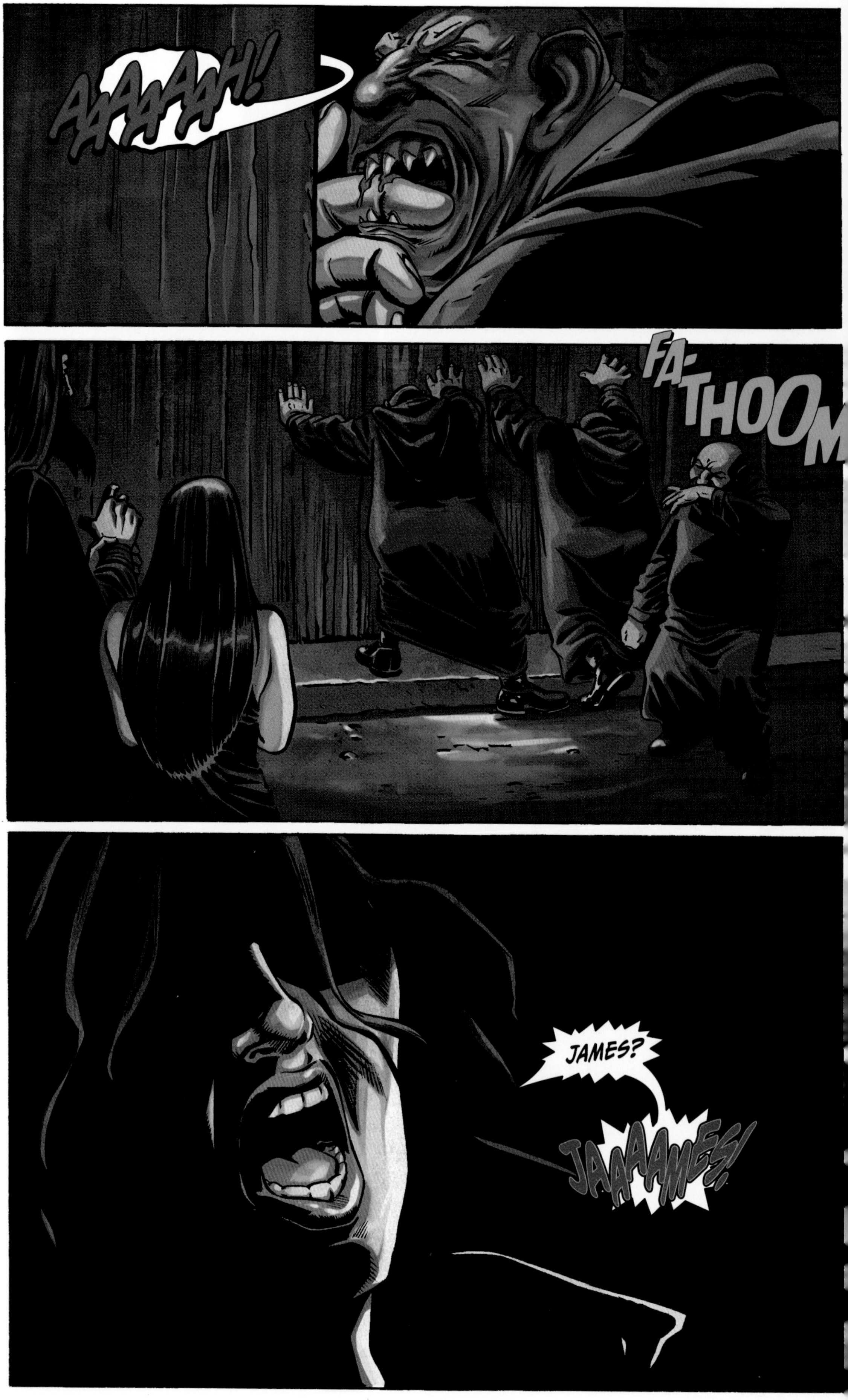
AAAAAAH!
FA-THOOM
JAMES?
JAAAAMES!

CHAPTER FOUR

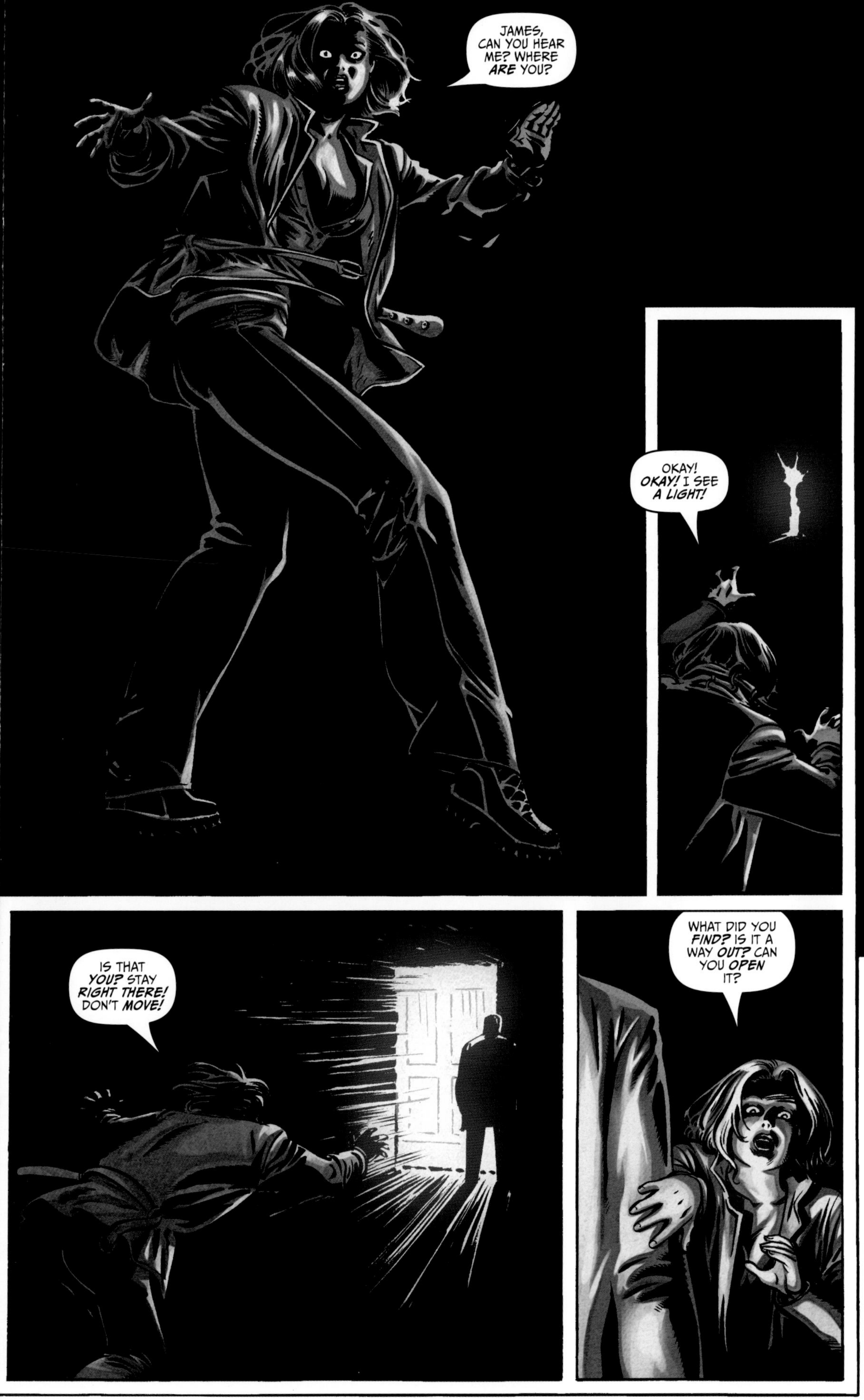
JAMES, CAN YOU HEAR ME? WHERE *ARE* YOU?
OKAY! *OKAY!* I SEE *A LIGHT!*
IS THAT *YOU?* STAY *RIGHT THERE!* DON'T *MOVE!*
WHAT DID YOU *FIND?* IS IT A WAY *OUT?* CAN YOU *OPEN* IT?

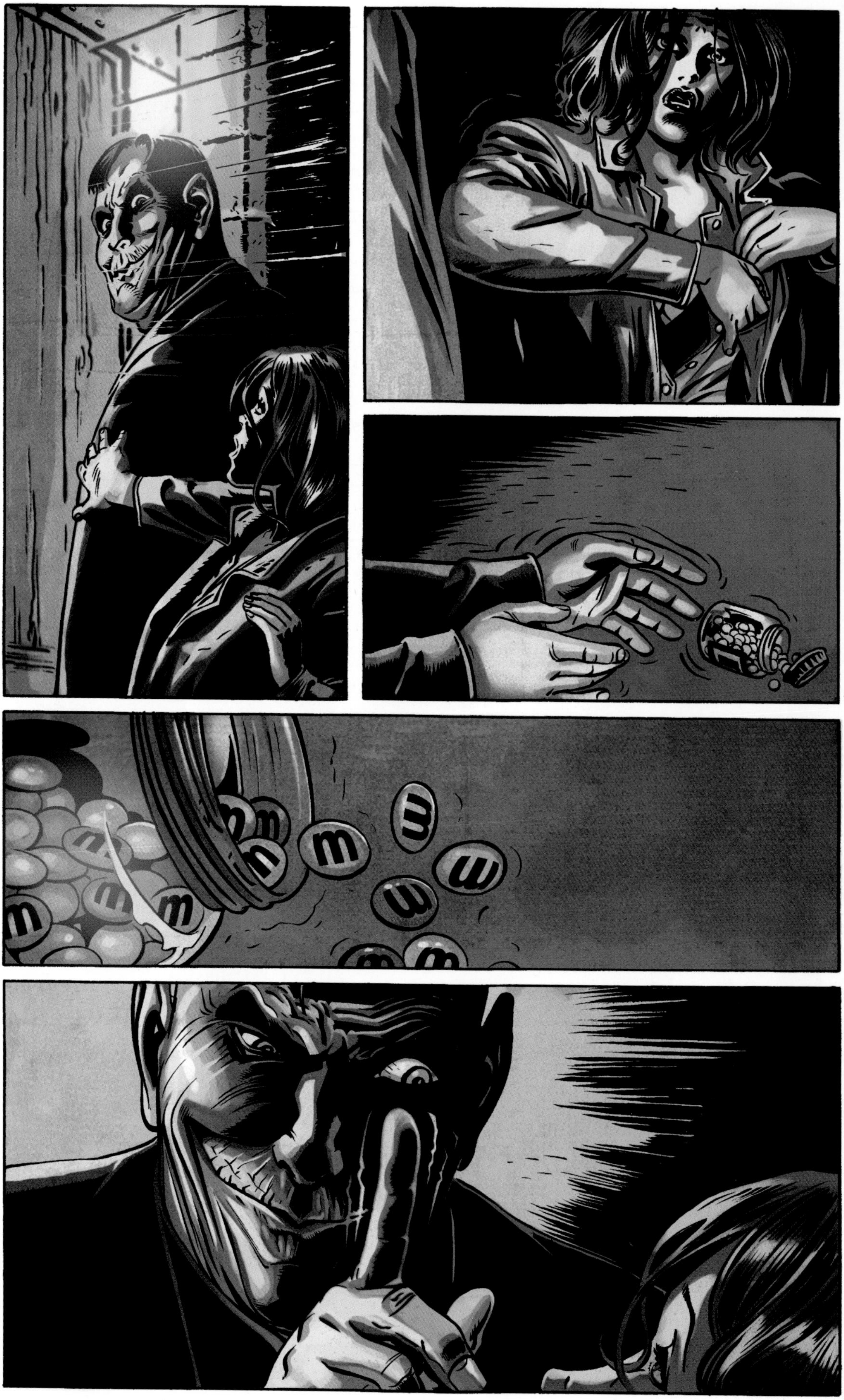

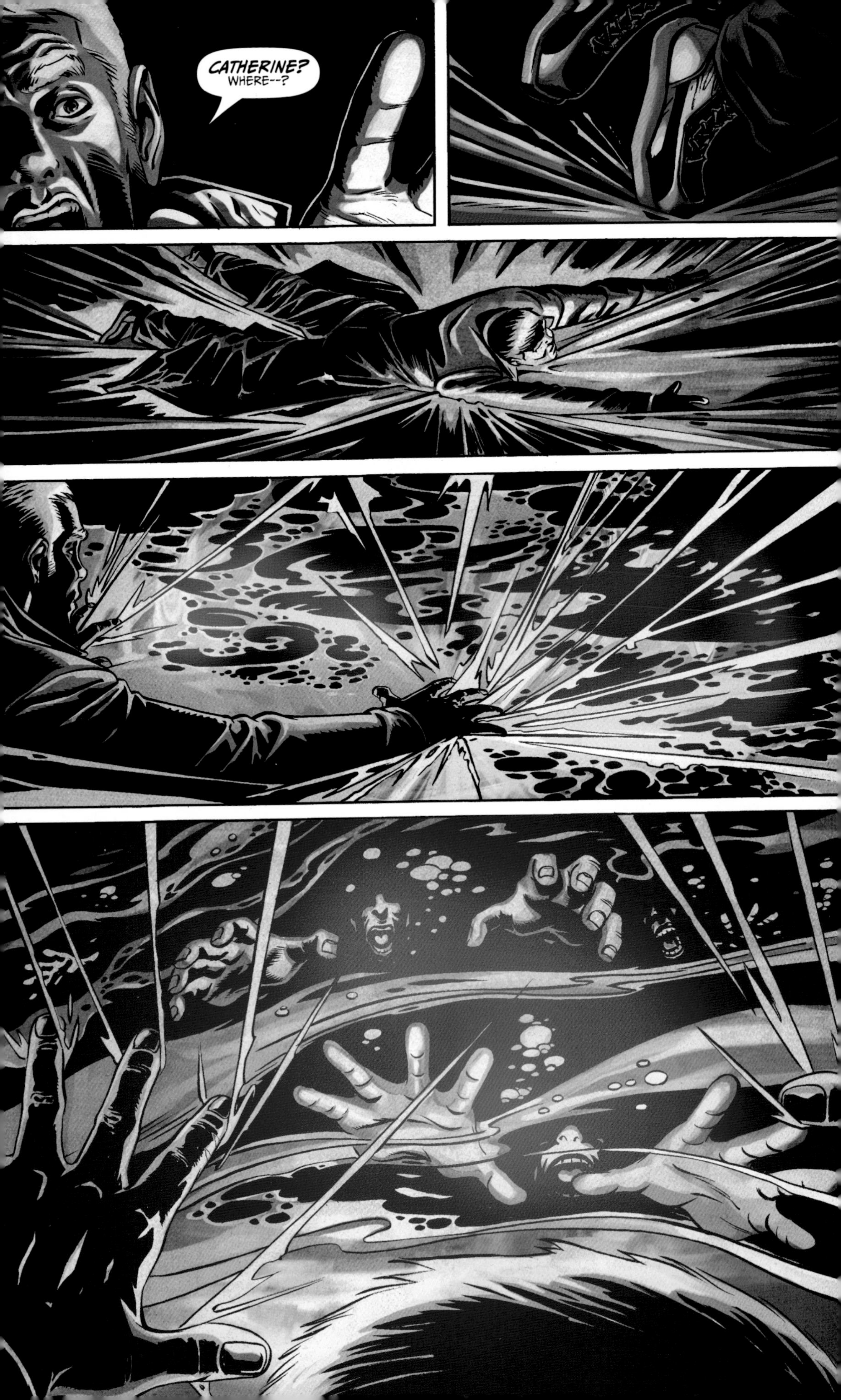
CATHERINE? WHERE--?

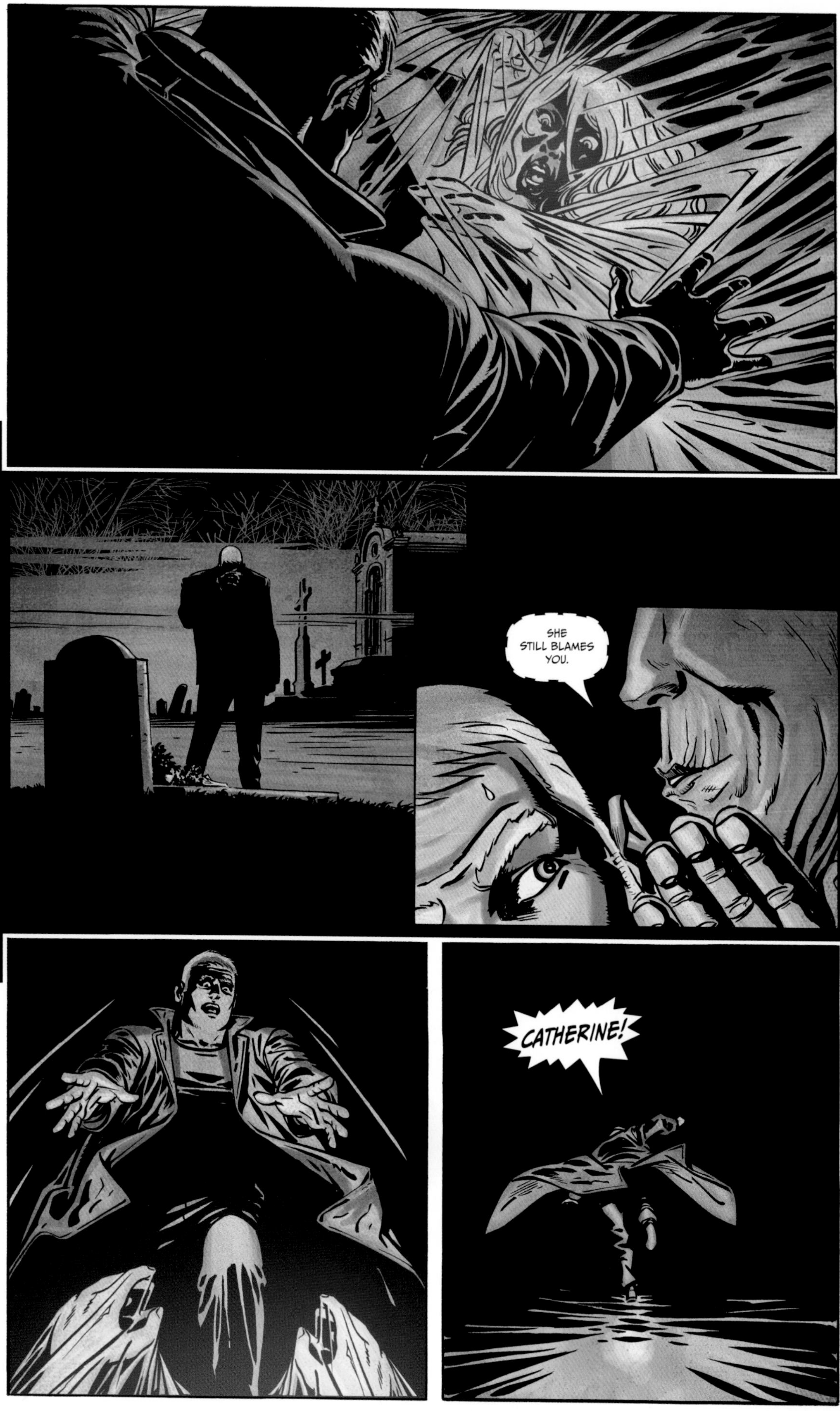
SHE STILL BLAMES YOU.
CATHERINE!

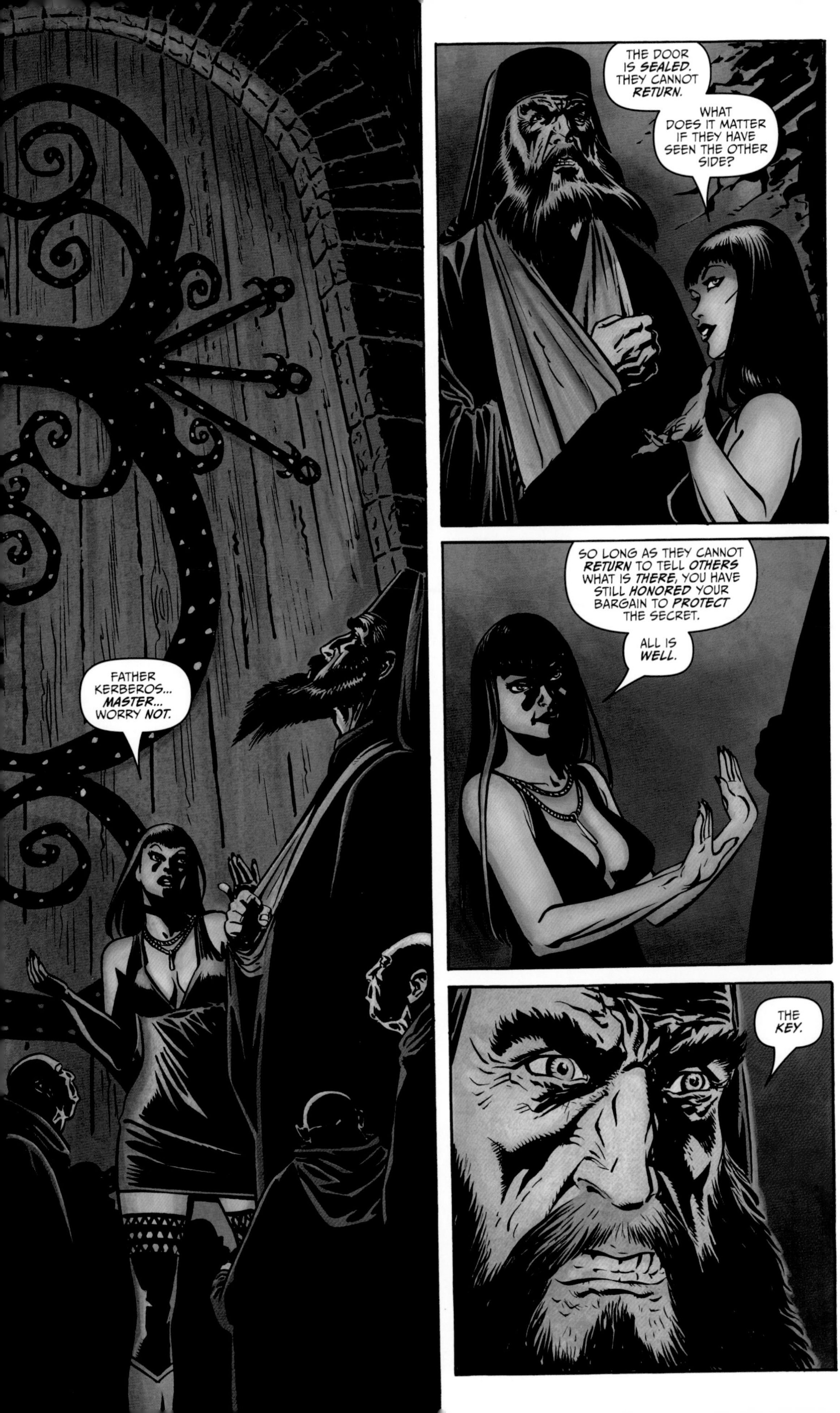
FATHER KERBEROS... MASTER... WORRY NOT.
THE DOOR IS SEALED. THEY CANNOT RETURN.
WHAT DOES IT MATTER IF THEY HAVE SEEN THE OTHER SIDE?
SO LONG AS THEY CANNOT RETURN TO TELL OTHERS WHAT IS THERE, YOU HAVE STILL HONORED YOUR BARGAIN TO PROTECT THE SECRET.
ALL IS WELL.
THE KEY.

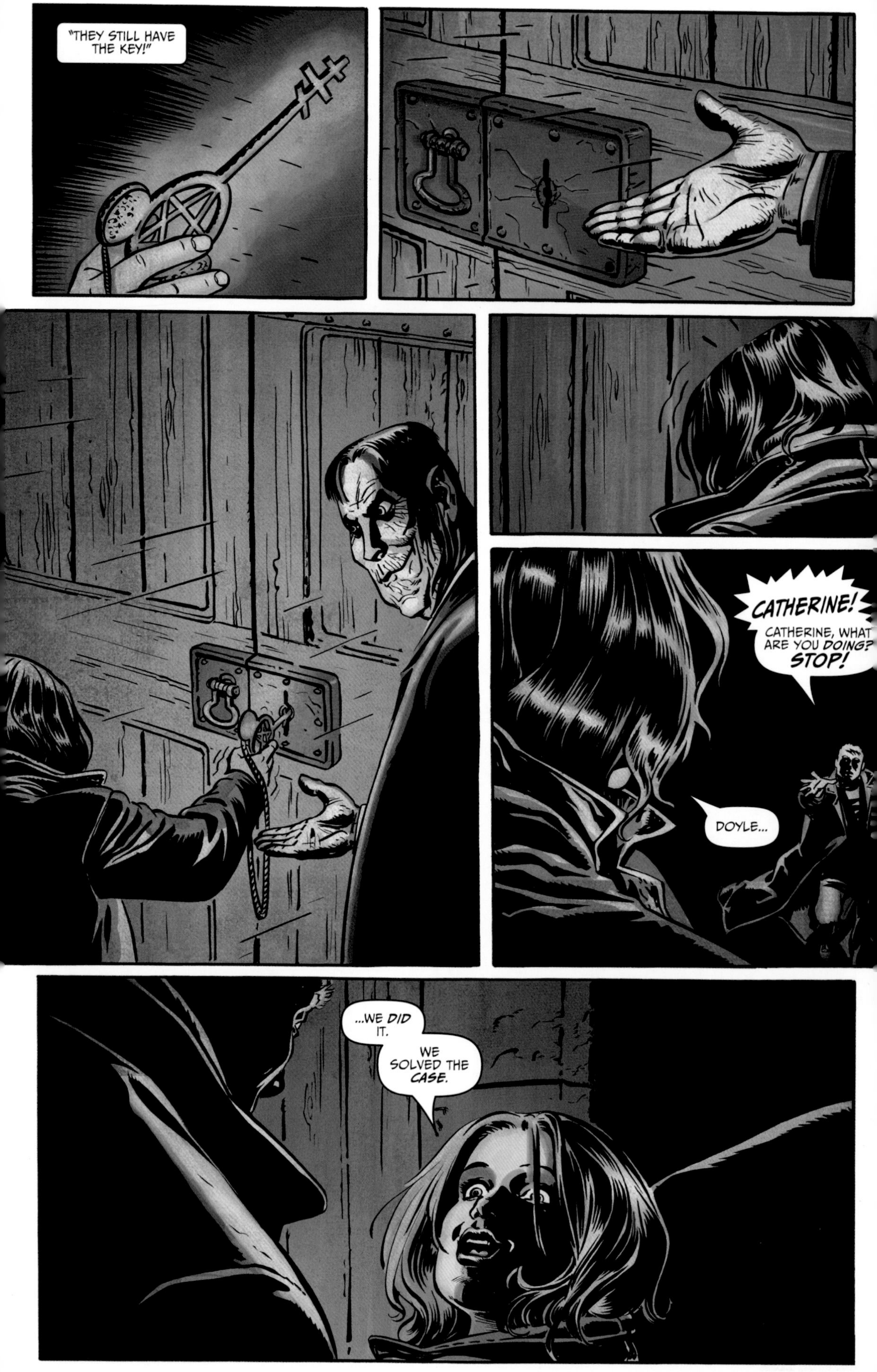
"THEY STILL HAVE THE KEY!"
CATHERINE!
CATHERINE, WHAT ARE YOU DOING? STOP!
DOYLE...
...WE DID IT.
WE SOLVED THE CASE.

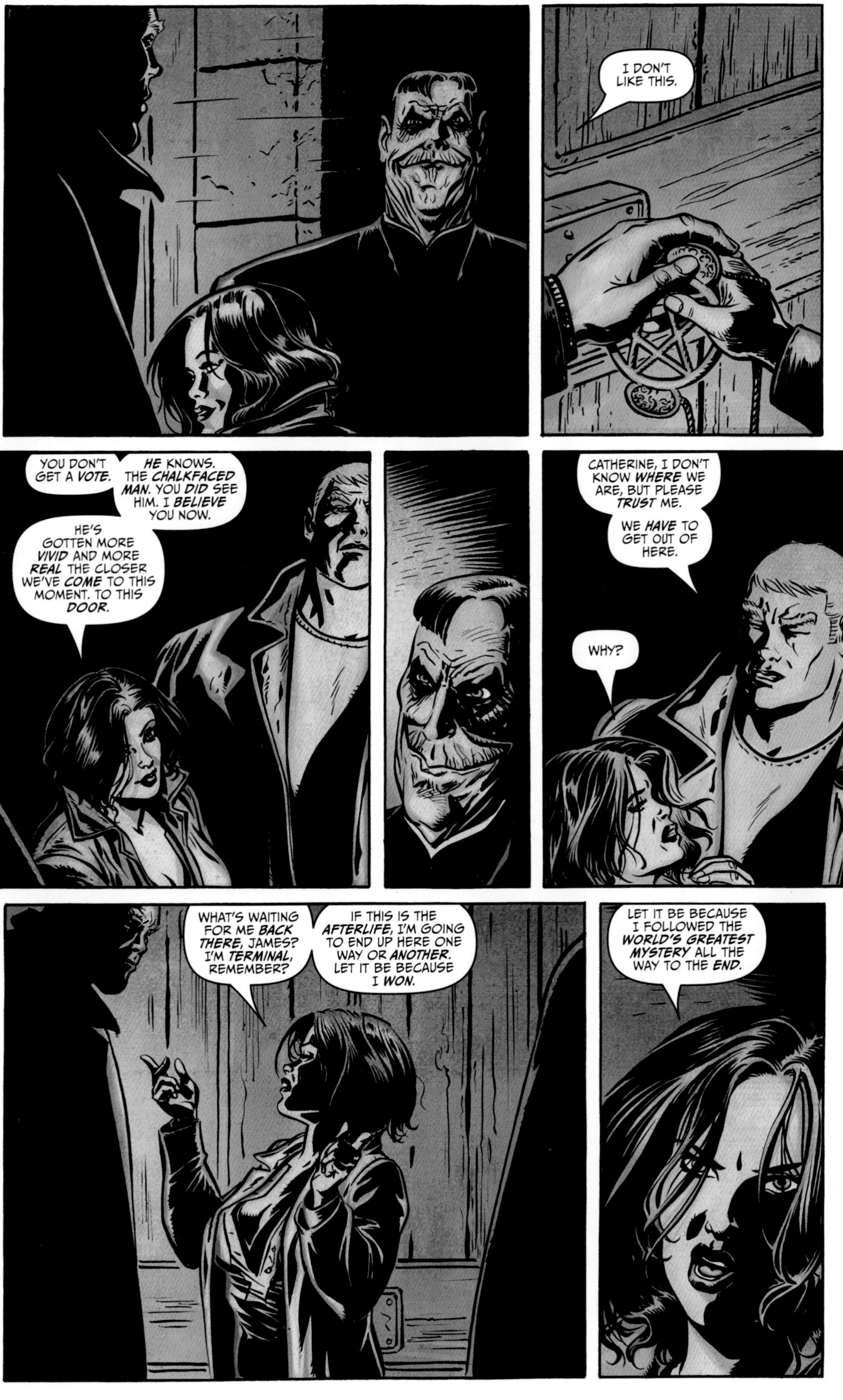

I DON'T LIKE THIS.
YOU DON'T GET A VOTE.
HE KNOWS. THE CHALKFACED MAN. YOU DID SEE HIM. I BELIEVE YOU NOW.
HE'S GOTTEN MORE VIVID AND MORE REAL THE CLOSER WE'VE COME TO THIS MOMENT. TO THIS DOOR.
CATHERINE, I DON'T KNOW WHERE WE ARE, BUT PLEASE TRUST ME.
WE HAVE TO GET OUT OF HERE.
WHY?
WHAT'S WAITING FOR ME BACK THERE, JAMES? I'M TERMINAL, REMEMBER?
IF THIS IS THE AFTERLIFE, I'M GOING TO END UP HERE ONE WAY OR ANOTHER. LET IT BE BECAUSE I WON.
LET IT BE BECAUSE I FOLLOWED THE WORLD'S GREATEST MYSTERY ALL THE WAY TO THE END.

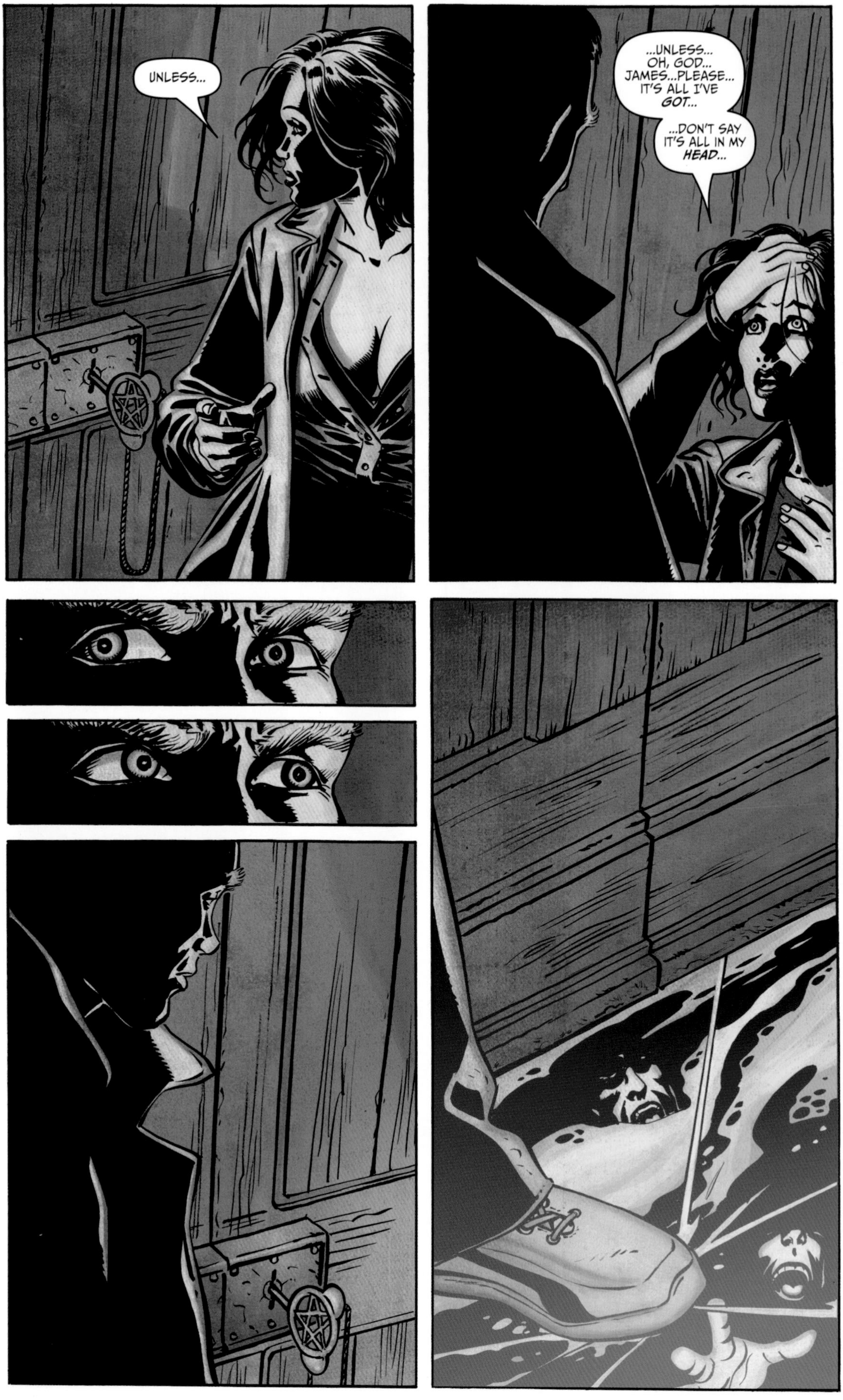
UNLESS...
...UNLESS... OH, GOD... JAMES...PLEASE... IT'S ALL I'VE GOT...
...DON'T SAY IT'S ALL IN MY HEAD...

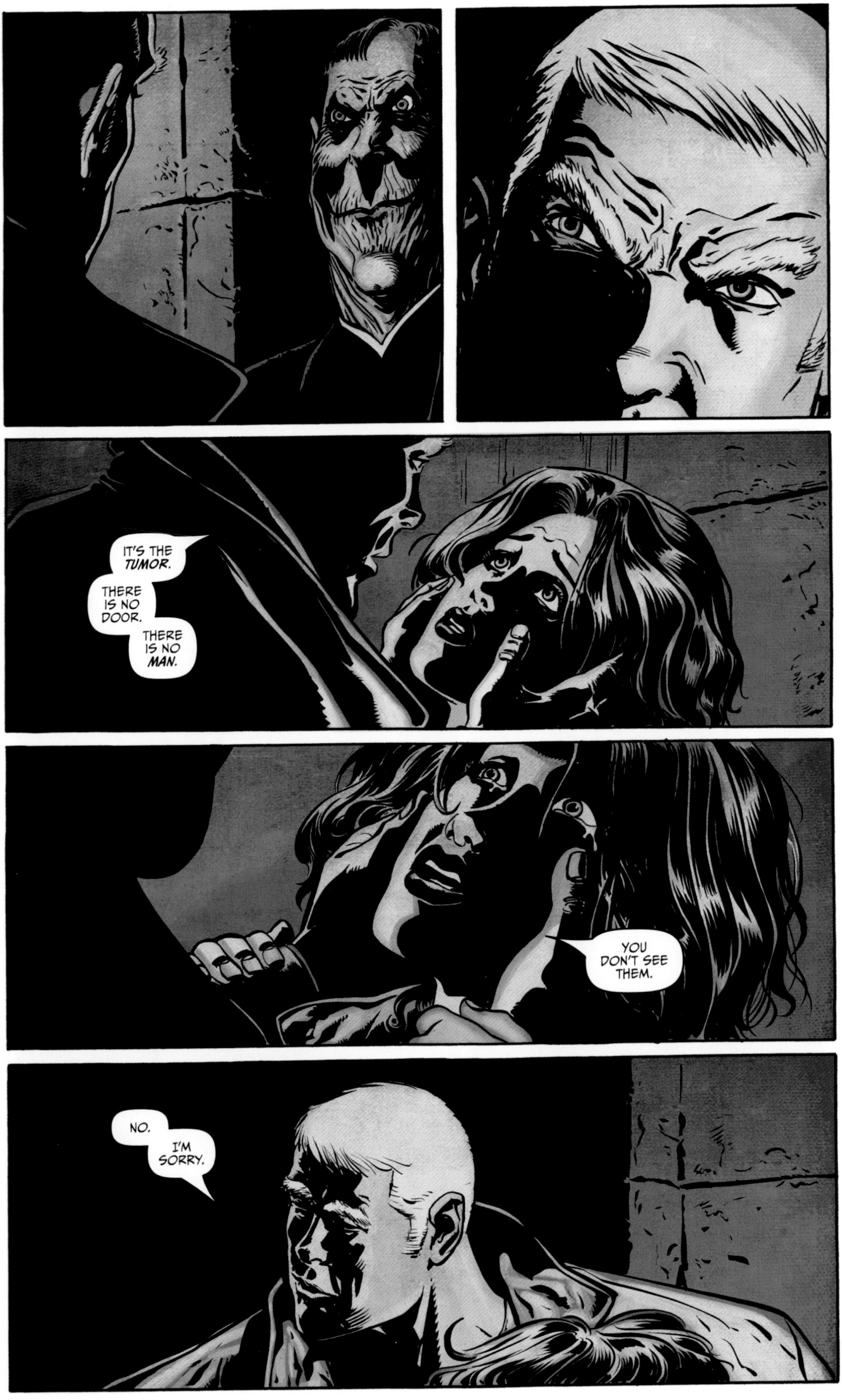

IT'S THE *TUMOR*.
THERE IS NO DOOR.
THERE IS NO *MAN*.
YOU DON'T SEE THEM.
NO.
I'M SORRY.

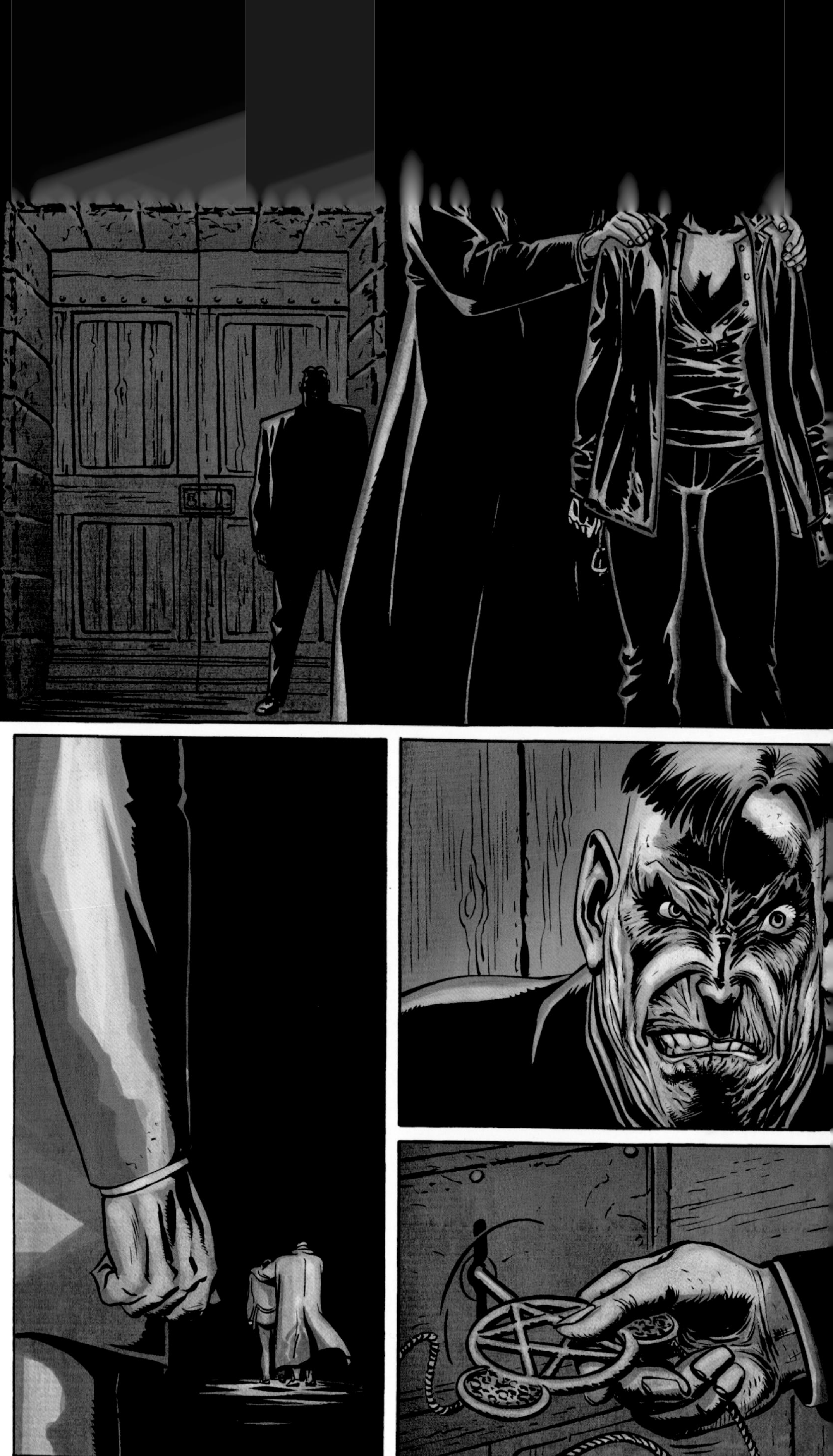

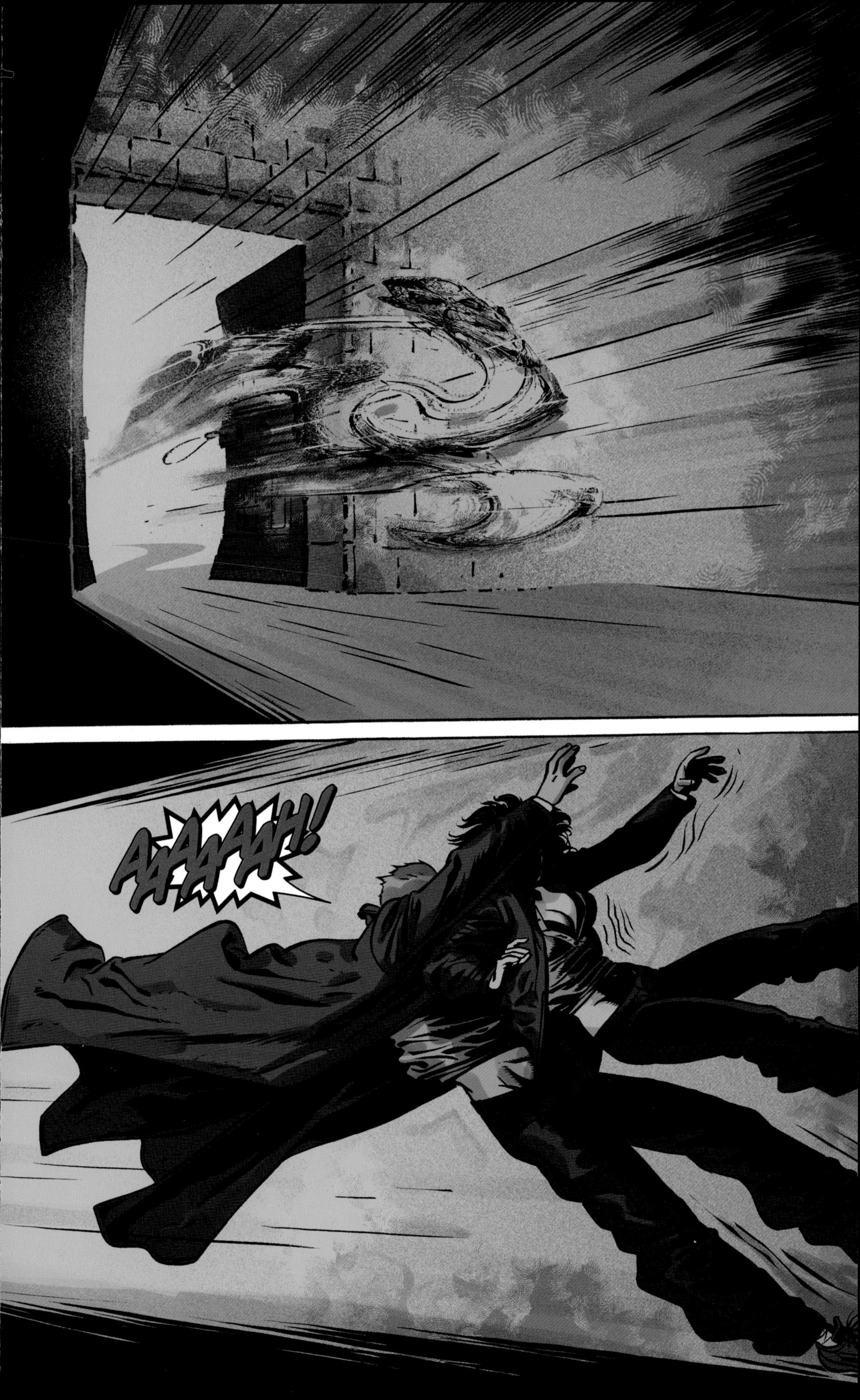
AAAAAH!

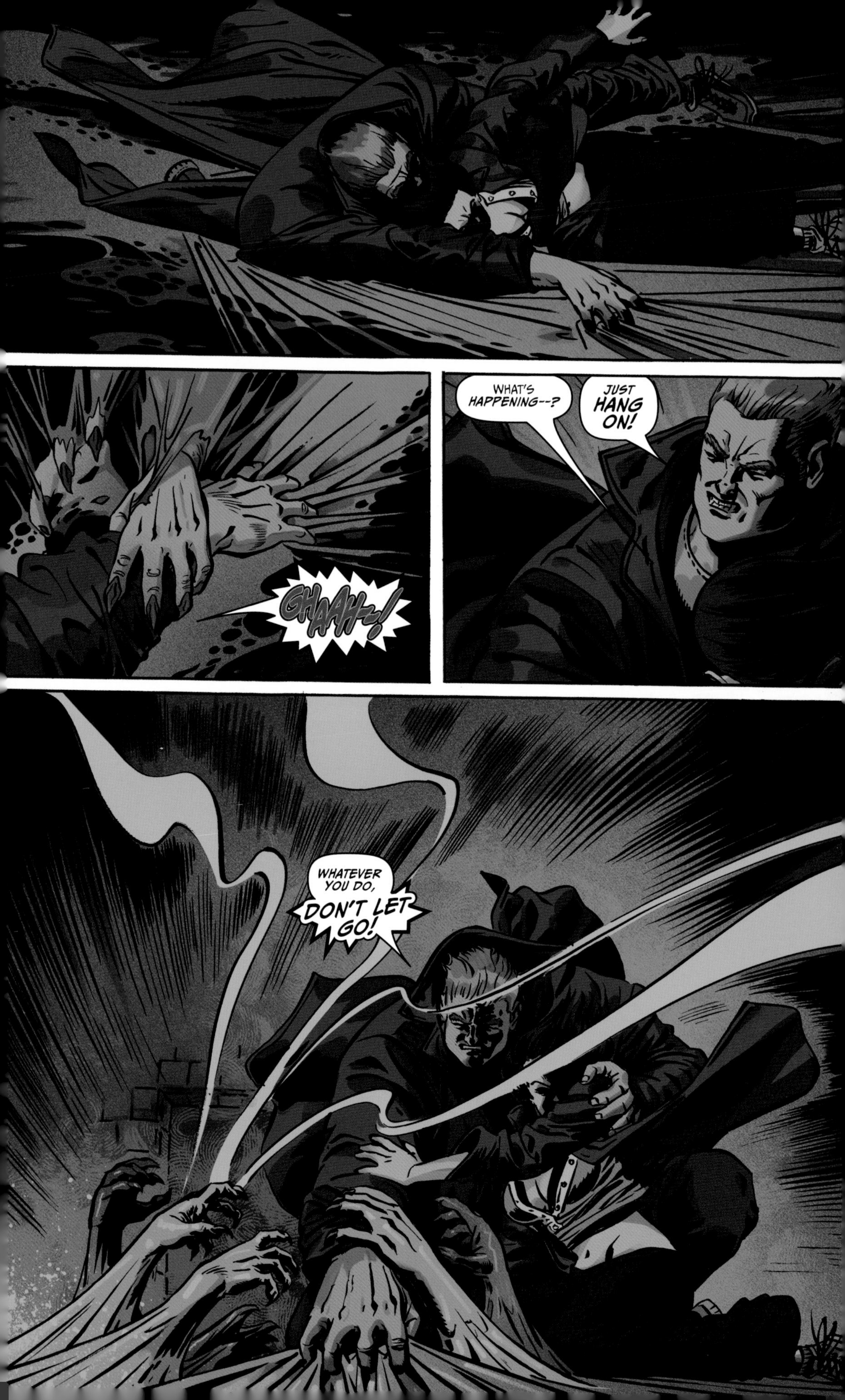
GHAAH--!
WHAT'S HAPPENING--?
JUST HANG ON!
WHATEVER YOU DO, DON'T LET GO!

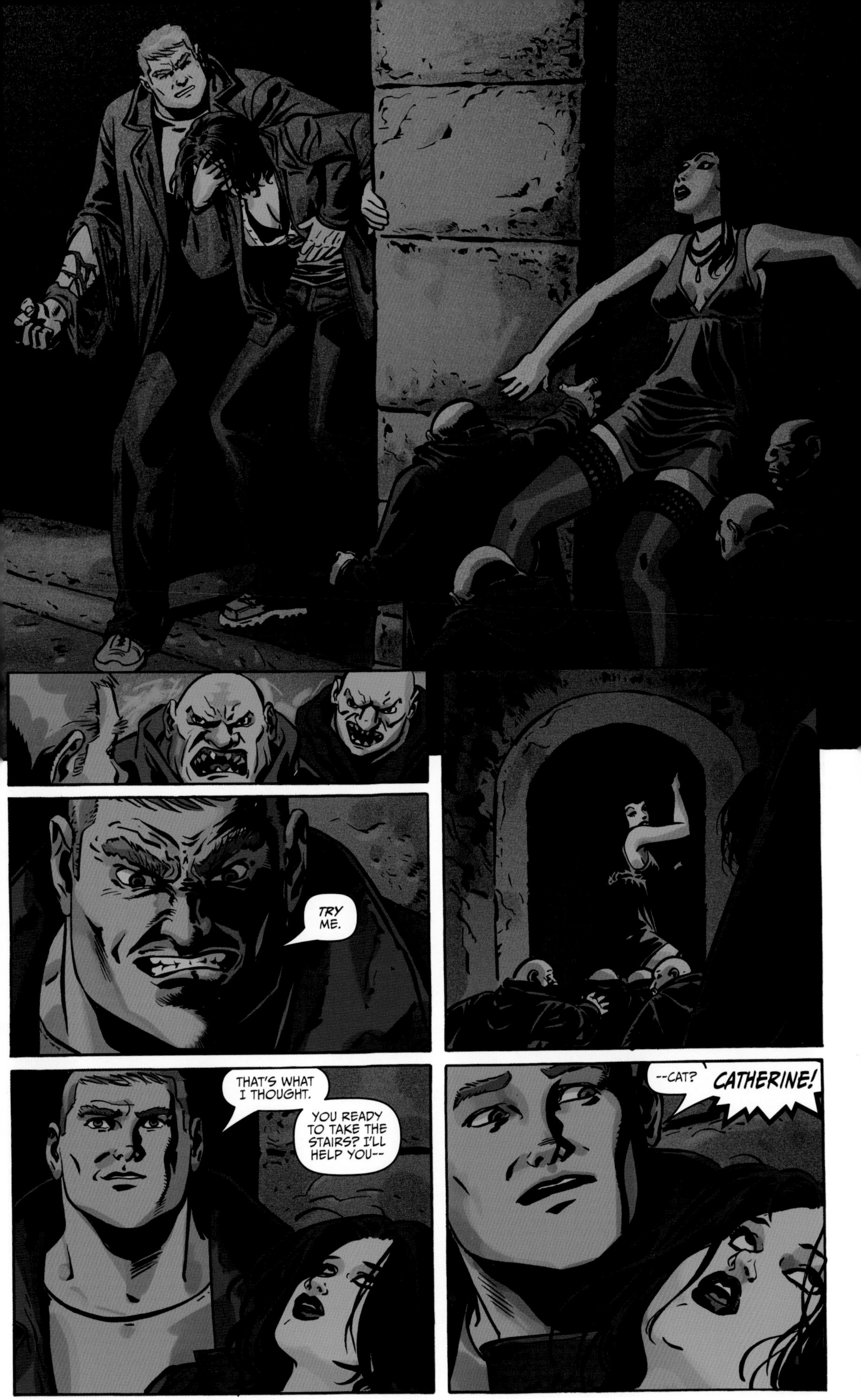
TRY ME.
THAT'S WHAT I THOUGHT.
YOU READY TO TAKE THE STAIRS? I'LL HELP YOU--
--CAT?
CATHERINE!

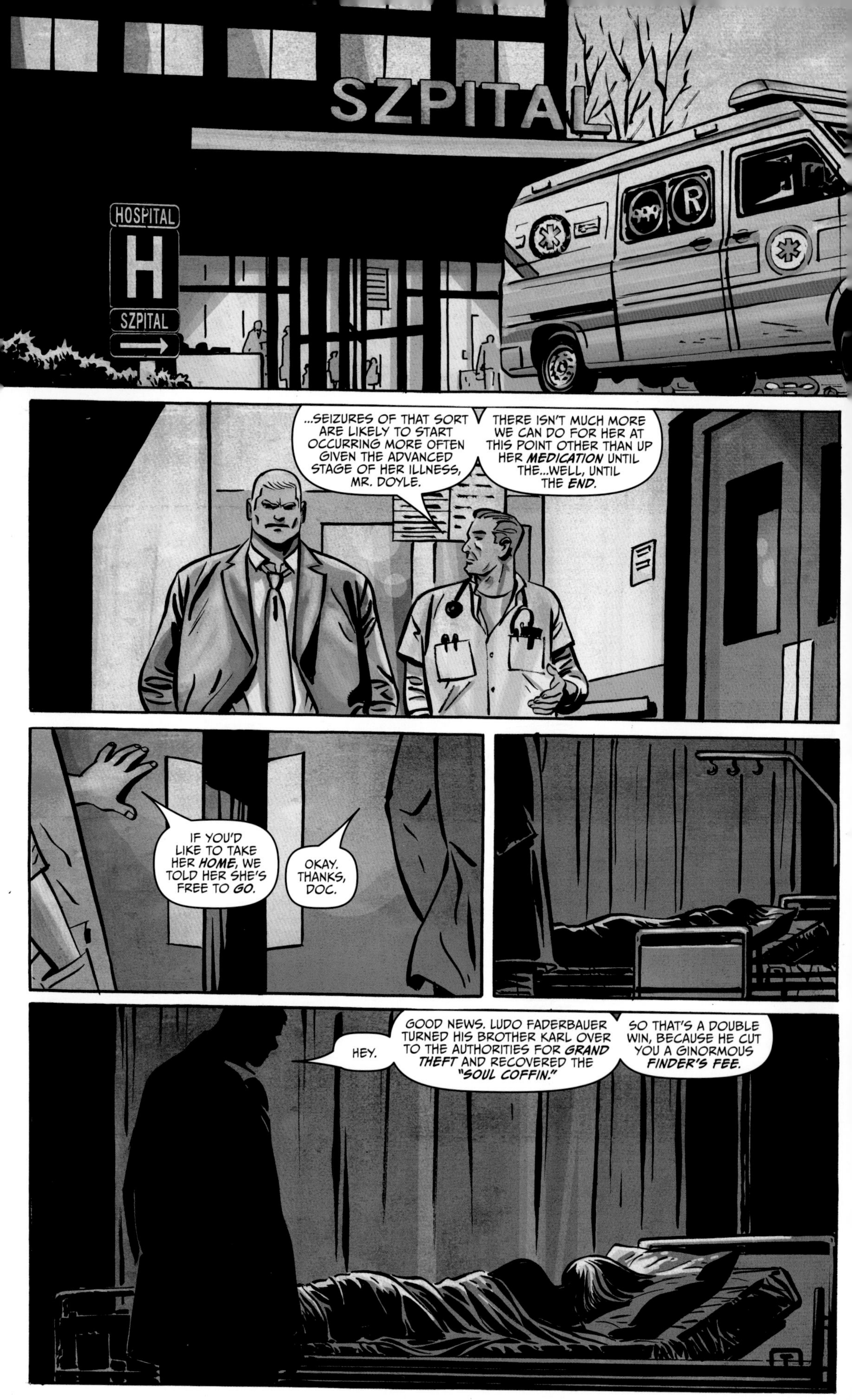
SZPITAL
HOSPITAL
H
SZPITAL
...SEIZURES OF THAT SORT ARE LIKELY TO START OCCURRING MORE OFTEN GIVEN THE ADVANCED STAGE OF HER ILLNESS, MR. DOYLE.
THERE ISN'T MUCH MORE WE CAN DO FOR HER AT THIS POINT OTHER THAN UP HER *MEDICATION* UNTIL THE...WELL, UNTIL THE *END*.
IF YOU'D LIKE TO TAKE HER *HOME*, WE TOLD HER SHE'S FREE TO *GO*.
OKAY. THANKS, DOC.
HEY.
GOOD NEWS. LUDO FADERBAUER TURNED HIS BROTHER KARL OVER TO THE AUTHORITIES FOR *GRAND THEFT* AND RECOVERED THE *"SOUL COFFIN."*
SO THAT'S A DOUBLE WIN, BECAUSE HE CUT YOU A GINORMOUS *FINDER'S FEE*.

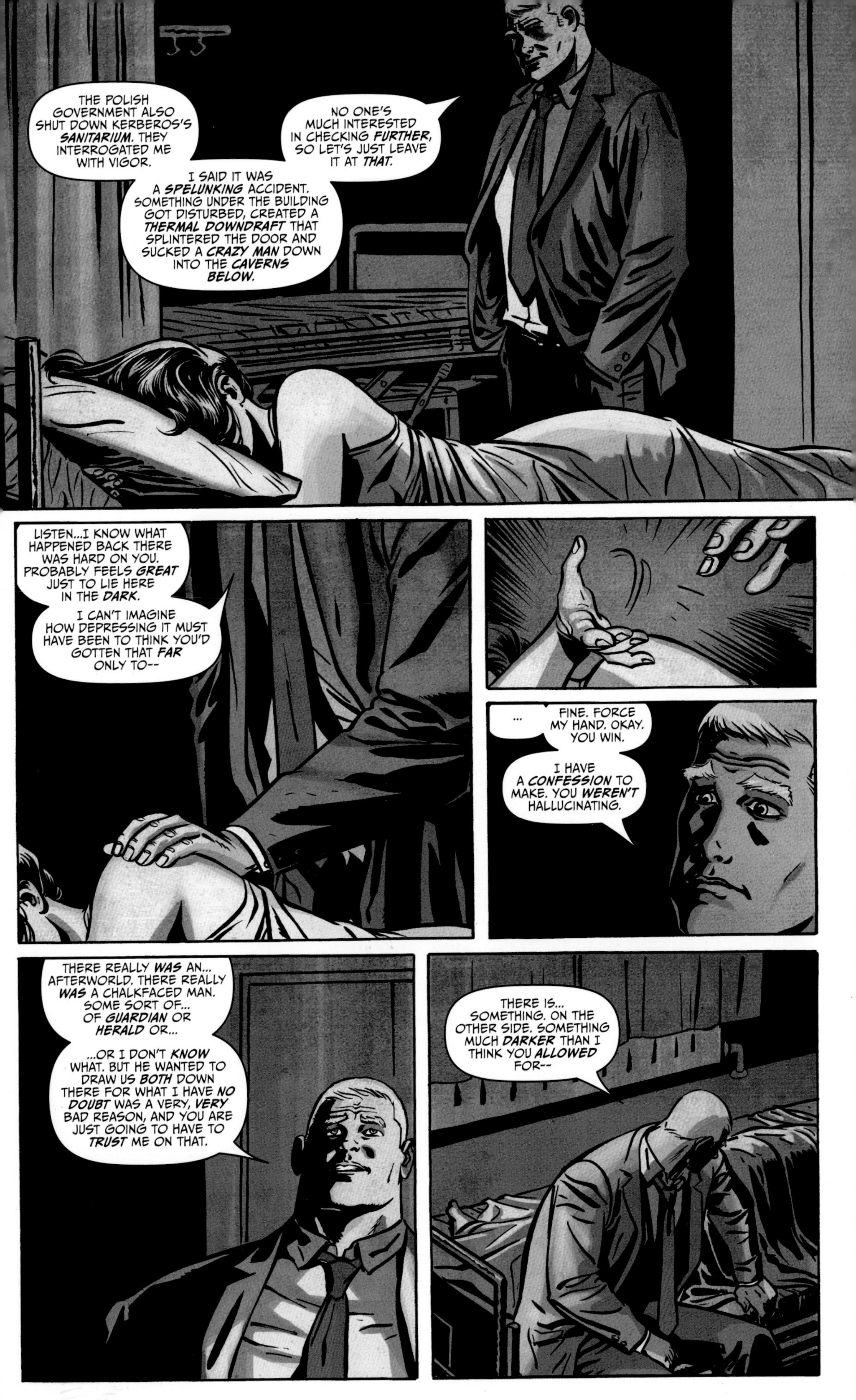
THE POLISH GOVERNMENT ALSO SHUT DOWN KERBEROS'S SANITARIUM. THEY INTERROGATED ME WITH VIGOR.
I SAID IT WAS A SPELUNKING ACCIDENT. SOMETHING UNDER THE BUILDING GOT DISTURBED, CREATED A THERMAL DOWNDRAFT THAT SPLINTERED THE DOOR AND SUCKED A CRAZY MAN DOWN INTO THE CAVERNS BELOW.
NO ONE'S MUCH INTERESTED IN CHECKING FURTHER, SO LET'S JUST LEAVE IT AT THAT.
LISTEN...I KNOW WHAT HAPPENED BACK THERE WAS HARD ON YOU. PROBABLY FEELS GREAT JUST TO LIE HERE IN THE DARK.
I CAN'T IMAGINE HOW DEPRESSING IT MUST HAVE BEEN TO THINK YOU'D GOTTEN THAT FAR ONLY TO--
...
FINE. FORCE MY HAND. OKAY. YOU WIN.
I HAVE A CONFESSION TO MAKE. YOU WEREN'T HALLUCINATING.
THERE REALLY WAS AN... AFTERWORLD. THERE REALLY WAS A CHALKFACED MAN. SOME SORT OF... OF GUARDIAN OR HERALD OR...
...OR I DON'T KNOW WHAT. BUT HE WANTED TO DRAW US BOTH DOWN THERE FOR WHAT I HAVE NO DOUBT WAS A VERY, VERY BAD REASON, AND YOU ARE JUST GOING TO HAVE TO TRUST ME ON THAT.
THERE IS... SOMETHING. ON THE OTHER SIDE. SOMETHING MUCH DARKER THAN I THINK YOU ALLOWED FOR--

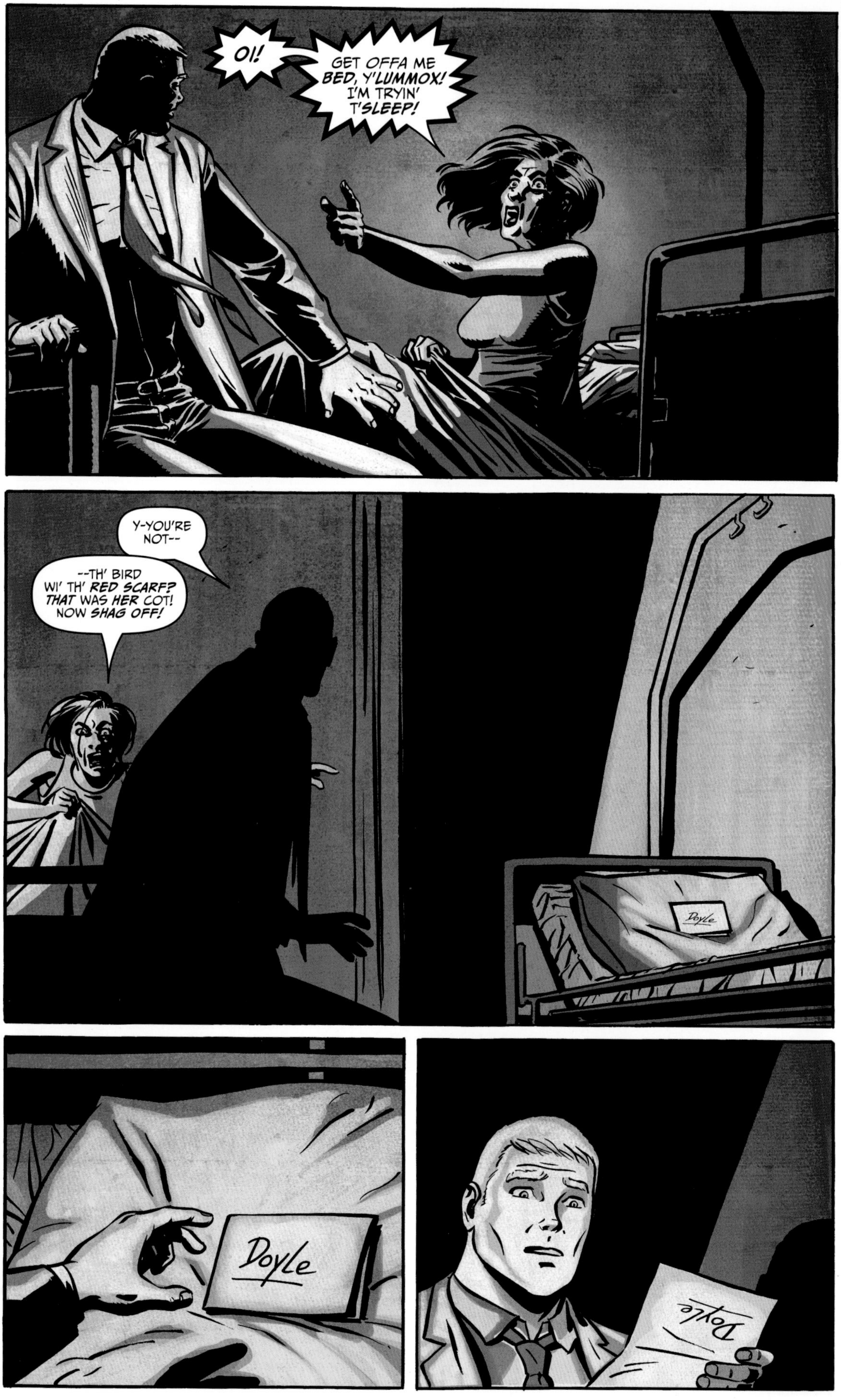
OI!
GET OFFA ME BED, Y'LUMMOX! I'M TRYIN' T'SLEEP!
Y-YOU'RE NOT--
--TH' BIRD WI' TH' RED SCARF? THAT WAS HER COT! NOW SHAG OFF!
Doyle
Doyle
Doyle

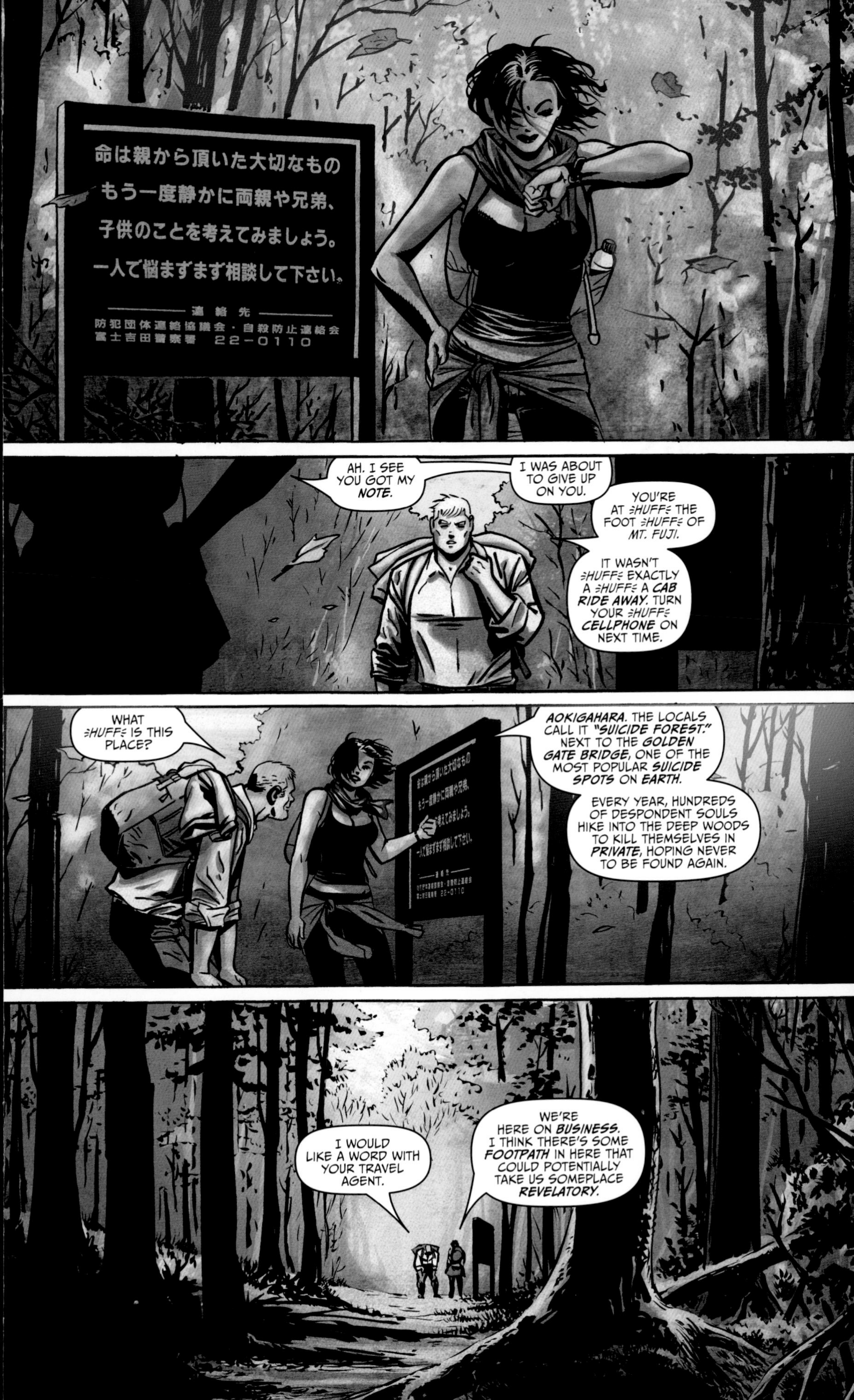
命は親から頂いた大切なもの
もう一度静かに両親や兄弟、
子供のことを考えてみましょう。
一人で悩まずまず相談して下さい。
連絡先
防犯団体連絡協議会・自殺防止連絡会
富士吉田警察署 22-0110
AH. I SEE YOU GOT MY NOTE.
I WAS ABOUT TO GIVE UP ON YOU.
YOU'RE AT =HUFF= THE FOOT =HUFF= OF MT. FUJI.
IT WASN'T =HUFF= EXACTLY A =HUFF= A CAB RIDE AWAY. TURN YOUR =HUFF= CELLPHONE ON NEXT TIME.
WHAT =HUFF= IS THIS PLACE?
AOKIGAHARA. THE LOCALS CALL IT "SUICIDE FOREST." NEXT TO THE GOLDEN GATE BRIDGE, ONE OF THE MOST POPULAR SUICIDE SPOTS ON EARTH.
EVERY YEAR, HUNDREDS OF DESPONDENT SOULS HIKE INTO THE DEEP WOODS TO KILL THEMSELVES IN PRIVATE, HOPING NEVER TO BE FOUND AGAIN.
I WOULD LIKE A WORD WITH YOUR TRAVEL AGENT.
WE'RE HERE ON BUSINESS. I THINK THERE'S SOME FOOTPATH IN HERE THAT COULD POTENTIALLY TAKE US SOMEPLACE REVELATORY.

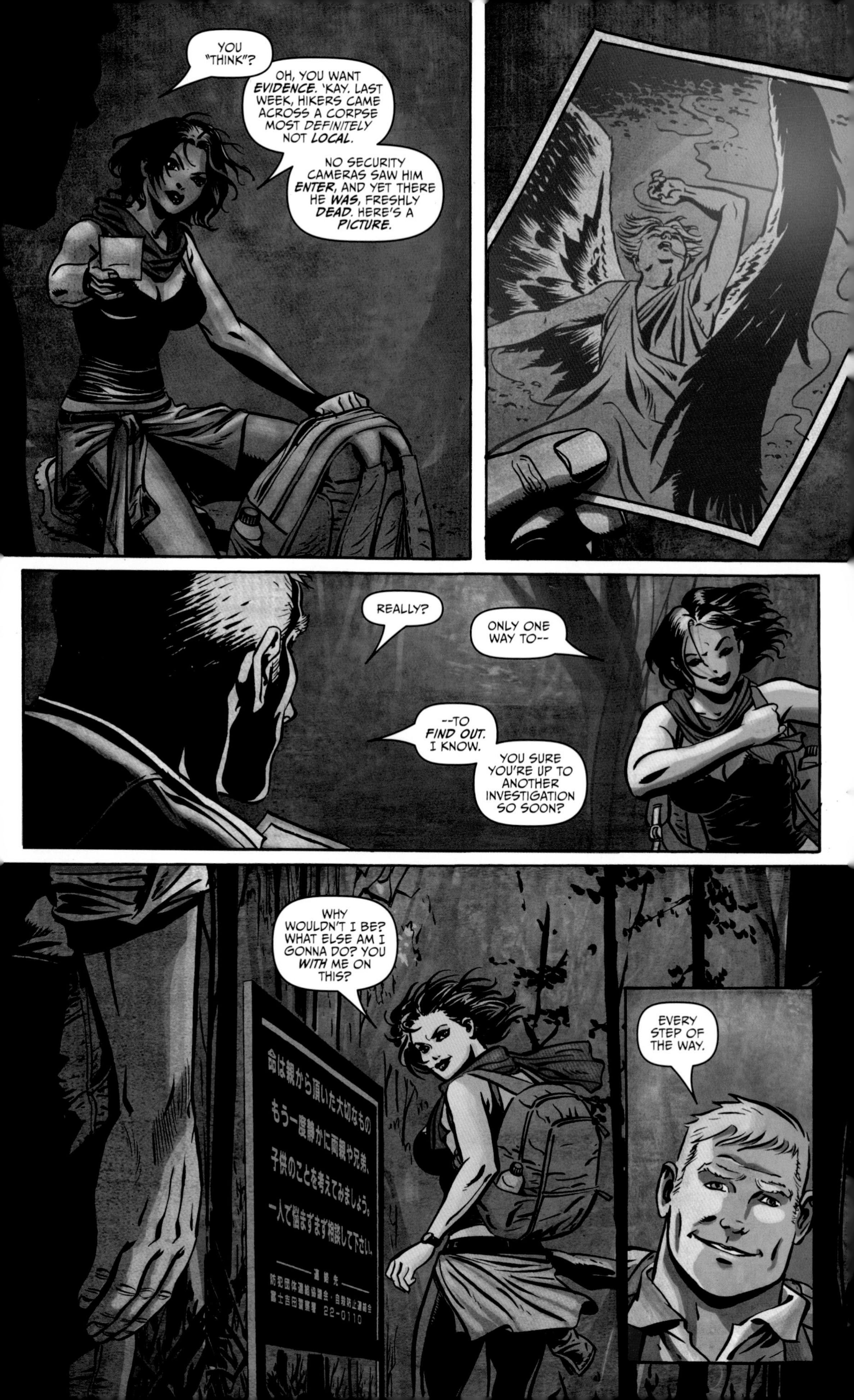
YOU "THINK"?
OH, YOU WANT EVIDENCE. 'KAY. LAST WEEK, HIKERS CAME ACROSS A CORPSE MOST DEFINITELY NOT LOCAL.
NO SECURITY CAMERAS SAW HIM ENTER, AND YET THERE HE WAS, FRESHLY DEAD. HERE'S A PICTURE.
REALLY?
ONLY ONE WAY TO--
--TO FIND OUT. I KNOW.
YOU SURE YOU'RE UP TO ANOTHER INVESTIGATION SO SOON?
WHY WOULDN'T I BE? WHAT ELSE AM I GONNA DO? YOU WITH ME ON THIS?
命は親から頂いた大切なもの
もう一度静かに両親や兄弟、
子供のことを考えてみましょう。
一人で悩まずまず相談して下さい。
連絡先
防犯団体連絡協議会・自殺防止連絡会
富士吉田警察署 22-0110
EVERY STEP OF THE WAY.

COVER GALLERY

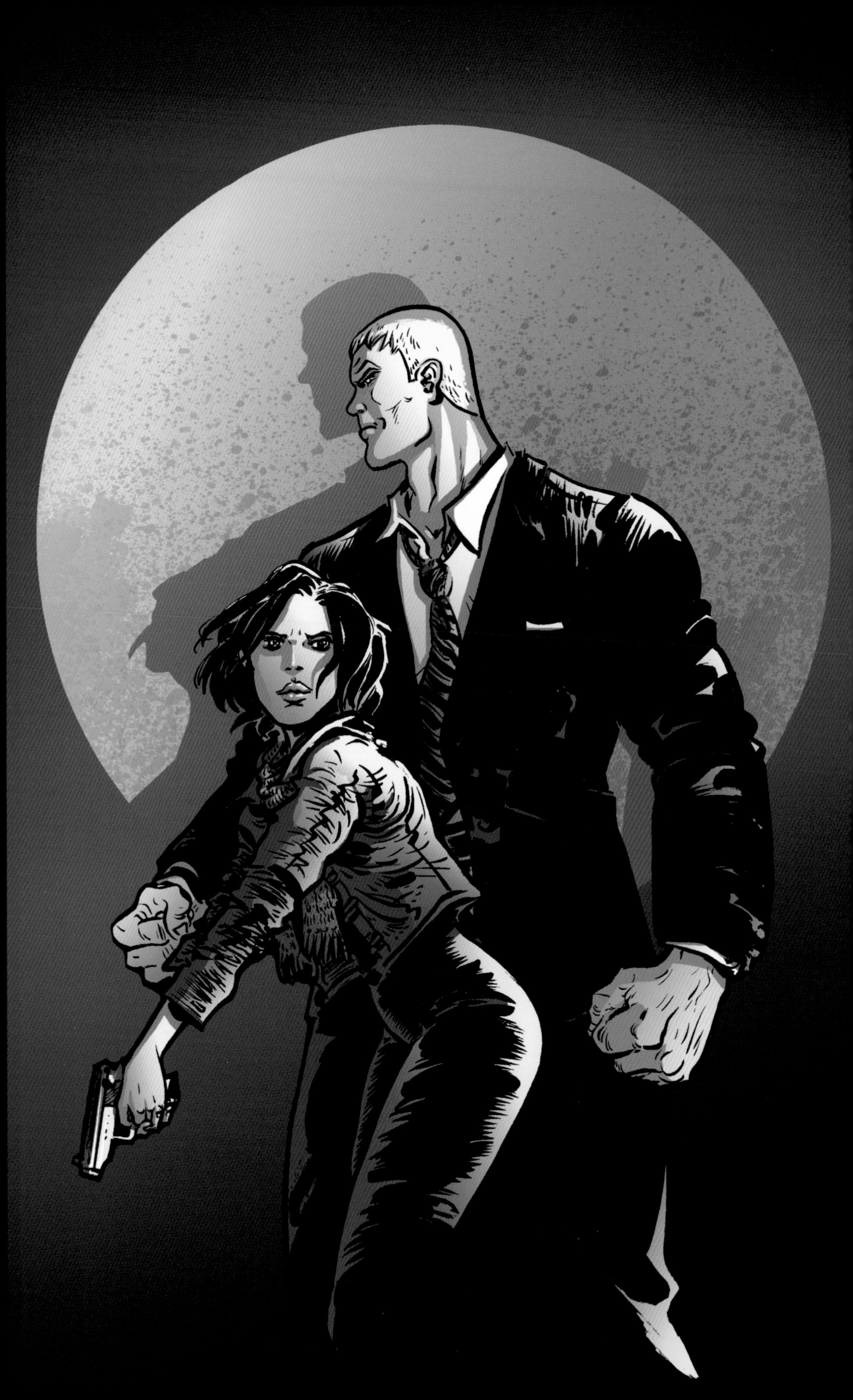

COVER 1
PAUL POPE / COLORS BY CRIS PETE

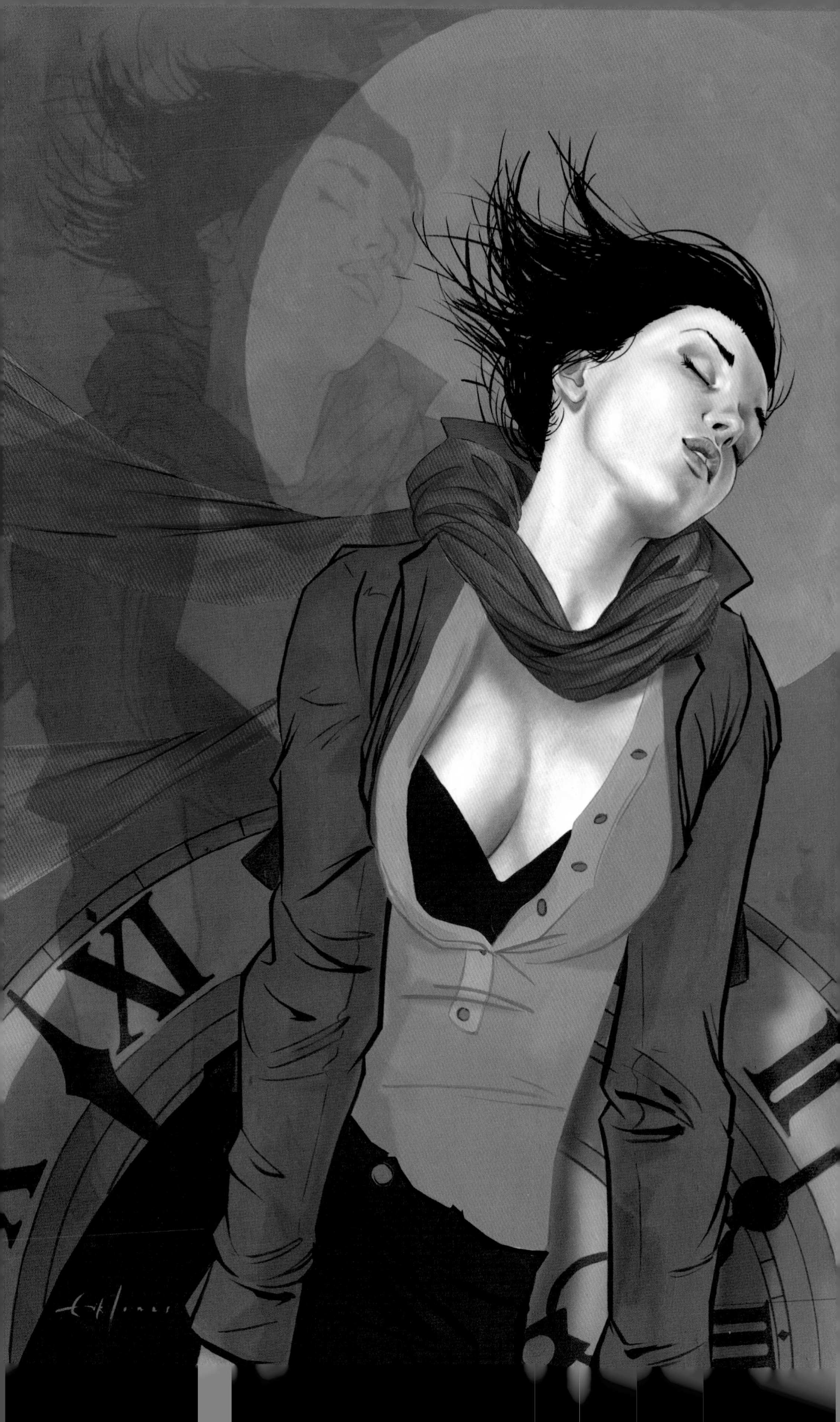

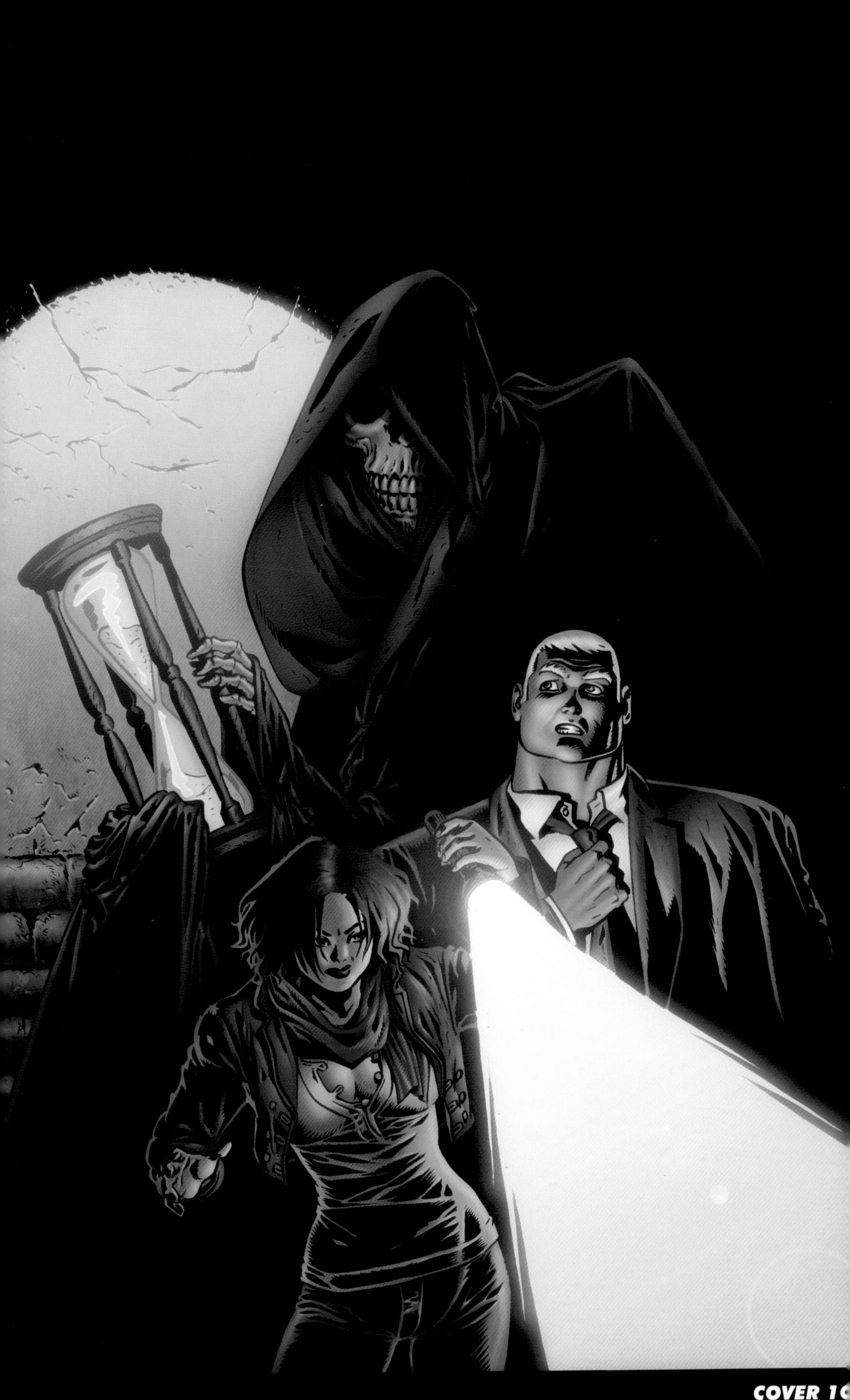

COVER 1
MINCK OOSTERVEER / COLORS BY ANDREW DALHOUSE

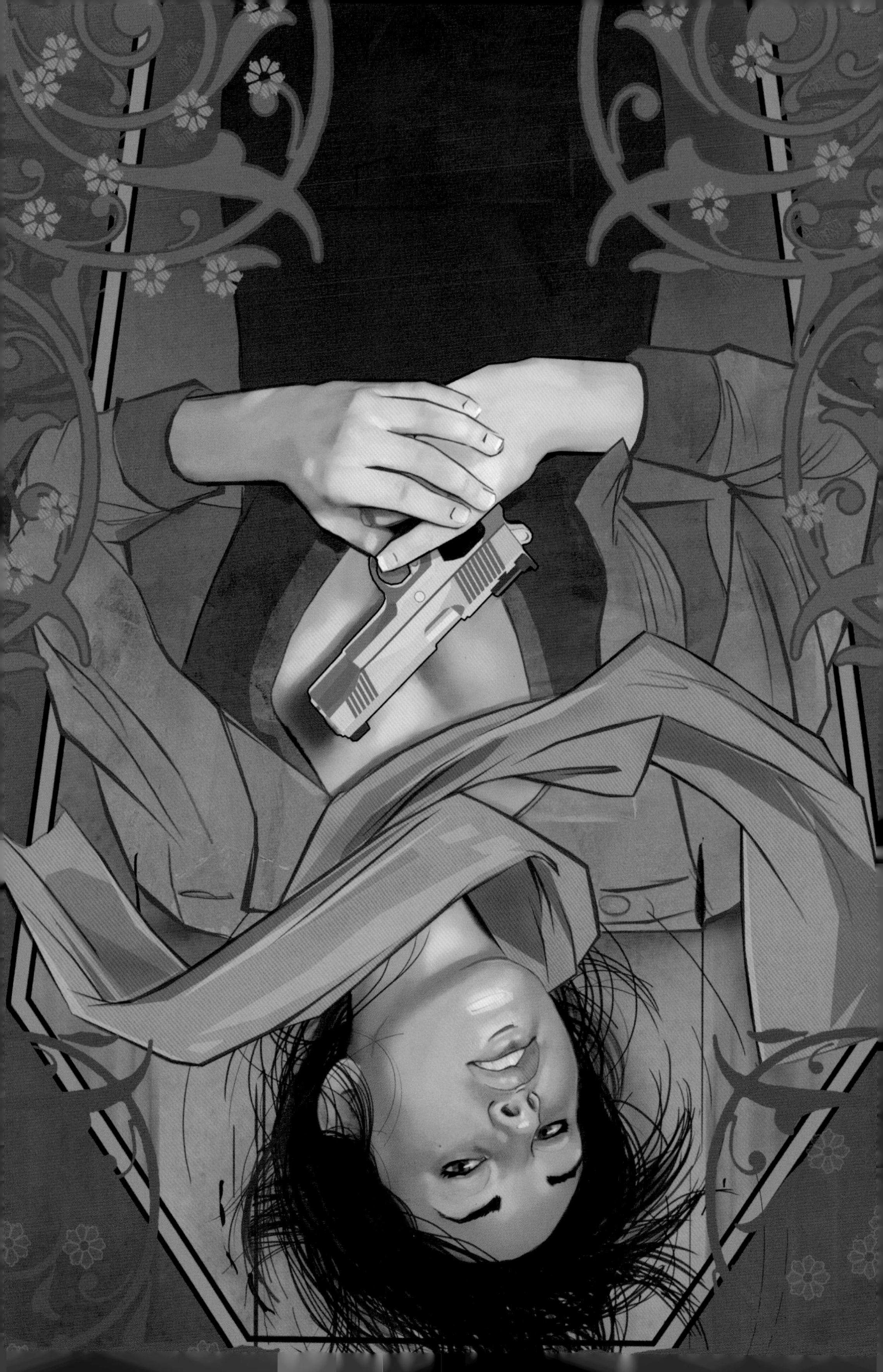

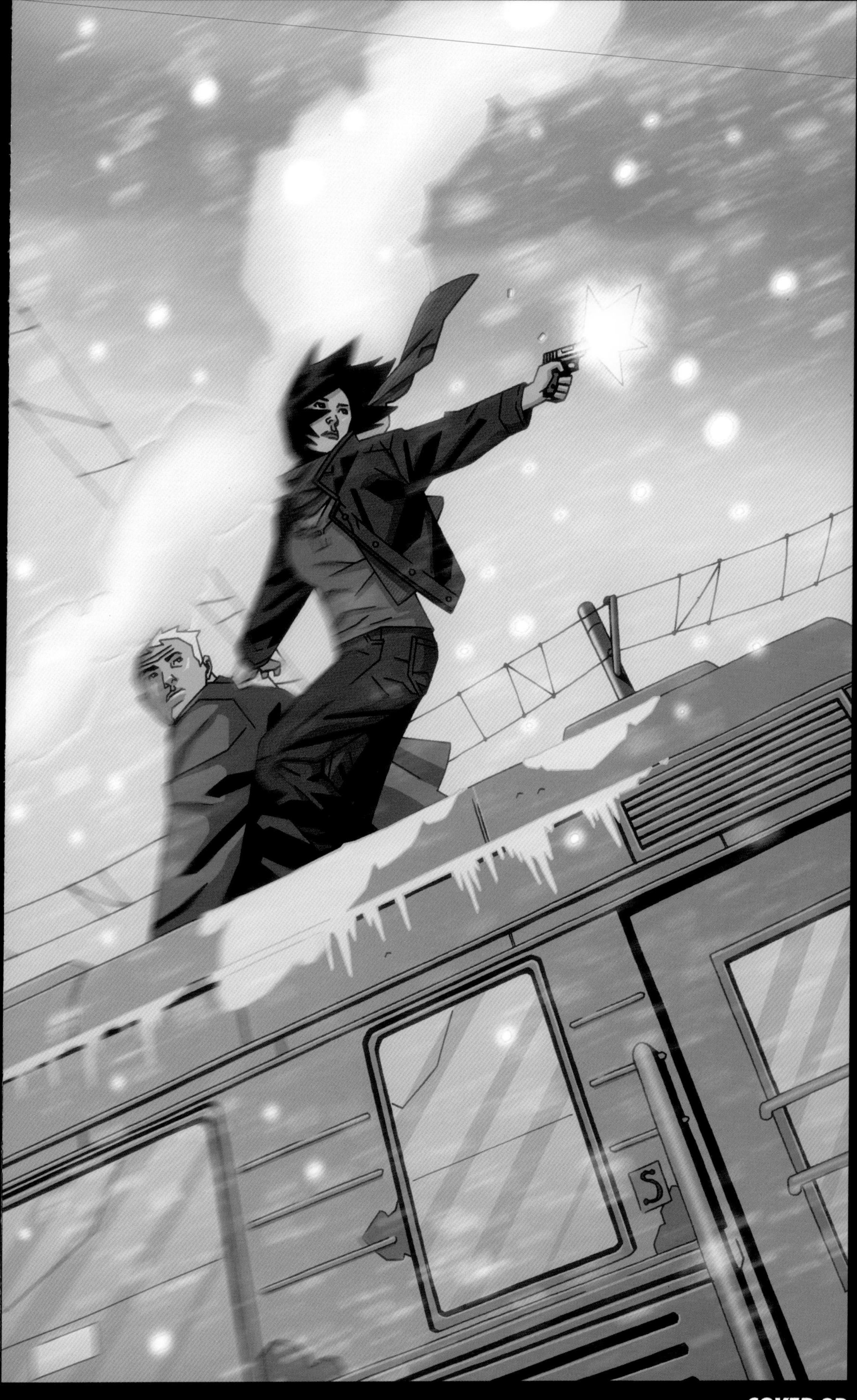
S

COVER 2B
MATTHEW DOW SMITH / COLORS BY ANDREW DALHOUSE

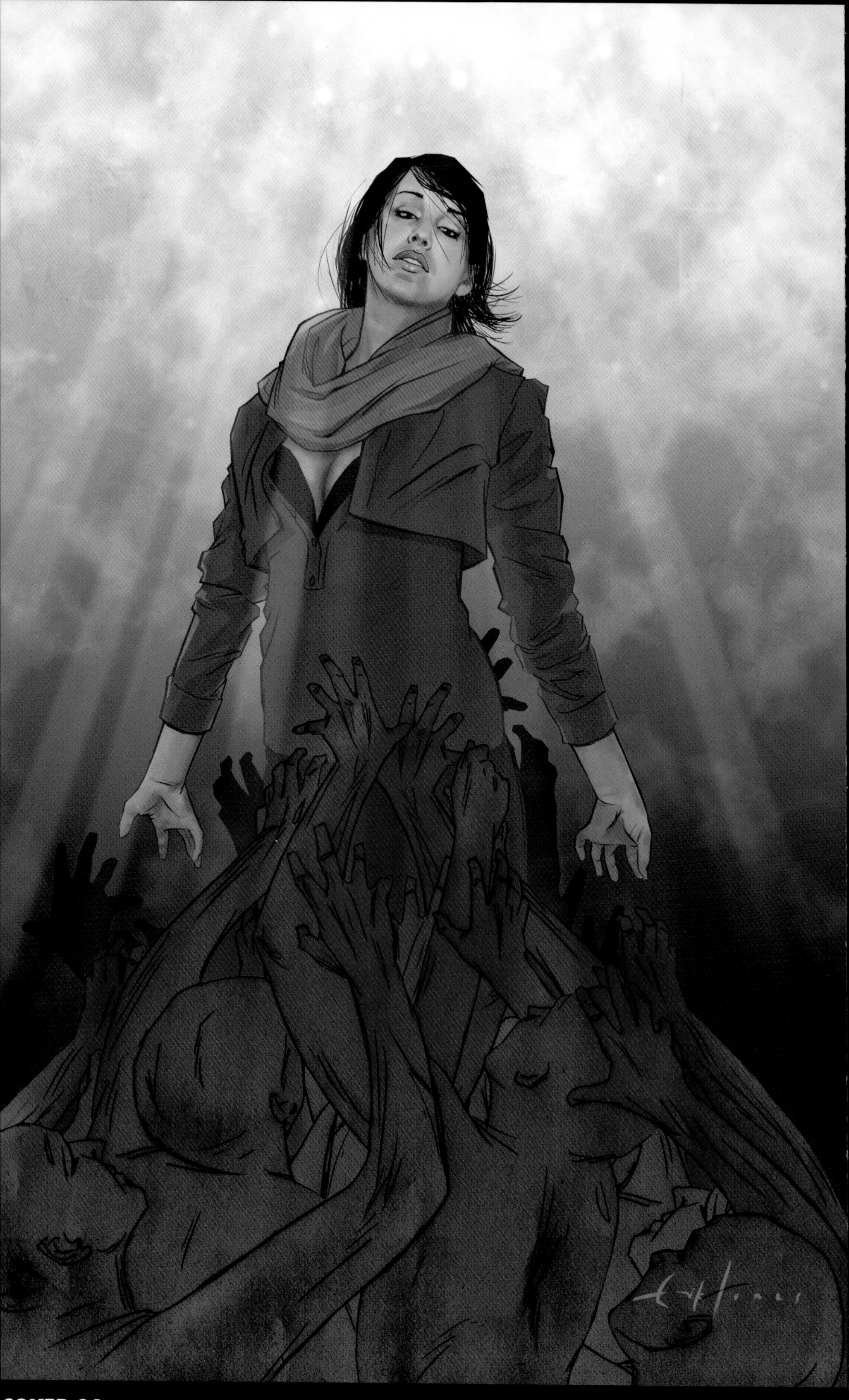

COVER 3A
ERIK JONES

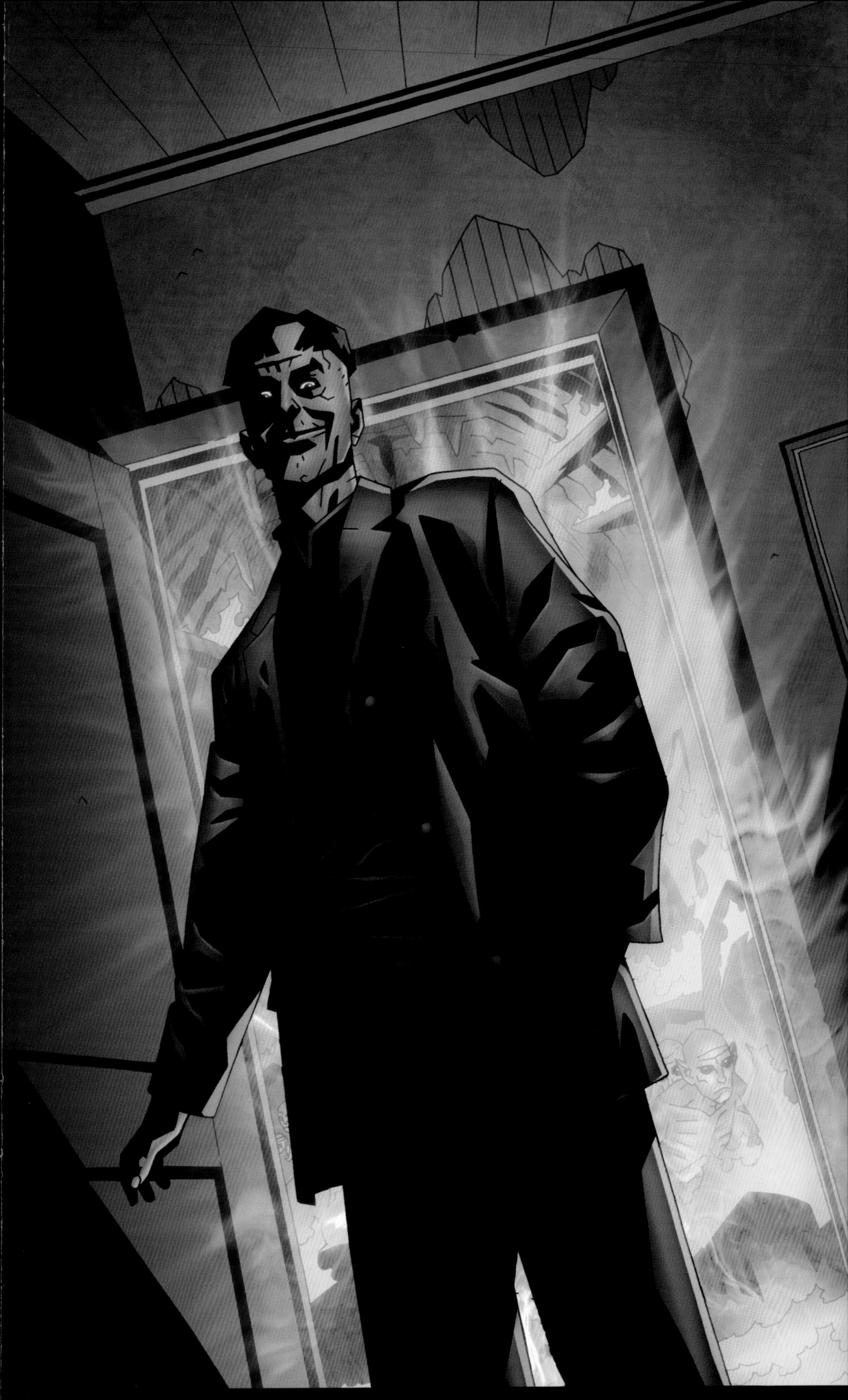

COVER 3B
MATTHEW DOW SMITH / COLORS BY DIGIKORE STUDIOS

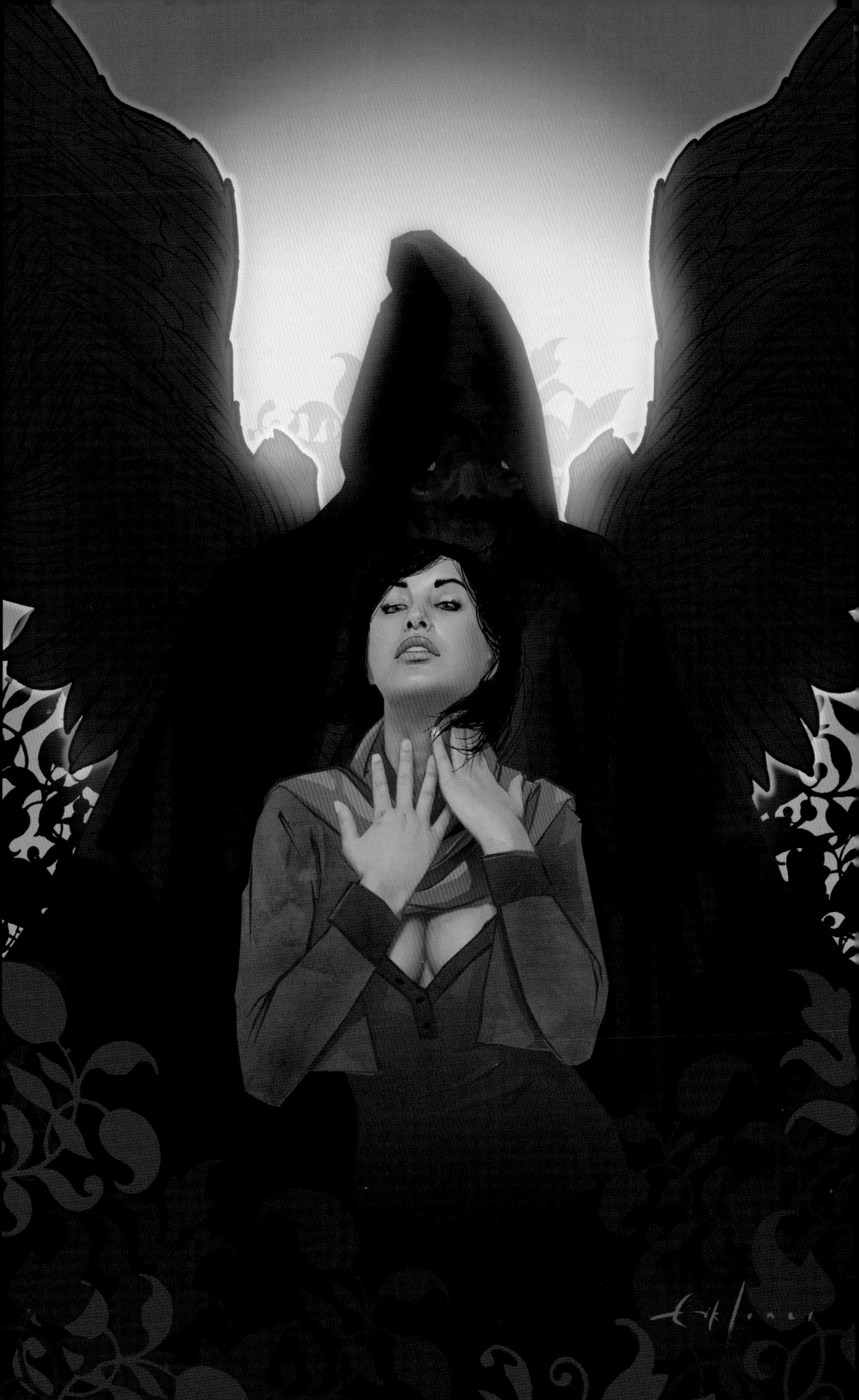

COVER 4A
ERIK JONES

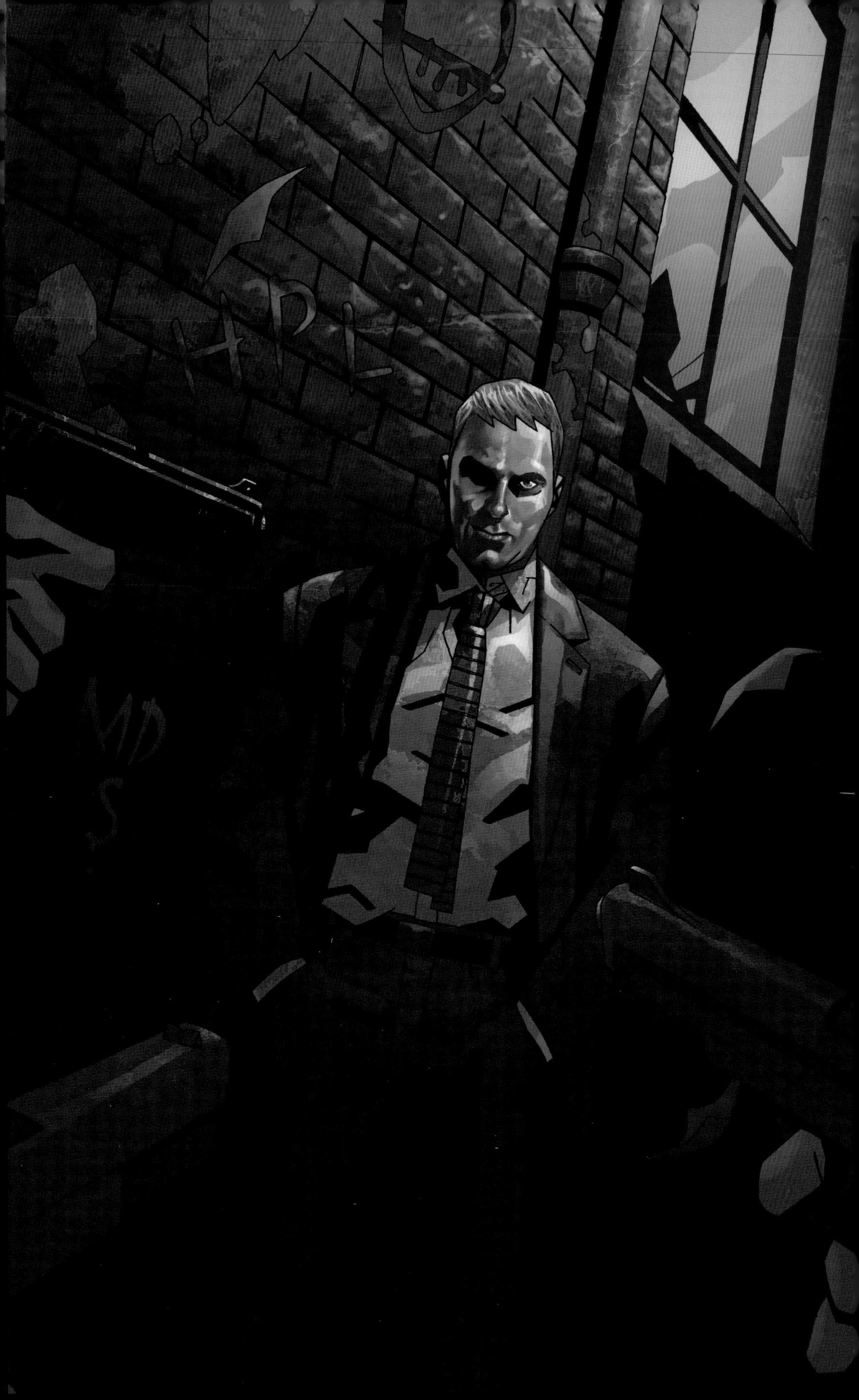

COVER 4B
MATTHEW DOW SMITH / COLORS BY DIGIKORE STUDIO

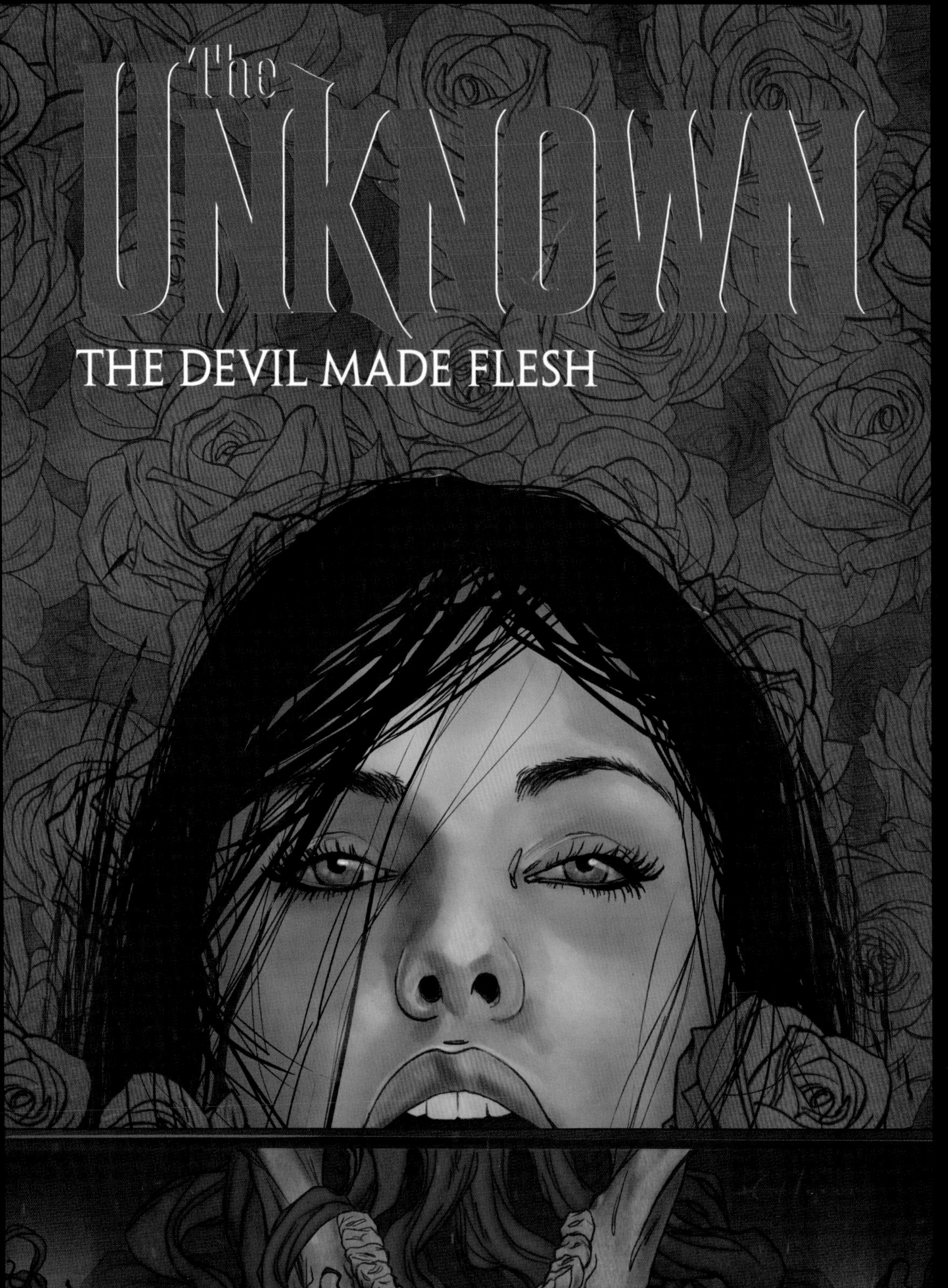
The UNKNOWN
THE DEVIL MADE FLESH

THE UNKOWN: THE DEVIL MADE FLESH

THE SAGA CONTINUES! CATHERINE ALLINGHAM IS THE WORLD'S MOST FAMOUS PRIVATE INVESTIGATOR. FOLLOW HER ADVENTURES AS SHE SETS OUT TO SOLVE THE ONE MYSTERY SHE'S NEVER BEEN ABLE TO CRACK — DEATH!